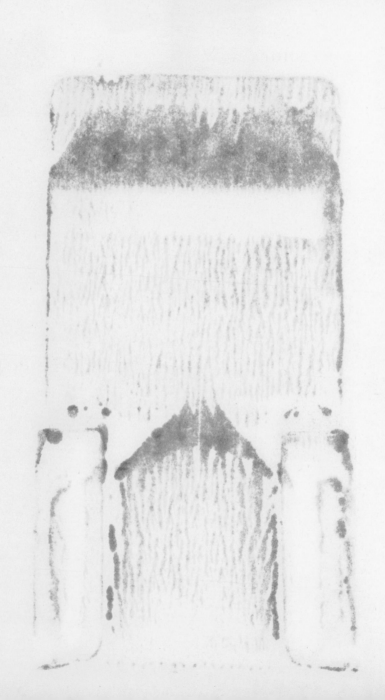

FAIRS, SHOPS, AND SUPERMARKETS

STUDIES IN SOCIAL HISTORY

edited by

HAROLD PERKIN

Senior Lecturer in Social History, University of Lancaster

◇◇◇◇◇◇◇◇◇◇◇◇◇◇◇◇◇◇◇◇◇◇◇◇◇◇◇◇◇◇◇◇◇◇◇◇◇◇◇

FAIRS, SHOPS, AND SUPERMARKETS

A History of English Shopping

by

Dorothy Davis

University of Toronto Press

TORONTO, 1966

First published in Canada 1966
by University of Toronto Press

© *Dorothy Davis 1966*

Published in Great Britain 1966
as 'A History of Shopping'

Printed in Great Britain

Contents

v

Illustrations

It would take too long to recount or enumerate the many and various Ways and Occasions that men and women have of spending and laying out Money, many of which are absolutely necessary unless we knew how to live without Meat or Drink or Apparel with other external Necessaries, as Horses, Armour, Books and the like—in a word, whatever may conduce to our Profit and honest Pleasure. Yet in husbanding our money in all these, there is a great deal of Caution and Discretion to be used. For most true it is that of all Nations in Europe our English are the most profuse and Careless in the laying out of their Money.

The Pleasant Art of Money Catching
Anon., 1737

Preface

ALL good scientists, I understand, are brought up not to ask questions to which there are no answers. This self-denying rule may be all very well for scientists, but nowadays it seems to be adopted by historians as well. This is a pity, for many of the most interesting questions about the past are only capable of a very partial and unsatisfactory answer and yet do not deserve to be entirely ignored. One such question is the history of retail distribution. Internal trade generally is so little documented that hardly anything is known about its past; the final stage by which goods reached the hands of the consumer is the least known of all. For the recent past, the existence of one substantial general study, the largely statistical classic by J. B. Jefferys *Retail Trading in Britain 1850–1950*, together with a handful of memoirs of individual organizations, do something to make the general outline clear. Before 1850, however, the subject remains a complete historical blank. It is on this blank space that this book aims to make some small impression.

Of course, it makes no claim to be a complete history of retail trade even for the years before 1850. Rather, it is a framework, a skeleton on which others, applying more detailed study, may in time put flesh. Moreover, scholars are few and general readers are many; I hope it may provide for the general reader who is little concerned with the more recondite problems of history an answer to the simple question: how did people do their shopping in the past?

In carrying the story over eight centuries, much has had to be omitted. My object has been to describe the situation that faced the consumer. The development of wholesaling and of the other ways in which retailers obtained the goods they sold find little place here. Of course, retailing has never existed in a vacuum; its character has always been determined by developments in the supply of commodities, in agriculture, manufacture

ix

and overseas trade. But I must beg to be excused from the attempt to combine a history of wholesaling with this study, for the shopper, as such, was not concerned with it. Prices, too, are only occasionally referred to. Although price levels are of vital interest to the individual consumer, they are largely irrelevant to the organization of retail trade and to the formation of shopping habits, and price histories have little to contribute to this subject.

But whereas I have left middlemen and prices out of the picture quite deliberately, it is only with reluctance that I have abandoned the attempt to give a more complete account of the coinage and of tradesmen's tokens. Histories of the coinage from the fiscal and antiquarian points of view are abundant enough, but no-one has yet tackled the more difficult problem of finding what was the small change of day-to-day business, the sorts and sizes and values of the common coins men were accustomed at different times to carry in their pockets. But for lack of space, I should have liked, too, to deal with the fascinating and specialized trade in horses. And I have not attempted to include Scotland's experiences; this I leave to the Scots.

For the rest, I have tried to select from this vast and virgin field what seem to me to be some significant aspects and periods that together present a coherent story. The selection is necessarily arbitrary. Another student of this subject might have told the story from a completely different selection of times and places, but would still, I hope, have come to much the same general conclusions.

I am indebted to Mr George Eland and Messrs Sidgwick and Jackson for permission to quote from the *Purefoy Letters*. I have to thank Dr Anthony Bridbury, Professor F. J. Fisher and Mr Peter Mathias for their kindness in reading parts of the text and making some useful suggestions, and my husband for much useful encouragement. Nobody but myself, however, is responsible for the faults that remain.

DOROTHY DAVIS

Glossary

There is some ambiguity about all the following terms, but I have found these to be the most usual meanings.

TRADESMAN. A skilled craftsman, until the eighteenth century, in the course of which the term came to include shopkeepers.

SALESMAN (SALES-SHOP). Eighteenth-century term for a shopkeeper who bought all his goods ready-made in those trades where they had formerly been made on the premises, especially in the boot and shoe, tailoring and furniture trades, where the general rule was still for the shopkeeper to have his goods made by outworkers.

FACTOR. The producer's general name for anyone who bought wholesale from him. There were factors in nearly all trades, both in food and manufactures, before the nineteenth century (sometimes with special names, 'badger', 'crimp', 'brogger', etc.) whose business it was to gather up the scattered production of small units and supply it in quantity to the merchants in London or other cities.

CHAPMAN. In medieval times, every travelling merchant. Later it became a Londoner's term for any kind of dealer outside London. In the seventeenth and eighteenth centuries it came to mean a settled shopkeeper in a country town, and the term 'petty chapman' was reserved for pedlars.

COUNTRY DEALER. A London dealer who sold wholesale on long credit to retailers in the country. Until the eighteenth century, country dealers were City shopkeepers with a retail trade as well. Thereafter, an increasing number kept only warehouses and did not trouble with retail trade for which, in the City itself, they had to take out their 'freedom'.

PEDLAR. A house-to-house retailer who travelled either on foot or with a packhorse about the countryside. Generally he both bought and sold for cash. 'Petty chapman' was a politer name for pedlar in the eighteenth century.

HAWKER. A street seller who cried his wares in a town, but often applied to country pedlars as a term of abuse.

MANCHESTER MAN, SHREWSBURY MAN, SHEFFIELD MAN, ETC. A wholesale travelling merchant trading between factory and shopkeeper, with his goods on packhorses. Sometimes independent, sometimes employed by the manufacturer. Often abused by London merchants (whose role he tended to usurp in early industrial times) as 'pedlar', 'hawker', etc.

SCOTCH DRAPER, SCOTCHMAN, ETC. Eighteenth century onwards. A house-to-house retailer who specialized in the new type of factory-made textile goods for payment by instalments. Occasionally independent; usually on commission for a small firm.

THE LATE MIDDLE AGES

I

$\diamond\!\diamond$

Town Markets in the
Late Middle Ages

$\diamond\!\diamond$

Thou, trader, shouldest trust God that He will find thee a livelihood with true winnings, for so much hath He promised thee with
His divine Mouth. Yet now thou swearest so loudly how good
thy wares are and what profit thou givest the buyer thereby. More
than ten or thirty times takest thou the names of all the saints in
vain—God and all His saints—for wares scarce worth five
shillings. Ye yourselves know best what lies and frauds are busy
in your trades.

> Berthold of Ratisbon, quoted in L. F. Salzman,
> *English Life in the Middle Ages*

T H E pattern of shopping in the middle ages reveals an attitude
to living that is in many ways the exact opposite of our own.
Today, we think of a personal standard of living as a matter of
getting an income and spending it, whereas then, people thought
primarily of what they could grow and make for themselves,
and only incidentally of what they could buy with money. For
though they were no less interested in worldly goods, the things
that money could buy were few in kind and limited in quantity,
while virtually everyone lived in close touch with the immediate
source of all wealth, the land itself. There were very few people
indeed who did not either own land or work on it; the vast
majority of the population were peasants. History in the middle
ages is dominated by churchmen and the nobility, but numerically

they were insignificant; trade belonged mainly to the occupants of towns, but they, too, were only a small minority of the whole country. The social conditions of all the nobility, all the church-men, all the merchants, their habits in diet and dress, the surpluses they could spend on castles or cathedrals or ships, their leisure for tournament or pilgrimage or pageant, all these things were rigidly determined for them by the nameless mass of peasants in the background about whose life we know so little.

There were all sorts of peasants, rich and poor. Some worked very much like wage labourers, except that they were paid largely in goods to supplement what they could manage to pro-duce for themselves. Others, more independent but not neces-sarily better off, had to grow or breed or catch nearly everything they needed, and their standard of living was then determined by how much land they worked and what rights they enjoyed to pasture animals, cut fuel, catch fish and so on. But rich or poor, they did not look far beyond the land for their supplies, and money, until the very end of the middle ages, played a limited part in their scheme of things. The peasant's dream of per-fection was not a chest full of coins to spend, but to farm wide acres in order always to have grain in store and malt to brew ale; to have cows and sheep, pigs and poultry among the village herds and flocks so as to eat meat in abundance, so that butter and cheese were plentiful and there was an unfailing supply of tallow for candles and leather for a hundred purposes; to have the freedom of the woods for hunting and for fuel and to see wool always waiting for the busy distaffs of his wife and daughters. In other words he did not work simply for money; he worked so as to avoid as far as possible the need for money.

But even the most self-sufficient peasant was no Robinson Crusoe. He had to find money for taxes, and there were some things he could not produce and needed to buy. This meant selling what he could spare in the local market. By the fourteenth century there was a market of some sort within a day's journey of even the remotest hamlet although in some of the wilder parts of the country a visit to market might take from dawn to dusk of a summer's day. The size and importance of market towns grew steadily throughout the middle ages, yet for many cen-turies after regular marketing had become commonplace for the whole population, the trade in markets remained poor and crude. The peasants' negative attitude towards buying was pervasive, and it died hard everywhere beyond London and a few large cities.

Most towns up to Elizabethan times were smaller than a modern village, and each of them was built around its weekly market where local produce was brought for sale and the towns-folk sold their work to the people from the countryside, and provided them with refreshment for the day. Trade was virtually confined to that one day even in a town of a thousand or so people. Any place of that size today centres upon a collection of retail shops; in the middle ages a town was a collection of craftsmen rather than shopkeepers. On market days they put up their stalls in the open air. The members of the shoemakers' guild in the important town of Beverley, for example, drew up rules in 1462 which include precise instructions on this point.

> They shall have and keep their tables for selling shoes in a lane called Shoemarket lane, standing in order on the south side of the said lane on market days and other markets and fairs . . . and every shoemaker shall stand in his priority as he entered the craft, beginning at John Danby's shop. . . .[1]

On one or two other days during the week, the townsman would pack up his loaves, or nails, or cloth, and set out early to do a day's trade in the market of an adjoining town where, however, he would be charged a heavy toll for the privilege and get a less favourable spot for his stand than the local craftsmen. Another chance for him to make a sale was to the congregation gathered for Sunday morning worship. Although no trade was allowed anywhere during the hours of the service (except at annual fair times), after church there would be some trade at the church door with departing country folk. Some towns, more proud and pious than most, expressly forbade their own craftsmen to go 'peddling at church doors' in outlying places.[2]

The trade of markets was almost wholly concerned with exchanging the products of the nearby countryside and the goods made by local craftsmen. Bread, meat, ale, cooked meals, fire-wood, candles, articles in leather, wood and metal, cloth and

---

[1] *Hist. MSS. Comm.*, *Beverley Town Manuscripts* (1900), p. 92.
[2] *ibid.*, p. 93.

B

linen, were the staple commodities of the weekly market. The producers and the consumers of these things met face to face and consequently the genuine retail trader, the man who bought only to sell again, had very little place. In all goods sold in the market but particularly in food, retail dealing was disliked and distrusted as a kind of profiteering. Even where there was enough trade being done to afford a livelihood to an enterprising man ready to buy wholesale and sell retail, town authorities would not allow it if they could help; middlemen might be unavoidable evils if goods had to be carried over a long distance, but otherwise they thrust an unwanted service between producer and consumer.

Yet there plainly were people who were tempted to 'forestall the market' by buying goods outside it, and to 'regrate' them, that is to resell them, at a higher price. The constantly repeated rules against these practices and the endlessly recurring prosecutions mentioned in the records of all the larger towns prove that people did these things, that the desire to trade could not be suppressed, that there were always people ready to take a chance with the law to make a profit out of consumers less well-informed or less sharp-witted than themselves.

Nowadays, shopping hours are restricted in the interests of the retailers, and not because of the scarcity of goods. It is one measure of the difference in their way of life that medieval people restricted the market hours in the buyers' interests, so that every buyer should have an equal chance to buy a fair share of whatever was going, and also to enable the authorities to keep an eye on all the transactions and make sure that no-one made a corner in some commodity and 'engrossed' it, that is, forced up the price. Buying before the market was officially open was a grave offence. At Yarmouth, no-one was to 'open either sak, pooke . . . or any other vessell wherein victualls or other things be' before the market bell. Norwich market was under starter's orders until the Cathedral bell rang for mass; Salisbury's, until 'after broad day'.[3]

Once the market was open, every aspect of buying and selling was hedged about by complicated regulations about where, when and by whom everything was to be done. Every town made its own laws, and if it was big enough to have craft guilds, these

[3] L. F. Salzman, *English Trade in the Middle Ages* (1931), p. 76.

regulated the business of their members and tried to enforce a strict monopoly of their own trades. Yet while the guild leaders, as craftsmen, followed fiercely protectionist policies directed to keeping all the trade of the market to themselves, at the same time, as leading townsmen, they wanted to see a big, busy market yielding a handsome revenue in various dues and tolls. Conflicts of interest led to endless, minute regulations, changeable, often inconsistent, frequently absurd. There was a time in the fourteenth century, for example, when London fishmongers were not allowed to handle any fish that had not already been exposed for sale for three days by the men who caught it [4]

Besides trying hard to keep out dealers and profiteers and to see that as many goods as possible, particularly food, came to their market, the authorities did what they could to establish their town's reputation for peaceful and honest trading. Everywhere there were long and bitter battles over the matter of weights and measures, which, as between one town and another and even within the same town, were in a general state of confusion. There were two sides to this problem. Many false weights and short measures were used for deliberate fraud, but there was much more trouble with perfectly honest local variation. To convert the literate and organized England of today to the use of the metric system would be a simple task compared with the job of persuading the people of the middle ages to abandon their traditional ideas about how big was a bushel or how heavy a stone. For example, at Bury St Edmonds the first effect of enforcing the use of the London standard weights and measures was to paralyse the town; no-one brought any more goods into the market for sale, preferring to carry them farther to sell in towns where they could see the measures they were accustomed to. [5]

Magna Carta declared emphatically that 'there shall be one measure of wine throughout our realm, and one measure of ale, and one measure of corn, namely the London quarter . . . and as with weights, so with measures'. A century and a quarter later, much the same thing was said in another statute. Ninety years on, it was said yet again and after another sixty-five years the same law was passed once more and this time members of parlia-

---

[4] E. Power & M. M. Postan, *English Trade in the Fifteenth Century* (1933), p. 278.
[5] Salzman, *op. cit.*, p. 43.

ment were given standard weights and measures to take home to their constituencies. But still local variations persisted.

Meanwhile, different tables of weights were used for different commodities; a 'weigh' of lead, for instance, or of wool, flax, tallow or cheese was officially 168 lbs., but a weigh of cheese in Suffolk was always 256 lbs., in Essex 336 lbs. and in several other places 224 lbs. Then there was the 'true' hundredweight of 100 lbs. and the common or garden hundredweight of 110 lbs. In some counties you might buy a hundred nails and get a 'long hundred' of six score and in others you might not, but everywhere you expected a baker to count thirteen to the dozen. For buying bulky things, grain, for instance, or salt or malt, not the weight but the volume was measured, tubs being cheaper to make than scales. The vat was originally the 'fat'—that is, a cheating or oversized bushel measure used by the buyer to measure grain. There was constant disagreement about whether a bushel measure counted as full when it was heaped up with as much as it would hold, or when the top was 'striked' or struck off level with the brim with a strip of wood. Pictures of medieval markets show corn tubs being levelled off in this way, but they omit the details of the surplus corn being pushed onto the ground among the general filth until it was shovelled carelessly back into the next measure.

Market regulations often instructed men 'not to sell by aime of hand'. Standard weights and measures—that is the local standard, as a rule—were hired out to the public, and were a source of considerable profit to the authorities. Only gradually did the use of private tubs and scales become general, because for a long time the town authorities discouraged them as untrustworthy. Officials were supposed to inspect private weights and measures, and seal approved ones with the town's seal, but there was a thriving trade in making false ones for unscrupulous traders. Leather black jacks in ale-houses, after they had been 'ensealed' by the officer, were often lined with pitch to reduce their capacity unobtrusively. Small quantities were often weighed on an auncel or steelyard, and as the peculiar advantages of this continental instrument became known it came into wide use. It was a kind of hand scale, a graduated rod, held aloft from a handle pivoted near one end. The operator placed goods in a pan hanging from the short end, slid a weight along the other end until the rod balanced, and then read off the amount from the markings on the rod. 'Another weight is called the auncel's shafte . . . a disseivable weight if a man cast himself to deceive the people and for to be false.'[6] Even a genuine instrument could be wilfully misread, and it was harder to catch the cheater than if he actually possessed false weights. At last it became such a notorious instrument of fraud that it was prohibited by law. (The Germans, however, in their privileged trading sanctuary in London, continued to use their native steelyard which gave its name to the site of their medieval trading post until the eighteenth century.)

The pound weight had a certain basic steadiness about it for the odd reason that Henry III linked it by statute to the silver coinage. The ounce, he said, weighed 20 pennies and twelve ounces were to make a London pound. In spite of some hesitations and backslidings this old money pound persisted, and formed the basis of the present avoirdupois pound. In its early life it was sustained by the fact that it could always be checked by the weight of 240 silver pennies, thin little discs the size of a modern sixpence. Then the coinage got worn and bits of silver were stolen off the edges, and since in those days it was the value of the metal rather than their face value that really mattered, the coins themselves came to be weighed, instead of counted, for large payments. Payment 'by weight and not by tale' meant enough to weigh so many lbs. of silver, often far more coins than the nominal 240 that sufficed when they were all new. So the coinage was first used to establish the national pound weight and then the weight, when universally recognized, came to be used as a check on the coinage.

How far all these complications and uncertainties about measurement affected the consumer we can only speculate. Most people bought always in the same local market or fair and probably the occasional great merchant or responsible town official was more troubled by them than the average consumer. The householder buying for his own use would judge by the eye and the feel of his hands, and haggle about the price of everything he bought, and would be more likely to feel ashamed of being outwitted than outraged at being swindled.

A more obvious nuisance was the shortage of small coinage.

[6] Arnold's *Chronicle*, quoted in Salzman, *op. cit.*, p. 60.

The chief coin, and for a long time the only one, was the silver penny; later there were some very rare halfpence and farthings. 'One of the minor problems of medieval life,' says one historian, 'is, how did the thirsty traveller pay for a drink of ale at the tavern when ale was a penny a gallon? The smallest recognized coin being a farthing, he could not, apparently, buy less than a quart of ale. And the same problem applies to other wares in the days when twopence was a good day's wage.' Part of the answer lay, no doubt, in the use of unofficial small foreign coins, French and Scottish, although not much is known about them. Silver pennies were sometimes indented with a cross for breaking into four quarters, but even so, it was as if almost no-one nowadays had less than a ten-shilling note in his pocket. Legal records and monastic chronicles do not record the minor inconveniences of the poor, but they, after all, concerned people who did not need small change because they did not buy trifles; when rich people spent money at all they bought in bulk or bought things of value.

But although the medieval customer seems to us to have been ill-served in national matters like weights and measures and coinage, when it came down to local government regulation his interests were in many ways protected with great skill and thoroughness. For example, bread and ale were two basic articles of diet regularly on sale in every market, and as both depended on the local corn crop which varied more precariously than nowadays with good and bad seasons, the prices of both were rigidly controlled by authority according to a sliding scale. The regular meeting of the town officials to fix bread prices and ale prices was known as the assize, and since it could not alter the amount of money to be charged for a loaf—for there could only be farthing-loaves, halfpenny-loaves and penny-loaves—it varied the amount of bread in the loaves. And similarly it fixed the strength of ale in the standard penny gallon. So although the customer always bought one loaf and one quart of ale for two farthings, in a bad season the ale would be half as strong and the loaf half as big as in a good one.

There is plenty of evidence that the assize was treated very seriously and that everyone, customers and town authorities alike, combined to try to keep the bakers and brewers up to the mark. But not every consumer could try the loaves he bought on a pair of scales, and bakers had very little margin of profit and were constantly tempted to cheat a little, so the records of all medieval towns are full of bitter complaints and savage punishments about the 'breaking of the assize'. In Coventry for instance in 1421 a Mayor's proclamation ran:

> That every Baker that baketh to sell, that he sell no less than four wastells for a penny and that they be of well seived flour and well baked and weighing up to the standard weight, upon pain, at the first trespass of 13s. 4d., at the second to lose 20s., and at the third to stand in the pillory, and at the fourth to forfeit the freedom of this City for a year and a day.[7]

Bakers also had an important trade in baking horse bread, for hay was scarce and generally needed for cattle and in towns the usual diet for horses was a coarse bread made of peas and beans 'without bran or refuse'. Again, it was common in towns, at least down to the time of the Civil War, for a well-run household to prepare its own dough at home and have it baked by the baker alongside his own loaves, and indeed a baker regarded it as his job to bake anything that was brought to him. Meat chopped small and pease pudding was a very common Sunday dinner baked at the baker's. An oven was a luxury only found in the houses of the wealthy, and in a village too small to have an independent baker, the only oven would probably belong to the lord of the manor who made a profit out of the villagers' use of it, in the same way as he often made a profit out of owning the only mill for grinding corn. Otherwise, the simple means of domestic cooking was the open hearth, and in an isolated cottage the loaves were simply charred among the hot ashes in the way King Alfred is said to have found so unsatisfactory.

During the summer when the next harvest was awaited and bread was becoming scarce and the loaves smaller and smaller, the poor often turned to horse bread or, indeed, to loaves made of practically anything that would grind up and stick together. The medieval poet described the summer not as men saw it with their eyes but as they felt it in their stomachs:

> What was detested by Dobbin was dealt to the hungry
> And beans made beggars obedient to work.
> The poor felt paid with peas for their wages . . .

7 M. Dormer Harris, ed., *Coventry Leet Book* (1907), p. 23.

But later on:

> By then harvest was nighing, new corn came to market,
> And folks were fain of it and fed hunger with the best.
> No beggar would eat bread if beans were in the baking,
> Only if it were morning white of the finest flour.[8]

Ale was the universal drink of all classes with all meals, although the well-to-do might drink nearly as much wine as ale. It was served to the wealthy nobleman alongside his wine, and to his children in the nursery for breakfast. It was simply fermented malt, innocent as yet of hops—the 'wicked and pernicious weed'—and generally speaking about as alcoholic as present-day beer. To drink water was not only dangerous, it was degrading, the last, wretched resort of the very poorest. Ale was brewed so easily it was done by all and sundry. All the bigger households made or bought malt and brewed their own, while in every town several housewives brewed at home for sale to all comers, either to drink on the premises or to carry away. So far from being restricted and regulated as it is now, brewing was one of the most casual and unorganized of medieval trades and was largely in the hands of women. In the City of London in 1309 there were 1,300 brewers for a population of well under 50,000.[9] Regulation in most towns took the form of insisting that anyone who offered their brew for sale must put out their sign, a pole with a bush of leaves attached as in many present-day Continental taverns, so that the officially appointed ale-tasters could come and sample the new brew before it was sold to the public and check that the tankards in which it was supplied were marked with the town seal. One set of regulations for ale-wives reads as follows:

> And that they sell it with measures enseled and not with cups nor bowls and with signs set out; and that they sell it forth out of their houses as well as within by measure enseled. Upon the pain that whoso shall make true plaint to the Mayor thereof shall have four pence for his trouble and a gallon of the best ale.[10]

The price of wine was fixed on a national basis every year, but probably only the larger towns took any notice of this. Apart

[8] N. Coghill, *The Vision of Piers Plowman* (1949), pp. 52–4.
[9] R. R. Sharpe, *Calendar of Letter Books of the City of London* (1902), Book D, p. 19.
[10] *Coventry Leet Book, op. cit.*, p. 25.

from this, and the bread and ale already noticed, the foodstuffs sold in the market were free of price control except for some unusually important occasion. After bread, meat was the most important food and by our standards it was cheap and abundant, usually costing only about half as much as, for example, cheese or butter. Most of the meat that was eaten never passed through the market, of course, because families kept some livestock of their own. Even town dwellers kept cows and sheep as a sideline on the town commons, while pigs and poultry were backyard stock to be fattened on household scraps. Nevertheless a good deal of meat was bought at the butchers' stalls in all markets. Big institutions bought their meat on the hoof and slaughtered it themselves so that the tallow and hide could be sent off to the chandler and tanner to make candles and leather, for these materials were as valuable as the meat. Substantial households bought sheep or pigs or even oxen by the half or quarter; but there is seldom any mention of small quantities like joints or mere pounds. Game was plentiful, but its enjoyment was confined to the landowning classes.

Only two things about the sale of meat interested the town authorities. First, they were always anxious that demand should not outstrip local supply, so they were inclined to welcome country people bringing in livestock to slaughter and sell, and they made curious regulations to discourage and delay the slaughter of town beasts, such as that no bull must be killed until it had been baited for sport. Their other concern was that meat should be fit to eat, 'good and wholesome for man's body', and so, for example, it had not to be sold by candlelight, and Thursday's leftovers had to be salted, and most important of all, meat must never be sold from an animal that had died of its own accord. 'Murrain cattle', and 'putrid and stinking sheep' figure in the charges that sent butchers to the pillory with dismal frequency.

In a diet where fruit and vegetables were scarce and poor, fish made a most welcome change and the whole population ate no meat on Fridays and fast days and all through Lent. Fresh fish was so dear that unless he lived by the sea the poor man probably never tasted it; and even salted or dried or smoked fish, much more widely eaten, was quite expensive. Salt herrings, the cheapest and most plentiful fish, were the universal standby.

The price of a pound of butcher's meat would, at a rough estimate, buy the same weight of salt herring—say from two to four fish including their heads. People who could afford the outlay bought their salt herring—or salt cod or haddock which cost a little more—by the barrel at the autumn fairs to store for winter and the following Lent. 'Mistress,' wrote a Norfolk bailiff to his lady one autumn, 'it were good to remember your stuff of herring now this fishing-time. I have got me a friend in Lowestoft to help me buy seven or eight barrels and they shall not cost me above 6s. 8d. a barrel. You shall do more now with 40s. than you shall at Christmas with 5 marks [66s. 8d.].'[11] For variety they would also store dried or 'stock' fish, which was cod or haddock split open and dried hard like a board or stock—the 'poorjack' of later times. But it did not keep so well as fish in brine and was usually eaten first before the damp got at it. There were no tins or airtight containers, of course, and indeed the whole principle of preserving dry goods by the exclusion of air seems to have been unknown, so that not only dried fish but the much more precious corn and barley tended to mould even in the driest garret in damp weather. But we read of someone claiming that he could keep dried ling wholesome for two years by putting it in thick straw and 'covering it with mats close and dry'.

Fresh-water fish was like game in that while it was eaten in greater quantity than nowadays, it was nearly all privately owned and little came on the market. Landowners whose tenants occupied stretches of river would often take part of their rent in fish, or in the work of building and maintaining weirs or stake fences to facilitate the catching, and bitter were the quarrels about the illegal practice of setting the stakes across the whole width of water and taking all the fish. The rivers were prolific; the crown, for example, had a big salmon fishery in the Thames at Richmond and sold the surplus pickled in barrels. We hear, too, of people obtaining occasional barrels of salted whale-meat from abroad, or seal-meat, 'fit only for the digestion of mariners'. Porpoise or 'sea-pig' tongue was an especial luxury. But these would all be private purchases that almost certainly never reached the public market. On the other hand, a big, rich city like Coventry boasting over five thousand inhabitants in the

11 J. Gairdner, ed., *The Paston Letters* (1900), III, 254.

fifteenth century attracted the wives of sea-fishermen all the way from the coast with panniers of live sea-fish in brine carried on pack-horses; they had a special pitch in the market, and were especially protected from interference by would-be middlemen. Their prices were no doubt exorbitant.[12]

One of the regular complaints of the London fishmongers was that fish—by which they meant salt fish—was sold all over the City by all and sundry. And this seems to have been the case in most towns. The demand for fish was so irregular that any tradesman who wished to do so was allowed to deal in dried and salt fish; it figures among the miscellaneous stocks of the so-called mercers and grocers of provincial towns.[13] Even the more lucrative monopoly of the fresh merchandise had to be relaxed in London, and probably in other ports, to the extent of allowing the fishermen to retail their own catches to the public, while the London fishmongers competed from their own stalls in the markets. Thames fishermen could sell from their boats tied up at Billingsgate stairs; other fishermen from stalls in the present Fish Hill Street and neither sort was 'to be so daring as to stand elsewhere'. A handful of recognized hucksters were allowed to 'carry fish through the City to sell to divers working men . . . but they are not to stand in any certain place to sell such fish'. There are endless twists and turns to the London regulations about the sale of fish throughout medieval times, and these reflect the struggles of one of the most powerful City guilds to establish its monopoly, and the determination of the rest of the Corporation to see that the citizens should not go hungry on fast days.

One more victualling trade remains to be mentioned, that of the cooks. The stock-in-trade of a cook was a big fire with spits and sometimes an oven as well. His customers were chiefly the hungry travellers who crowded into the town for market or fair, and it was one of the boasts of London that in Cook's Row in Eastcheap it was possible to get a good meal of roast or boiled fish or meat or a hot pie at any hour of the day or night. Cooks would also take the customer's meat, when required, and turn it into a hot pie. As might be expected, they were often accused of using poor ingredients. In Coventry in 1421 they were expressly forbidden to re-heat meat already cooked or to buy dead

---

[12] *Coventry Leet Book, op. cit.*, p. 646.
[13] Power & Postan, *op. cit.*, pp. 290-1.

eels or pike for their pies.[14] And in London a proclamation of the Mayor said:

> because that the pastelers [i.e. pastry-cooks] of this City of London have heretofore baked in pasties, rabbits, geese and garbage not befitting and sometimes stinking, in deceit of the people, and also have baked beef in pasties and called it venison ... that no-one of the said trade shall buy ... at the hostels [i.e. town houses] of the great lords of the cooks of such lords, any garbage from capons, hens or geese to bake in a pasty and sell.[15]

Shortly after the Black Death, when prices that had been steady for generations except for seasonal fluctuations were showing a mysterious tendency to rise, the Lord Mayor of London issued the following price-list for cooks, which shows their varied menu; such variety would not be found outside London, and even there might not all be available at any one time.

Best roast pig 8d.	Best roast river mallard 3½d.	Best roast plover	2½d.
— — capon 6d.	— — snipe 1½d.	— — heron	18d.
— — pullet 2½d.	— — partridge 3½d.	Ten — finches	1d.
— — goose 7d.	— — pheasant 13d.	Three— thrushes	2d.
— — hen 4d.	— — curlew 6½d.	Three— pigeons	2½d.
— — rabbit 4d.	— — bittern 20d.	Five — larks	1½d.
— — teal 2½d.	— — woodcock 2½d.	Ten eggs	1d.
For the paste, fire and trouble upon a capon 1½d.			
— — — — — — — a goose 2d.			
The best capon baked in a pasty 8d.			
— — hen — — — 5d.			
— — lamb roasted 7d. [16]			

These, then, were the principal victualling trades, the bakers, the brewers, the butchers, the fishmongers and the cooks. Although only bread and ale were directly price-controlled, all the victuallers were carefully watched by the town authorities in markets big and small to prevent the three great crimes of medieval retailing, 'forestalling, engrossing and regrating', that is speculating, hoarding and profiteering, for if local supplies failed it was usually impossible to get food from farther afield. Consequently, although their crafts were important the victuallers were never allowed to make big enough profits to enter the

[14] *Coventry Leet Book, op. cit.*, p. 26.
[15] H. T. Riley, *Memorials of London and London Life, in the 13th, 14th and 15th Centuries* (1868), p. 438.
[16] *ibid.*, p. 426.

ranks of the leading citizens from whom were recruited the mayors and the sheriffs of their towns, and their guilds always came well down the list in order of precedence, as they did in London. Only the fishmongers, whose trade contained an element of speculation in buying wholesale supplies of salt fish from distant places, ever achieved any sort of status among the townsmen of the middle ages. And yet the victuallers were fairly numerous in the towns. How numerous it is not easy to say because they are often omitted or under-represented in the surviving lists of tradespeople contributing to pageants or defence or taxation. But among the almost complete lists of freemen enrolled in York in the early fifteenth century they averaged from 12 per cent to 14 per cent over the years.[17]

The last word on medieval victuallers might perhaps be left to the author of *Piers Plowman* who, whether his strictures be true or not, summed up his contemporaries' view of them. Notice that he says it is the poor who buy retail and form their chief customers:

> Punish in the pillories and stools of repentence
> The brewers, the bakers, the butchers, the cooks,
> For these are the men that do the most mischief
> To the poor people that buy by the parcel.
> They poison the people privily and often
> Getting rich by retail and buying up rents
> With what the poor people should put in their bellies.[18]

Those people who could afford dairy produce bought it direct from the farmers on market days. Eggs, butter, cheese and milk were sometimes available all the year round, but except in spring and early summer they were scarce and dear. Cheeses were bought whole, but a well-to-do town household would often hire a cow for the summer to supply itself with cheese for the coming months, the conscientious housewife preferring the home-made article to the product of the farm. Butter came in gallons, that is, in gallon tubs although not necessarily liquid. Along with lard, which was dearer, butter was used not only for food but for all sorts of lubrication—to oil cartwheels for example; oil of any other kind for domestic purposes was almost

[17] J. N. Bartlett, 'Some Aspects of the Economy of York in the Later Middle Ages' (unpublished London Ph.D. thesis, 1958), *passim*.
[18] N. Coghill, *op. cit.*, p. 32.

unknown throughout the middle ages. In early Tudor times the practice spread downwards from the rich of using olive oil from Spain for cooking. Perhaps an exception ought also to be made of herring oil, for although its chief use was for dressing sheep-skins, it is also recorded that 'men annoint therewith shoes'.

Fuel meant wood, and that too was bought and sold in the market, in bundles by the hundredweight, or in loads of regulation size. There was 'small wood' for kindling and 'great wood' or logs. Countryfolk collected their own, and townsfolk some-times bought the underwood of so many acres of forest from a nearby landowner and hired men to cut it and bring it to the house as required—another instance, like kneading their own dough and making some of their own cheese, of the tendency of town dwellers to model their domestic economy on that of the self-sufficient peasants all around them.

Victuals and firewood could be bought in the market of any town; a very small market might have nothing else, a big one might have a fair selection of medieval production, in leather, wood and metal. But the smallest town would have by the fourteenth century at least one genuine retail shopkeeper. He might call himself a mercer or a grocer or a haberdasher, for outside the biggest cities these names were unimportant, the shopkeeper's speciality being not any particular class of com-modities but simply any goods brought from far away. In London, Bristol, York and Coventry, merchants specialized sufficiently—barely sufficiently—to justify these names, but elsewhere the local merchant dealt in whatever he could get of cloth and linen, drugs and spices, hardware and miscellaneous small manufactures. Consider, for example, the inventory of the stock of a so-called mercer in Leicester in the fifteenth century:

This man was at the same time draper, haberdasher, jeweller, grocer, ironmonger, saddler and dealer in timber, furniture and hardware. Even this does not describe him adequately, for he had a small stock of wool, wool-fells and skins on hand, and he could have offered you ready-made gowns in taffeta or silk, daggers, bowstrings, harpstrings, writing-paper, materials for making ink, and seeds for the vegetable garden.

His resources were greatest in the drapery department which comprised twenty different kinds of British and imported cloth, belts, ribbons, skeins of Paris silk, children's stockings, silk coifs, and kerchiefs for nuns. In the way of hardware he had everything from cutlery and candelabra to coal scuttles and horse-shoes. Provisions he had none beyond honey, raisins and salt . . .[19]

There were probably two or three such general merchants serving a population of something under three thousand in Leicester itself and market-day visitors from a wide area around. The range of stock here looks impressive at first sight, but it should be remembered that these goods do not represent 'lines' he regularly dealt in (except, perhaps, for English cloth) but rather a miscellaneous assortment of bargains that had been picked up at fairs. It would be a haphazard and no doubt jumbled collection crowded into the cellar and ground-floor room of his own house. And most of it had probably been there for a long time, for the rate of business would be exceedingly slow; in a society with a low standard of living it did not take much trade to yield a livelihood.

The 'gowns' that this merchant had for sale would, of course, be second-hand. Clothes were very expensive, were worn a long time and never thrown away. If they were not given away as presents or bequeathed in wills, they were sold, and at second-hand aroused none of the distaste that would be felt in a more squeamish age. In the bigger towns, dealing in second-hand clothes was a full-time trade for the 'Phelipers' or fripperers. The Lord Mayor of London in 1365 made an order

. . . that the phelipers who buy old clothes, or budges (short cloaks made of a single piece of lambskin) or furs, linen-lined . . . shall sell the same budges and linings with the collars on when repaired, the furs or linen being attached to the same budges and lined garments in the same manner as they have bought them. That so, people may have full knowledge that the same things are old budges and linings and not new . . .'[20]

Many of the features of the medieval market for local produce have survived into the English country markets of modern times. When we see the farmer's wife, as we still do today in York and many other north-country towns, sitting on an upturned box at the edge of the Saturday market with her home-made butter, her few chickens and fresh eggs, or the independent

19 Power & Postan, *op. cit.*, p. 291.
20 H. T. Riley, *op. cit.*, p. 324.

small-town butcher bidding for a beast from the side of the cattle pen, we are seeing something as old as English civilization. But these accidental survivals do not mean that present day markets bear any resemblance to their medieval forerunners. The truer comparison would be with the present markets of the East, with the bickering and fraud, the jostling and noise, the narrow lanes and confused traffic of men and animals, the dirt and the smells.

It was comparatively late in the middle ages before Coventry, not only one of the largest but one of the best regulated of English cities, began to turn its attention to the amenities of its streets and some of the rules it made are very revealing. 'No man to have no Swine . . . nor no Ducks . . . nor no great Hounds nor Bitches going in the High Street.'[21] Sellers of various different commodities were assigned to particular places and bidden to stay there and not walk about. Cloth sellers were not to spread the stuff out so as to 'obstruct the light'. In the street of the fish sellers, if they chose not to sell from a tub on the ground but to put up a board or trestle it was to be 'holden firm and stable' and to leave what is described as a 'reasonable' space of one yard between it and the house-front for horse or man to pass between. The narrow streets in which the markets were held were lined with tall, narrow houses, oversailing above and open-fronted at street level for they were house, warehouse, workroom and shop in one. Business was done with the customer standing in the street and dealing over the dressing board or counter which at night was pulled up and fastened to act as a shutter. It was tempting to make this board as wide as possible, but in Coventry and no doubt elsewhere it was supposed to be narrow enough not to project beyond the eaves of the house.

In these shops the householder and his apprentices did their work, and at least in Coventry, if that work happened to be butchering then they did that too. When they were forbidden to tie live sheep and cattle to their doors and slaughter them in the street, they slaughtered them in their shops, but each butcher was commanded to carry away his own offal to a pit outside the city instead of leaving it in the street, and to 'keep his door clean from blood and other filths'. In another burst of good resolutions, the Coventry corporation forbade anyone to wash entrails or

21 *Coventry Leet Book, op. cit.,* pp. 24–5.

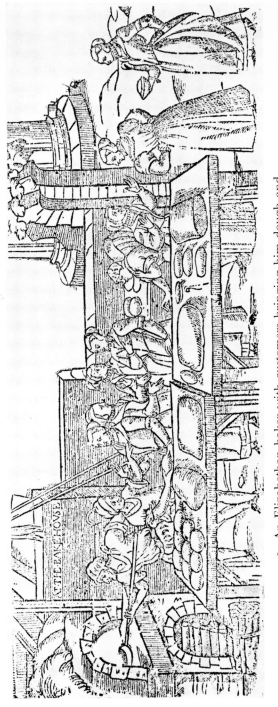

1. An Elizabethan baker with customers bringing him dough and pies.

2. A small fair in Elizabeth's reign.

vessels or to singe hogs or do 'any filthy operations' in the market and ordered traders who threw garbage or entrails under their boards to remove it by four o'clock. Fishwater, however, was only to be thrown into the street after dark or else 'one penny to the constable for finding it', and 'no person within this City shall from henceforth sweep their streets in any Rain time, whereby to pester the River with filth and muck'.[22]

If the disposal of rubbish was a perennial problem in a medieval town, a very much bigger one was the maintenance of law and order. Every market was obliged to have a summary court for the enforcing of the assize of bread and ale and the use of honest measure, and in every market stood pillory and stocks for the humbler offenders who could not profitably be fined. The same machinery was used to punish breaches of the peace, but even so public safety was only precariously maintained. It was usually forbidden to carry swords in the market (lords sometimes being allowed as a favour to have their weapons carried by a page), or to drive beasts with long sticks which might encourage their owners to a readier brawling. Drunkenness and quarrelling, violence and even sudden death were certainly common enough, in spite of the fact that markets were held in the very shadow of the market cross put there for the express purpose of reminding a turbulent world of the need for a truce of peace and honesty in which to transact business.

Where so much is known about medieval life in its legal, administrative and economic aspects, we are curiously ignorant about many homely details concerning its inland trade and particularly about its markets. We can only infer from indirect evidence that they were of every kind and size, from the most meagre village exchanges of the more backward regions, through the relatively ample and varied furnishing of the special meat-days, fish-days and corn-days in proud cities like Bristol, Coventry or Norwich, to the full glory and wonder of London's multiple markets operating at full strength every day of the week. But we have no idea, for example, in what typical quantities goods were bought. The wealthy, with large households and long purses, we know to have bought all their needs in what we should call wholesale quantities. How lesser people bought we can only guess from casual references, from what we

---

[22] *Coventry Leet Book, op. cit.*, pp. 24–5.

c

know of the shortage of small change and of the difficulty and expense of weighing small quantities, and by remembering the long distance most people outside London had to travel to and from the market. From all these, it would seem certain that quite humble people commonly bought what we would think of as large quantities at fairly long intervals. It is noticeable that while there are constant references to 'mouldy' or 'diseased' or 'stinking' provisions being sold, there is never a mention of rancid butter, stale bread or merely jaded meat. Why should there be? Were they not still butter, bread and meat, luxuries to many and to all 'good food, honest and wholesome to men's body' —that is, not obviously poisonous? Monotony of diet was taken for granted at all levels and no doubt when poor people bought half a pig or a tub of butter or a cheese they made it last a long, long time. In the popular tale, the miser who half-starved his family bought a whole cheese at a time, marking it with a pen to measure consumption, until a waggish visitor helped himself to a generous portion, 'two or three pounds at least', and wrote a rude comment on the remainder.

We know, too, that nothing was wrapped or packaged with the exception of barrelled goods. We can picture a townswoman taking an apprentice or servant to the market, with a linen cloth to wrap the meat in, a sack for corn from a corn-monger or farmer or perhaps meal from the miller; she might tuck a length of cloth under her arm, but the poultry would dangle by the legs and the whole fish, candles, pepper-corns, spices, sugar-loaf and all would be at large in a basket. Ale, milk and fresh water would all have to be fetched to the house in her own containers. It is alleged that butterbur got its name because its great, thick leaves were once used to wrap small quantities of butter—what a vision of waste and mess in hot weather—and the 'old woman' in the nursery rhyme may quite probably have been addressing her winter's supply of pickled pork when she pleaded 'Piggy, please get over the style or I shan't get home tonight!' Again, the miser of fiction provides a revealing picture; an important London citizen buys his wife a pullet in Gracechurch Street and has it plucked on the spot before remembering that he has no-where to put the feathers. Ingeniously, he puts them in the crown of his hat. On the way home, he meets the Lord Mayor, who 'would needs speak with him. Then my Master moved his hat up and down a little with his hand and my Lord Mayor held him in talk so long till at last the feathers began to fly out about his ears forth of his hat. "What," quoth my Lord Mayor, "have you got a bird's nest in your hat that the feathers fly about so?" '

Two things, however, are certainly true about all markets. They were predominantly, though not exclusively, for food sales. And, because of this, they were invariably held in the open air, where the authorities could see that supplies were sufficient and went to the right people. Victuallers were always being ordered to make their sales 'in the open market', and not 'conceal in their houses' the food they had to sell, or store it from one market to the next. Where butchers or bakers or fishmongers were allowed to sell over their shopboards in their own houses, this was because the market itself was in the street before their doors. When they visited other markets, they sold from their packs on the ground, or perhaps set up trestles which they stored in a nearby house. As Stow remarked of London, 'The foreign butchers [that is the country butchers] for a long time stood in Lime street twice every week, namely Wednesday and Saturday, and were some gain to the tenants before whose doors they stood and into whose houses they set their blocks and stalls. But that advantage being espied, they were taken into Leadenhall, there to pay for their standing to the Chamber of London.'[23] Even so, it was their storage, not their actual sales, that were 'taken into Leadenhall'; they almost certainly continued to trade in the street outside the gate like all the other market people.

The City of London, although its streets were so 'pestered', was always particularly opposed to citizens storing up food in 'shops and other obscure places'. The Poultry, it is true, took its name from the houses of the poulterers. (It was formerly Scalding Lane, from the practice of scalding the birds in the street before plucking them.) But the poulterers always sold their goods in the open Stocks Market on the site of the present Mansion House until their trestles were moved farther up their own street to make more room for the 'foreign' poulterers from the countryside. Cheapside, once the biggest London market of all, is still surrounded by Bread Street, Milk Street, Friday Street and so on, streets named, not after the occupations of their residents, but because the middle of these thoroughfares was the

[23] J. Stow, *Survey of London* (Everyman edition), p. 268.

space reserved for the bakers from Stratford, the fishermen from the Thames, and the milk-sellers from the suburbs to come and set down their stalls and baskets and hold their markets. It was as late as 1302 that the old London rule was revoked which said 'Let no baker sell bread in his own house or before his own oven, but let him have a basket with his bread in the King's market'. And for long after this, the sellers of all other foods carried them forth into the London throng, and cried them aloud and thrust them on passers-by. If they had 'been so bold' in medieval times as to skulk in their shops waiting for customers to come to them the city authorities would probably have come first and put them out of business for hoarding.

In the non-food trades, craftsmen were much freer of municipal control. They managed their own affairs through their guild organizations, and their own affairs consisted chiefly in regulating entry into their trades and discouraging outsiders from spoiling their town market. They were probably free, as a rule, to sell from house or stall as they wished, although except in the few largest towns towards the end of the fifteenth century they would have been lucky to be able to sit at home all week and get enough customers to make a living. The place to sell things was in the market. A craftsman's workshop in the middle ages, albeit open to the casual passer-by, was typically known as his 'house'; his 'shoppe' was a trestle on the cobbles under the open sky, week by week in his local market and, when the season came round, at the fair.

II

◇◇◇

Fairs and Their Customers

◇◇◇

The merchants were damp and wet from the eddying storms which were frequent as is usual at that season. They were hungry and thirsty, their feet were foul with mud and their wares were ruined by rain. . . . All who came or remained there were afflicted with weariness. For during all the time that the crowd came, remained and went away, torrents of rain soaked everything; so that all, muddy, damp, tired and jaded, felt wretched. For, the bridges broken down, the fords became, through traffic, hardly passable, the roads hardly usable, the city muddy beyond words, food and other necessaries scarce and dear, and all involved in wretched inconvenience.

Matthew Paris, Chronicles, v. 29

F o r winter stores, for craftsmen's products of a more or less durable kind, or just for 'a bunch of blue ribbons to tie up my bonny brown hair' people outside London went to the fair; and it made a yearly outing as well. By about 1400 there were some two or three dozen annual fairs in the whole country, and though they differed greatly in size, each must have seemed as if all the world and his wife had come together to build stalls, open packs on the grounds, and set up shop for the few days or weeks that the fair lasted.

Every known article came to the big fair; everything that could normally be bought in the market and a great deal more besides. Nothing was too bulky, or too costly, or too common-place to find its way there somehow, by wagon or packhorse or

25

barge. Iron from Sussex, tin and copper from Cornwall, lead from Derbyshire were sold all over the country by means of fairs. So was the skilled work of London craftsmen, especially in costly fabrics and in gold and silver. So too were barrels of herring and cod for the winter months, and the countless varieties of goods that travelling merchants bought in one fair to sell in another. The biggest fairs of all were international markets. Merchants from overseas came to buy bales of the famous English wool or fine woollen cloth, and they brought with them luxuries from abroad. There were exotic silks and velvets, glass and jewellery brought from the Italian traders in London; there were Flemish linens and French wines; there were spices in astonishing variety, and great quantities of almonds from the Levant; there were fine furs from the Baltic, and tar from Norway for treating diseases in sheep. Even an occasional piece of eastern porcelain or an uncut precious stone might change hands in the back of a booth after being traded from fair to fair, almost haphazardly, across the width of the world.

But though one aspect of the fairs was the bringing together of trader and trader to exchange goods each would sell again, great numbers of people thronged to the fair to fill their own needs. Knights bought the finest armour from Milan, and horses bred in Spain to carry them when they wore it. They could choose the makings of costly robes from the best English cloths and the richest fabrics from abroad. Their choice was crude and lively; the brightest colours, the showiest textures, the most dazzling contrasts were the way to proclaim rank and riches, and even among the poorest in their coarse homespun clothes of wool or hemp the most popular wear was in harsh reds and yellows, greens and violets from the crude vegetable dyes. Ladies of rank, besides buying cloth and furs, looked for such things as the frames of gold wire on which they draped their fantastic headdresses, precious needles for embroidery, silk and linen sewing thread, as well as pins, buckles and ornaments. The stewards of great houses and the wives of country gentlemen would count on a visit to the fair to lay in stores of all kinds for months to come, not only of salt, food and wine, but also rushes for the floor, tallow and wax for candles, and all kinds of non-perishable goods that were not only cheaper bought in bulk at the fair but were of choicer quality than the local markets could normally supply.

The great monasteries and convents sent emissaries to buy at fairs. The canons of Bridlington Priory laid in their supplies of cloth, wine and groceries at Boston Fair in Lincolnshire, eighty miles away. Oxford colleges sent to the Cambridge fair at Stourbridge in September for their stock of winter fish, spices, wax and salt. We might pause to wonder why Oxford did not simply buy in London, which was quite as near, and whence many of the things they needed—spices for instance—had already been carried to Cambridge. The answer is that during the short period it lasted, Stourbridge Fair was a better all-round market than London itself. The best of everything from all over the country, including the capital, was gathered there annually for a few brief hectic days. One year when New College had for some reason failed to lay in a proper stock of pepper, an unexpected visit from the king's brother drove the bursar in hurried search for a supply which was essential to any banquet; a messenger scouring Oxford as a forlorn hope found a merchant who agreed to let him have a pound; but the price he had to pay was three times the college's normal price for it.[1] It was an expensive mistake not to victual at the right times and places.

The royal household also got some of its requirements from fairs. Its officers had the right—known as purveyance—to take the pick of any market or fair, taking precedence over all other buyers and paying—or promising to pay—arbitrary prices. Towards the end of the middle ages these prices gradually became standardized as 'the king's price' at an agreed level below current market prices, and purveyance was gradually restricted to basic foodstuffs, so that it became in effect a tax on their producers. Meanwhile attempts were made from time to time to prevent the king's officers from abusing these powers of pre-emption. Petitions to the king declared that his minor officials made a practice of earmarking for the king's use goods they had no intention of buying—perishable food, or horses, for example—solely for the sake of being bribed to release them again. Royal custom, far from being coveted, was evaded whenever possible, if necessary with a fat bribe.

[1] J. E. Thorold Rogers, *History of Agriculture and Prices in England* (1866), IV, 154.

Quite as numerous as the customers who came to the fairs to buy for their own use were the craftsmen who frequented them to get the materials for their trade. The town millers came to do business with big landowners selling their surplus corn, smiths to buy iron from far afield, clothmakers to have a choice of the best wool in the country. Above all, the town mercers, grocers and drapers relied on the fairs to obtain their miscellaneous stocks of foreign goods—spices, cloths, and small wares such as ribbons, knives, mirrors, purses and so on. Regular traders at the biggest fairs gave and received credit from one fair to another, so that these fairs became important settling days. In the fourteenth century, St Giles at Winchester, in the fifteenth, St Luke's in Huntingdon, Stourbridge at Cambridge and St Bartholomew's at Smithfield in London, were the most important fairs, but there were several others nearly as big.

Fairs changed their fortunes over the years. Some fairs flourished while others declined; new fairs were inaugurated and others suppressed. Though all were general markets, many had their own specialities. St Giles at Winchester was famous for wine and spice, St Bartholomew for English cloth, Stourbridge for luxury fabrics, Yarmouth for fish. But there was no distinction between what we should call wholesale and retail selling, between small purchases and big ones, between the customer buying for his own use and the tradesman buying for his business. The sellers had also come to buy; the buyers had very often brought something to sell.

The whole organization of the medieval fair must be regarded as a triumph over the adverse circumstances of the time. First there was the general scarcity of goods; there were not enough to stock any large permanent centre of trade outside London. It is as if nowadays the shops in our major cities—and only those— had enough goods to open for a few days once a year. Fairs brought what goods there were briefly within reach of a large part of the population.

Even if we allow for some exaggeration in the many stories of violence, of high-handed lawlessness on the roads, it remains true that merchants travelling with valuable goods and money were obvious prey to plunderers. But in the fairs themselves, as on a smaller scale in markets, special efforts were made to secure peaceful conditions for business; Salzman describes them as 'oases of commercialism in a wilderness of militancy'. Most fairs had begun as gatherings for religious festivals, and many of them not only bore the names of saints but were actually run by churches or monasteries, and the strong influence of the medieval church helped to develop the conception of 'the peace of the fair', the idea that commerce deserved some sort of special immunity from violence. Many fairs were held in and around churchyards and monasteries, the trade often carried on in the church itself, and the public scales or 'beam' fastened to the wall of the church while the fair was on. In 1285 Edward I tried to have fairs moved out of church premises, but it was not easy to break the habit of treating the parish church as the parish hall. Two centuries later it was still being said that merchants came to Exeter Fair 'to lay open, buy and sell divers merchandises in the church and cemetery'.

Some centuries before the King's Peace came to be automatically extended to the country at large, it had been expressly conferred on many fairs. But the best guarantee of the blessings of law and order on the fair-ground, as in the market, was that in every case the fair or market had an owner, and that owner was powerful and directly interested in its prosperity and good name. It was impossible to hold a market or fair except by royal permission: 'None in the realm is permitted to have a market without the licence or goodwill of the king'. This was granted specifically as a money-making privilege, sometimes to towns or individual nobles, often to churches or monasteries.[2] St Bartholomew's Hospital in London was originally endowed with the annual proceeds of Bartholomew Fair. Successful fairs were lucrative properties, as their owners were free to make what they could out of them. As in markets, there were tolls for hiring booths, tolls for building stalls, and tolls for laying out goods on the ground. There were charges for the hire of weights and measures (which was compulsory) and a tax from both buyer and seller on every transaction. Equally profitable was the right to administer justice and impose fines and forfeitures for the breaking of the assize, breaking the peace, for using bad language or trading out of hours; even, in one case, on merchants arriving late at the fair. The Bishop of Winchester, who owned St Giles' Fair in that town, took over the keys of the town gates

[2] L. F. Salzman, *English Trade in the Middle Ages* (1931), p. 145.

every year while his fair was in progress, and with much pomp and ceremony installed his own bailiffs in place of the Mayor and Corporation, who went into temporary retirement. The Archbishop did the same thing at York. The University of Cambridge shared the proceeds of its great Stourbridge Fair with the town council, the town taking the rents of the booths and stalls, and the proctors of the university getting the lion's share of the bargain by holding the court and administering the fines.[3]

The frequenters of fairs seem to have acquiesced cheerfully enough in the owners making their own rules, administering their own justice and enforcing it with their own armed constabulary, pillory and stocks, and making profits out of fines and forfeitures. All justice was rough and ready, and a rule that ensured peace and security at the fair was acceptable at any hand. Moreover, there are indications that despite the regulations that were solemnly proclaimed in public on these occasions, the ignominy of the pillory was on the whole reserved for the humbler offenders, while more important or influential people contravened the regulations for the price of a fine.

For the settlement of what we should now call civil disputes arising out of the trade of the fair—for example, non-payment of debts, or claims that goods handed over were of poorer quality than those displayed at the time of purchase—a special tribunal was held in every fair. It was known as the Pie-Powder Court (from *pieds-poudrés* or dusty feet) because it served temporary visitors and travelling merchants who wanted quick settlements and could not wait for the lengthy proceedings of the common law. The adjudicators on these tribunals were themselves visiting merchants who had obeyed a summons, no doubt often with reluctance, to leave their own business in their stalls or booths and serve in the court for a spell. Usually they would find that they had been chosen because of a dispute involving a fellow-townsman and that they shared the bench with other merchants sympathetic to his opponent. Although this arrangement sounds like a formula for persistent deadlock, the Pie-Powder Courts were famous and popular for their speed in coming to decisions. The quality of their judgments is less certain. Any substantial purchase which was not for immediate delivery and payment was

3 C. Walford, *Fairs Past and Present* (1883), p. 76.

supposed to be made in the presence of two witnesses who could afterwards swear to the terms of the contract, and sealed with the payment of a token coin or 'God's penny'. In practice, the taste for prolonged bargaining and the scarcity of written agreements or receipts gave ample opportunity for misunderstanding and sharp practice of all kinds. The records of the time are full of cases like the barrel of spices with earth in the bottom, the roll of cloth folded or even sewn up so as to hide defects, the 'iron' pots that melted on the fire, and the debts that were repudiated.

Corporate pride among traders from the same town, and above all the members of the great London guilds, has often been quoted as proof that these gentlemen kept one another up to the mark, affording a protection to the consumer against fraud or shoddy workmanship. Certainly there are numerous instances of fellow-guildmen or fellow-townsmen denouncing the faulty materials or bad workmanship in goods on sale at fairs. Many London Companies, including the Embroiderers, Goldsmiths, Horners, Leathersellers and Pewterers exercised the right to search for and confiscate 'false wares' not only in any premises in London but on the booths and stalls of anyone selling goods of their crafts anywhere in England—an indication, by the way, of how largely Londoners dominated the fair trade in these lines.

The occasional conflicts which are recorded between the wardens of London guilds and the owners of fairs, over which of them was to have the benefit of the forfeited 'false goods', show that searches for inferior goods were actually made. But how thorough or regular these inspections were it is impossible to guess; the one certainty is that it was not only the consumer's welfare that was being so vigorously protected, but also the principle of making life uncomfortable for anyone who threatened to trespass too freely on the quasi-monopoly of the London guilds. Piers Plowman, when he wanted to personify Covetousness, chose a London draper; his description is evidently the stock figure of that trade:

> I was put as an apprentice to make profit for my master.
> First I learnt to lie, little by little,
> And to falsify weight, my very first lessons.
> But for the grace of guile in the grading of my goods,
> They had been unsold these seven years, so help me God.

I was drawn into drapery, and by devious tricks
Learned to lay out linen so that it looked longer
Till ten or twelve yards told out thirteen.[4]

Another writer has a grudge against a whole group of crafts.
(Clothing here, of course, means cloth, not clothes.)

> Ye that work in clothing, silkes, wool and fur, shoes, gloves or
> girdles, men can in no wise dispense with you; men must needs
> have clothing and therefore should ye so serve them as to do your
> work truly, not to steal half the cloth or use other guile, mixing
> hair with your wool, or stretching it out longer whereby a man
> thinketh to have gotten good cloth, yet thou hast stretched it to
> be longer than it should be and maketh a good cloth into useless
> stuff. Nowadays no man can find a good hat for thy falsehood; the
> rain will pour down through the brim into his bosom. Even such
> deceit is there in shoes, in furs, in skins; a man sells an old skin
> for a new, and how manifold are your deceits, no man knoweth
> so well as you or your master the devil.[5]

The volume of this sort of pious denunciation of 'false goods',
as well as the crudity and variety of the frauds that court records
reveal, is eloquent testimony of the low commercial morality of
the times and the difficulty of establishing standards. Even
allowing for the medieval writer's love of dramatic exaggeration,
the impression grows on the reader that men and women had to
be very wide awake indeed when they set out to re-stock their
larders or wardrobes or farms at the annual fair, if they were not
to return home with their trust betrayed, their ignorance exploited, and their pockets picked.

The general appearance of fairs no doubt varied a great deal,
but certainly at the major fairs the booths were laid out regularly
in 'streets', some of which were reserved, at a price, for particular
trades. There would be 'Goldsmiths' Row', 'Saddlers' Row',
'Skinners' Row', and so forth. Some had areas assigned to
merchants from each of half a dozen different countries. About
the year 1300 the proprietor of the Lenten Fair near Nottingham
was charging the traders from that town a preferential rate of
twelvepence for the hire of a booth in a special position. Those

4 N. Coghill, *The Vision of Piers Plowman* (1949), p. 40.
5 Berthold of Ratisbon, quoted in L. F. Salzman, *English Life in the Middle Ages*
(1926), p. 240.

selling coarse cloth could pay eightpence for the hire of the framework only, and cover it themselves if they wished. An iron merchant was only charged fourpence for a booth near other iron merchants, or twopence for one not in a special position, and tanners and shoemakers from Nottingham—which was a leather centre—could come and put up stalls for nothing. Some fairs left booths standing from year to year as permanent fixtures, while some traders owned booths outright, or the sites of them, and bequeathed them in their wills.

The traders with booths were the aristocracy of visiting merchants, but most of the ground was covered by tents or trestle stalls, and many small local craftsmen or itinerant pedlars opened their packs on the ground or tried to hawk their goods among the jostling crowd—though this last was specially forbidden for fear that some sales might escape paying toll. Prominent everywhere were the food- and ale-sellers, supplies pouring in from the surrounding countryside to feed the swarms of visitors and to be consumed by all in the enormous quantities appropriate to a gala occasion. Once more to quote Piers Plowman; his 'fair field full of folk' might well have been inspired by the fairs of his time:

> Barons and burgesses and bondsmen too
> I saw in this assembly as you shall see later
> Bakers and butchers and brewers galore,
> Weavers of wool and weavers of linen
> Tailors and tinkers and tax-collectors,
> Masons and miners and many other craftsmen,
> Cooks and their kitchen-boys calling 'Hot Pies!'
> Geese and good gammon! Get a good dinner!
> Advertising taverners told the same tale
> With a 'white Alsatian wine! Red wine of Gascony!
> Rhenish and claret give relish to a roast!'
> All this I saw sleeping and seven times more![6]

But although the highlights of the scene are easy enough to visualize, there must have been less pleasant aspects of fairs which that coarse, lusty, comfortless society took in its stride. At Stourbridge, for example, at least part of the fair was held on cultivated land; there was an agreement that if the corn was not

[6] N. Coghill, *op. cit.*, p. 20.

off the ground by 24 August it could be trampled down by those who came to build booths. It is hard to imagine the conditions underfoot when thousands of visitors swarmed about stubble fields in a wet season churning them into mud. Again, where did all these people sleep? The towns where the big fairs were held were far too small to accommodate all the visitors with even the most elementary comforts, allowing for the fact that to sleep several in a bed and many in a room was an everyday occurrence for the well-to-do and that a bed on a heap of straw on an earth floor was no hardship to the majority. Many traders must have slept beside their goods on the fair ground if only for safety's sake, for although the lord of the fair might tell off some of his men to act as watchmen at night, these were often negligent, and robbery was a serious matter for a merchant in days when insurance was unknown. Many visitors must have slept where they could, wet or cold notwithstanding, but when a monastery or convent was near at hand, lay-persons of good standing as well as visiting monks and nuns could hope to find space there.

But to medieval writers these were unimportant and sordid details rarely worthy of mention, and, indeed, fairs must have been extraordinarily stimulating and exciting to the people from the countryside, most of whom spent their lives cut off from the outside world, without news or books or entertainment, in a laborious monotony it is nowadays hard to imagine. Although the fair that was dominated by entertainment, by side-shows of jugglers and sword-swallowers and two-headed calves, belongs properly to a later age, the medieval trading fairs must have been even more wonderful to the people who came to them. They were the common meeting-ground of all classes, the places where men heard news of national events, compared their grievances and caught the first breath of new ideas.

We know nothing useful about the volume of business done at typical fairs and markets, or about the degree of competition in selling different commodities. We know hardly anything about profits, about credit, about stock and capital, at the retail level. Perhaps most intriguing and most elusive of all is some picture of growth; we know that the economy was growing, despite war and pestilence and bad harvests, and that constant new developments were slowly knitting together the inland trade of England, but the reflection of these secular movements in the retail structure and shopping habits of the fourteenth and fifteenth centuries is little recorded. No customs or taxation yields, no family papers or court records, will enable us to reconstruct in modern economic terms the business of the medieval butcher or baker or candlestick-maker, still less the turnover of market or fair.

Some light can, however, be thrown on the retail trade of the time by considering first a few of the more important things bought at fairs, and then the buying habits of various kinds of customers. Although there are plenty of records surviving from the middle ages to show what things cost, it is hard for our minds to extract meaning from the figures of prices. Nobody takes home corn, or cartwheels, or iron bars from the shops today; but people did so then, to grind their own flour or make a cart with their own timber or to hand over to the smith to make ploughshares. And it was the price of such things that was important to medieval people rather than the prices of what we nowadays call 'consumer' goods. What connection can there be between the price of a loaf today and at a time when most people grew some corn for their own use? Or again, the field labourer of 1300 commonly earned twopence for his day's work; but before we set this beside modern labourers' wages and say that money prices should be multiplied by 140, we must remember that the labourer of those days lived in conditions of hunger, cold and cheerlessness which have no parallel in modern England. In other words, medieval patterns of expenditure and the whole social structure were so different from our own that it is misleading to compare the prices of any individual article without looking at it carefully in its medieval context.

Two classes of goods, however, were unmistakably of great value and expensive to buy because their production with primitive tools needed a great deal of skilled handwork. These were all goods made of cloth and all goods made of metal. Medieval inventories show this very clearly. We find that in a gentleman's house the most important items are the bedding, the kitchen utensils and the table silver, and pewter; by comparison with these, the wooden furniture, for example, simply does not count. Consider, some of the purchases we find recorded for a Warden of Merton College, Oxford.[7] The cloth for his

[7] Rogers, *op. cit.*, I, 577, 585.

robes cost from three to five shillings a yard, perhaps a twentieth of the price of similar cloth made today by prosperous workers on modern power-driven machinery. But by contrast, his shoes cost only 8d. a pair, and an undergraduate at the same time paid only 2½d. a pair—no more than a two-hundredth part of the price of a surprisingly similar pair of 'winkle-pickers' in the 1960's. Add a pair of metal spurs to riding boots, however, and their price goes up from about 8d. to 3s. 4d.

We can make no modern comparison with the price of a knight's armour at £6 or £7 a set, but the more domestic forms of hardware bought at the fair seem expensive in modern terms— a brass jug at 6s. 8d. and a brass ewer and basin at 5s., representing, again, products of an industry since extensively mechanized.

Lady Stonor, the wife of an Oxfordshire gentleman in the fifteenth century, bought 38 yards of a green satin known as sarcenet for which she was charged 5s. a yard, and the merchant's letter about it survives in the family papers:

> Madam, the sarcenet is very fine. I think most profitable and most worshipful for you, and shall last you your life and your child's after you, whereas harlotry [cheap, showy stuff] of 3s. 4d. or 3s. 5d. a yard would not endure two seasons with you. Therefore for a little more cost, me thinketh most wisdom to take of the best . . . I win never a penny in that.[8]

When textiles were so dear to buy, it is no wonder that, like most wealthy people, the Stonors clad their children and servants in homespun, that is, in cloth from their own wool, spun in the house and woven and dyed for them in the nearest town. But this was probably of a very loose, poor texture; the sort that Piers Plowman describes, 'unless a louse could have leapt a little she could never have walked on so thread-bare a weave'.

One of the most important commodities that brought people to fairs was wine, which was cheaper and more widely drunk then than it has ever been since. It has been estimated that those favoured officers of the Duke of Clarence who were entitled to take wine with their meals drank, in 1461, about a gallon a week per head. It was sold retail in taverns in the larger towns

[8] C. L. Kingsford, ed., *The Stonor Letters and Papers* (Camden Society, 1919), II, 90.

3(b). Trade card of Benjamin Cole, about
1700.

3(a). Trade card of Susannah Fordham,
about 1700.

4. New Exchange in 1772.

both for drinking on the premises and for carrying home, just as ale was sold in ale-houses although it was not so common as ale. But the price this way ran at around 18d. a gallon, and it was much cheaper to buy it by the barrel at the annual fair. The wine nearly all came from Gascony, for many centuries a province of the English crown. Some Rhine wine was drunk and a little of the rather dearer Spanish and Greek wines. For instance, that same Duke of Clarence whose servants drank a gallon of wine a week was the one who was murdered in the Tower by the future Richard III; his 'butt of Malmsey', in which Shakespeare found it convenient to drown him, was choice Cretan wine, most suitable for a Duke. More ordinary folk, however, only bought the sweet wines in small quantities from the apothecary for use as medicine.[9]

Wine-making was a crude affair in those days, and because it could only be stored in the cask it was a perishable commodity. We read of whole grapes and much lees going into a cask and of its continuing to ferment after sealing and having to be thrown away after a few months because it 'boiled and stank'. Spanish wine was exceptional, sometimes keeping for two or even three years, but most was sour and feeble after a year, so there were laws forbidding taverners to keep old stock in their cellars after the new wine arrived. In a bad year it was said to be common for a taverner to have to throw away as much as half his consignment because it had gone bad, and 'corrupt' wine was often confiscated to be given, in easy charity, to the poor, or (what was much more fun) poured over the taverner's head as he stood in the pillory.

So the competent housewife needed to understand what she was buying from a wine merchant—or from any merchant, for many people dealt in wine. Prices varied with every grape harvest, and they rose steeply and permanently in 1453 when new customs-barriers marked the conquest of the vineyard area by France. But local varieties meant nothing as yet to the English consumer, and the common Gascony wine, red or white, cost the same from anywhere in south-west France. The main difference was between the 'vintage' or new wine, brought over in hazard of the winter gales as soon as it was made, and the 'racked' or

[9] John Taylor, the Water Poet, 'The Life of Thomas Parr', C. Hindley, *The Old Book Collector's Miscellany* (1873), III, 26.

matured wine which had been allowed to settle, had the lees removed, and been sent over the following April, its slightly enhanced
price being generally offset by the cheaper summer voyage. So
most people bought their supplies at the late autumn fairs or the
summer fairs. But like everything else at that time, wine was
often tampered with by unscrupulous dealers. White wine was
dyed and doctored to fetch more money sold as red Spanish wine.
Spanish, in its turn, was treated with gum and resin to give it
the characteristic taste of the still more expensive Greek product.
In 1419 the City of London proclaimed against the sellers of
'broken, sodden, reboiled and unthrifty wines . . . when they are
enfeebled in colour and nought in value, put in divers butts and
other vessells that are razed [scratched] and gummed with
pitch, cobbler's wax and other horrible and unwholesome
things, for to produce and bring again, in deceit of the people, a
pleasant colour to the sight and a likely manner drinking of
Romney to the smell and taste'.[10] *Caveat emptor.*

In the middle ages, the wife of a country gentleman of substance had to work and plan very hard indeed to feed and clothe
her family and servants, for she could not simply lay out a cash
income to buy all she needed; she was expected to make full use
of the produce of scattered farms or estates from which her
husband was entitled to draw supplies and only supplement these
resources by purchases in the local market and annual fair—and
occasionally, if she lived near enough, from the capital. One
difficulty about laying in stores at the fair was that the private
person was expected to pay cash, and ready cash seems always
to have been in short supply even in families which, by the
standards of the day, were quite wealthy. William Stonor was
constantly in debt to his tradesmen and servants, and he once
pawned the family plate with the local parson, although we know
that he was rich, a big landowner, sheriff of the county, member of
parliament and trusted servant of the king. Here is how one of
his servants wrote to him after he had been on a visit to London:

> . . . Furthermore, sir, your mastership shall understand that the
> ale-brewer calls on me daily sore for money, the which I have
> written unto your mastership aforetime. The sum is £5 and odd
> money, the which he beseaches your mastership he may have some

[10] H. T. Riley, *Memorials of London and London Life* (1868), p. 670.

money in hand unto the time that your mastership shall come unto London. Also sir, I beseach your mastership that you will remember your bread baker in London, for he calls upon me daily for money, the which sum is 35s. 3d.[11]

Other families of rank and importance suffered this same chronic shortage of ready cash in spite of owning much real wealth and it must have added considerably to the difficulties of housekeeping.

The annual buying spree had one feature very curious to modern eyes; the overwhelming majority of the goods people bought were consumables, food and drink, clothes and candles, raw materials to be expended in the coming year. Durable goods, on the other hand, figure very little in the surviving literature. Part of the reason, no doubt, was that objects in metal and wood were more usually commissioned from local craftsmen to be made from the customer's own materials, than bought ready made. Nevertheless it is abundantly clear where the heart of the medieval housekeeper lay; if he had little money he spent it all on his stomach; if he had plenty, he lavished most of it on his stomach and the rest on his back. Far below these in importance came the beauty and comfort of his surroundings, which seem to have made little claim on his purse. If he thought of his heirs, he thought of land; but such things as silver and porcelain, sculpture and carving, tapestry and stained glass were considered more suitable for the house of God than the house of man.

Take, for example, lighting. There were two sorts of lighting in common use, wax candles and tallow candles. The former, made from imported material, cost about 6d. or 8d. a pound but gave a clear, brilliant light. Tallow candles, on the other hand, cost only 1d. a pound but were very inferior. Nevertheless, wax candles were burned in churches and private chapels and the tallow ones were used at home. William Stonor spent as much as $3\frac{1}{2}$d. a week, on the average, on wax candles for his private chapel; what his domestic lighting cost we do not know for he probably made his tallow candles at home like most people. In short, the prevailing attitude to domestic comfort in general is nicely implied in a remark from Fitzherbert's famous *Book of Husbandry* warning people against sitting by the fire in the

[11] *The Stonor Letters and Papers, op. cit.*, II, 61.

evening; he takes it for granted that this will not be done for pleasure. 'Consider in thy mind whether the work that thou, thy wife and thy servants shall do be more advantage to thee than the fire and candle-light meat and drink that they shall spend.'

Although the houses of the well-to-do as revealed in household accounts and inventories seem bare and insufficient to modern eyes, we should not forget the state of the vast majority of the homes of the time. These were damp, draughty huts, built by their occupiers of wattle and daub, with earth floors, without window or chimney, and for kitchen, an iron pot and a spit over the open hearth. Beds were a heap of straw or bracken on the damp floor, fuel often scarce, and cleanliness unheard of and impossible. These were not their hardships—merely the ordinary circumstances of the poorer peasants. The English were said to 'live like lords' compared with their opposite numbers in Europe, but the comparison probably referred to their diet rather than to their other circumstances. 'Hardship' was hunger, and it was familiar not only to the sick and the widowed and the specially unfortunate, but intermittently to most of the poor who lived precariously from one harvest to the next. If they had any money to spare after selling a beast or some of their corn at the local fair and buying essential tar or salt or malt, they spent it on a hot feast at the cook's stall and then on some hard or pickled fish for the fasting days to come. If the peasant had a few sheep he might take some wool of his wife's spinning to a weaver to have it woven to make clothes. If he were a little more prosperous, he would buy shoes, linen, and perhaps some spice.

Between the mansion and the cottage, houses of the middling sort were relatively scarce; apart from those of the occasional parish priest and other minor clergy, the landlords' bailiffs or agents and a few prosperous peasants, they were mainly the houses of the better sort of town craftsmen and merchants. The lives of this middle class are not so well recorded as those of their social superiors, though they probably relied more on shopping for their daily needs, and less on the resources of their own lands than any other class of people. In many towns, the leading citizens still owned land around the city walls, grazed animals on the town common and shut up their shops to go harvesting until well into the fifteenth century. Even while towns and trade were growing, the preference for self-sufficiency died hard. Yet it was possible for those living in or near a town to buy all their needs if they wished, and a record has survived of one middle-class household that did so.

Miss K. L. Wood-Legh has reproduced the account books of two priests who lived with their single manservant in a minor chantry in Dorset.[12] Their housekeeping cost about £11 10s. a year, a comfortable sum for two elderly men with few visitors. They owned a garden with a pigeon cote, a vine and some fruit trees in which they probably grew some vegetables for they once bought onion seed. Everything else was bought, including even bread and ale, and the sums spent were noted down each week. Here are two typical weeks in October:

> 3rd week after Michaelmas, Bread 9d., Ale 12d., Meat 10d., Fish 6d., Total 3s. 1d. 4th week after Michaelmas, Bread 6d., Ale 10d., Meat 10d., Fish 6d., Oatmeal 3d., Candle 1d., Total 2s. 11d.

Two weeks in Lent, by way of contrast:

> 1st wk. after Ladyday, Bread 7d., Ale 9d., Fresh fish 10d., Total 2s. 2d. 2nd wk. after Ladyday, Bread 8d., Ale 10½d., Fish 10d., Total 2s. 4½d.

These were their regular weekly purchases. Luxuries through the seasons of the year went something like these for 1457–8:

> *October*, none. *November*, Raisins & Eggs 1d. *December*, Eggs 2d., Pork brawn 12d., Piglet for Christmas 5d. *January*, Raisins & Eggs 3½d., Piglet 3d. *February*, Figs 14d., Cinnamon 2d., Mustard 1d. *March*, plenty of fresh fish, apparently as gifts. *April*, Milk & Butter 2½d., Cheese 5½d., *May*, Milk & Butter & Cheese 10d., Eggs 2d. *June*, Milk & Butter 2½d., Cheese 5½d. *July*, Cheese 7d., Honey (half gallon) 8d. *August*, Whiting 12d., Peas, Beans & Pears 1½d., Cheese 2d. *September*, Crabapples 2d., Cheese ½d.

Wine was bought only for mass in chapel and to entertain their occasional visitors, and a ½d. or 1d. worth of rushes for the floor came four times a year. Altogether a wasteful and extravagant method of attaining a very modest standard of living.

12 K. L. Wood-Legh, *A Small Household of the Fifteenth Century* (1956), *passim*.

Far removed from peasant or humble priest or even substantial gentlemen like William Stonor was the wealthy nobleman or prelate with a large establishment of retainers, living in a style modelled on that of the royal household. Even up to early Tudor times when rents and feudal services had nearly all been converted into money payments of hard cash, a really big household found it difficult to live permanently in one place and buy everything needed in the open market without exhausting the supplies. The medieval practice for a large establishment was to keep it constantly on the move, using up the resources of the various farms in turn:

> Every year at Michaelmas, when you know the measure of all your corn, then arrange your sojurn for the whole year, and for how many weeks in each place, according to the seasons of the year and the advantages of the country in flesh and fish. And do not in any wise burden by debt or long residence the places where you sojurn, but so arrange your sojurns that the place, at your departure, shall not remain in debt but something may remain on the manor whereby the manor can raise money from increase of stock, and especially cows and sheep, until your stock aquits [pays for] your wines, robes, wax and all your wardrobe . . .[13]

One such wealthy nobleman was the Earl of Northumberland who lived at the end of the fifteenth century on his estates in Yorkshire, Durham and Northumberland. 'The North knows no prince but a Percy' it was said. His Household Book[14] describes the housekeeping for 166 people. This huge number—and the great estates that it implied 'with everything proportionable'—was the status symbol of the 'top person', more significant than either rank or income. The head officers of the various departments of the household were all knights each with several personal servants and a page of his own, for while real wars and pitched battles were rare events in a man's life, responsible people had to be found all the year round to help with estate management and running the daily life within the castle walls. When household 'shopping' was to be done, these were the people who did it. The purchasing of supplies fell into two parts.

[13] Walter of Henley, *Husbandry* (ed. E. Lamond, 1890), p. 145.
[14] Thomas Percy, ed., *The Northumberland Household Book* (1905).

There were the basic necessities bought in quantity at long intervals, and there were the small extra luxuries that were sought for the family and members of the High Table, and 'shopped around' for week by week.

For the basic necessities, the Head Clerk of the Household, the most important of the officials, would take a few servants and ride out, seven or eight times a year, to attend not merely one fair but several. It is probable that the fairs in the north country were smaller affairs than in the more populous south. The highlights of the medieval calendar, Michaelmas and Allhallows, Christmas and Candlemas, Easter and Whitsuntide, brought round the fairs that were the occasions for these journeys. At Candlemas, in February, salt fish for Lent was the chief objective for which he would probably go to the coast to get as many varieties of pickled and dried fish as possible. He may have dealt with the same sellers year after year, but he certainly sniffed and poked and haggled, knowing he would have to justify every penny he spent when he got back. This was also the season for buying a dozen or so good-looking lean pigs, a few here and a few there, where they could be driven to the various residences and put to fatten until required on stubble or in woods. A few specially fat ones would be marked for cosseting through Lent with household leavings, with pea-husks or even with corn, ready for the Easter rejoicings. Finally, three-quarters of a ton of white English-mined salt was bought for the table from a merchant who must have carted the heavy barrels over the Pennines from Cheshire; a barrel of Spanish olive oil for frying Lenten fish, this time probably from a merchant from London; a few hops from across the North Sea for summer beer; and a barrel each of foreign figs, raisins and spices for Lent.

At Easter, a six months' supply of wheat, a hundred-odd quarters, was needed, and this probably drew him south to Yorkshire or beyond. Wheat bought in quantity at this season needed careful choosing for it might be going bad. Then a dozen tons of malt for half a year's ale and three dozen lean bullocks and a hundred-odd sheep for fattening. The sheep on offer were the spring throw-outs from flocks kept principally for their wool —that is, the ageing or weak or diseased; healthy sheep in their prime were scarce and sold for breeding, not for food. So the Head Clerk needed to have with him on this trip a good sheepman who could judge which sheep would survive the long trek home and stay alive to fatten without trouble. A hundred-odd pounds of beeswax from the Baltic for chapel candles; half a ton of coarse Bay salt (that is sea-evaporated) for preserving; fifty quarters of oats for summer horse-fodder, all pasture being needed for stock in those sparse north-country meadows; and more barrels of whatever spices he could get completed the Easter business at the fairs.

By Whitsuntide the wine left in the various cellars was getting sour, and the best racked wine, newly over from France, was finding its way about the country. About twenty hogsheads were due to be sampled, haggled over and finally bought, probably from a number of different merchants. Two hundred hard salt cod, fifty new lambs, and forty-five gallons of crabapple juice, known as verjuice, constituted the rest of the Whitsun shopping, except for the usual search for spices.

At midsummer he went out again for the new hops for his lordship's special beer, more Bay salt and spices, and then he watched the harvests, and the prices in his local markets, assessing the chances for Michaelmas when he set off on his travels in earnest to undertake the really large-scale buying of the year. Wheat, malt, oats, all in quantity for the winter. Beef cattle this time were wanted fat, since feed was scarce in the winter; he wanted over a hundred of them and seven hundred-odd fat sheep and a few pigs, all to be driven home. Most of the year's purchase of pigs took place in the spring, when they could be fattened cheaply on plentiful feed, whereas sheep and cattle were bought for food largely in the autumn when they had fulfilled their other uses as draught animals or wool-bearers or milk-givers for the season and were to be had most cheaply. The autumn was not a time for the wholesale slaughter of animals, but it was the time for the weeding out of old and unproductive stock and selling it for food, and while much of this was butchered and salted at once, a large establishment such as this one would try to keep as much as possible of its food stock alive until wanted, according to the severity of the winter and the availability of hay, oats, corn and horse bread.

The rest of the Michaelmas buying included more Bay salt for preserving, more fine white English salt, and dried salt cod and salmon in great bulk for the winter fast days. A six months' supply of the vintage wine was also required, barrels of Baltic honey and wax, and some cotton for making the wicks of next year's candles. Finally, he needed more mustard, verjuice, and a really big effort with the everlasting spices to make all the rest eatable. Christmastide was not an important buying season, but some luxuries were in order; resin for festive torches, more wax for a special brilliance of candles even in the private chambers, more honey and oil. And the Christmas festivities would last until Candlemas and the preparations for Lent came round once more.

This was the yearly round for whoever was Head Clerk, and a strenuous and responsible one it was. He was not encouraged to delegate the job to a subordinate: '. . . if he may possible, shall be at all Fairs where Gross Empcions [wholesale purchases] shall be bought for the house for the whole year, as wine, wax, beefs, muttons, wheat, malt, etc. and if he may not, then to appoint the Clerk Controller with such other Persons as he thinks good to go to the said Fairs . . .' We can only guess what personal commissions his less mobile colleagues—to say nothing of the ladies—thrust upon this busy man, so constantly in touch with the great world, while in between his fair-going he would have to see that his purchases were brought home and stored in safety and issued methodically.

On each return from an arduous journey he had to sit down in his chambers in Wressle Castle or wherever they were living and take out his box of coloured counters and reckon up his sums before presenting detailed accounts to the Earl. The use of counters or the occasional abacus for doing figures should not raise a smile in the days of adding machines. Even a straight-forward long multiplication was a tongue twister in roman numerals, and there was nothing straightforward about quantities in long-hundreds, scores and dozens instead of units, tens and hundreds, nor about prices quoted in pence, marks (13s. 4d.) and nobles (6s. 8d.), with a scattering of continental coins in the money bag for good measure. Only the reader who can reckon up easily how much he would owe for cciiijxx gallons of ale at a halfpenny and a farthing a gallon and, without resorting to arabic numerals, get the correct answer of three nobles,[15] can afford to feel superior upon learning that medieval account

[15] Long hundreds, of course.

books are full of errors (like that in the extract from the Dorset priests' journal, quoted above).

From time to time, the Earl's household equipment, such as linen, stone jars or brass pots, needed replacement, with which, no doubt, the steward or some minor official was entrusted. The Comptroller of the House, and the Clerk of the Kitchen were jointly charged with the hiring (from whom, there is no mention) of a long-hundred dozen of 'rough pewter vessels' each year, forty dozen each for the festivals of Christmas, Easter and Whitsuntide, at the rate of fourpence a dozen, to replace the home-made wooden trenchers and leather drinking jacks in normal use. The occasional outright purchase of pewter or silver for the High Table might well have engaged the attention of the Earl himself, as it was not attributed to anyone in particular. Nor was the buying of fuel, which was apparently a low-grade, routine job; it consisted of coal from the coast nearby, great wood, kindling ('which is because coals will not burn without wood'), and faggots from the forest for brewhouse and bakery.

The Earl was obliged to trust his highest officials to bargain wisely at fairs, but he himself kept an eye on any large purchases made by the less exalted Clerk of the Kitchen:

> Afore they make any manner of Grosse Empcion . . . that they make my Lord privy thereto, afore the bargain be concluded, to the intent that they may know whether his lordship will agree to the said prices or not . . .

The Clerk of the Kitchen and his 'Cator' or caterer were responsible for the fresh provisions; the markets rather than the fairs were their province. Dairy produce, poultry, wild birds, game, and fresh fish all ranked as luxurious extras and it was the caterer's job to buy these in small quantities or 'parcels' for immediate consumption. He collected what he could from the Earl's own land and he bought the rest in the local markets. But instead of having a budget within which to use his own initiative, he was restricted by a long list of 'don'ts'.

> Capons to be bought only for my lord's consumption when not above 2d. each lean, and fed in the poultry. Chamberlain and Stewards to be served with capons only when entertaining guests. Pigs only to be bought at the rate of 3d. or 4d. each, at the rate

of one pig to four persons. Chickens to be bought for my lord's consumption only, or when ½d. each for Chamberlain and Steward only . . .

Maximum prices were fixed for thirty-one birds all told, domestic and wild, including several unlikely sea-birds such as oyster-catchers. As in all medieval accounts, small game were far less important than birds; hares were never mentioned and rabbits seem dear at 2d. While there were several popular ways of catching birds—snaring, shooting and hawking—men may have been less skilful with small wild animals.

The Chief Caterer's standing orders also included the following:

> It is thought good that all manner of wildfowl be bought at the first hand where they be gotten, and a Cator to be appointed for the same. For it is thought that the poulterers of Hemmyngburghe and Clyfe hath great advantage of my Lord, yearly, of Selling of Cunys (rabbits) and Wildfowl . . .
>
> The Cator to go abroad in the country weekly for buying of stuff in such places as is thought it shall be best cheap, and to buy it seldomest about where my lord lieth, except it may be had as good cheap there as other where.

Although the Caterer's accounts show a lot of fresh food as if it were purchased at current prices, there is no doubt that much of this is only book-keeping and that it came in fact from the Earl's tenants or the bailiffs of his own farms. He kept two falconers and a huntsman whose main business was probably sport, but they supplied, among other things, forty-nine deer each year for the table. There was no dairying done; butter and cheese are not mentioned, and in the (presumably unlikely) event of any eggs or milk being bought, the Caterer was bidden to present a bill at the year's end. Fruit and vegetables were also ignored except for a ban on buying any 'seeing that the Cooks may have herbs enough in my lord's gardens'.

This shopping list reveals a diet of appalling monotony. Though ample by any standards, and lavish by the standards of the time, it only allowed the majority of the household to share in the fresh meat delicacies of the High Table at the three chief feasts of the year. At other times it showed an overwhelming preponderance of salt meat and salt fish with a virtual absence of fresh fruit or vegetables. It is not altogether surprising that scurvy was a common complaint. Root vegetables like potatoes, carrots and parsnips were unknown and cabbage, peas and beans were fit only for animals' food or for beggars. There used to be a popular notion that medieval barons dined invariably on succulent roast joints and enormous sirloins, but these dishes really came in much later times. A little plain roast meat was eaten, but most of it was not tender or fresh enough for roasting. Moreover, the prevailing taste in food, as in so many other things, was crude almost to the point of barbarity, and the most appreciated dishes were highly coloured and strongly spiced. 'The prevailing desire of the medieval cook,' it has been said, 'was to reduce everything to a fine pulp—hew it small and grind it well.'[16] So the fashion was for stews and purées of minced and sieved meats, hotly flavoured and coloured violet, red or yellow to resemble the original ingredients as little as possible and not remind the eater of the stringy oxen worn out at the plough, the stockfish dried hard like a board, that were the common foundation of ordinary meals.

The annual shopping list for this household that is reproduced here is incomplete in several ways. For example, no allowance is made for the very valuable leather and sheep skins he would get from the slaughtered animals and which was certainly put to a thousand uses, although he 'buys' the tallow from the slaughter-house for making domestic candles. He allows 'rent' to his own meadows for fattening stock for the larder, but does not include the true cost of his own fresh fish and swans and venison although there are hints that he allows for these in his reckonings with his bailiffs and tenants. It is, in fact, one more illustration of the fact that medieval organization cannot be forced into the strait-jacket of modern accounting. Nevertheless, on its own terms it is businesslike enough and when, as here, we see a clear and intelligent mind planning the buying for a big household, it is obvious that the primitive state of trade and the prevailing scarcity of supplies, so far from simplifying matters, posed problems of a complexity that the modern householder would gladly be spared.

[16] Anon., 'Old English Cookery', *Quarterly Review*, CLXXVIII, (1894), pp. 82–104.

A YEAR'S SHOPPING FOR 166 PERSONS FROM THE NORTHUMBERLAND HOUSEHOLD BOOK (1512)

		£	s.	d.	£	s.	d.
1. Meat							
Beef,	109 fat						
	34 for fattening	86	5	4			
Sheep,	906	68	12	2			
Pigs,	25	50	0	0			
Calves,	28	46	8	0			
Lambs,	60	2	11	8			
					253	17	2
2. Fish							
Stockfish, (dried) 140		1	13	3			
Salt cod, 1,600		18	14	0			
Salt herring, 19 barrels		4	10	0			
Red herring, 10 barrels		3	3	4			
Salt sprats, 5 barrels			10	0			
Salt salmon, 200		5	0	0			
Salt sturgeon, 3 firkins		1	10	0			
Salt eels, 30 (bunches)		1	0	0			
					36	0	7
3. Wheat							
59 tons					78	16	8
4. Drink							
Malt, 27 tons		49	16	6			
Hops, ½ ton		3	13	4			
Wine, 42 hogsheads		49	0	0			
					102	9	10
5. Salt							
3¾ tons					3	6	0

Carried forward

6. *Seasoning*	£	s.	d.	£	s.	d.
Honey, 1½ barrels	1	13	0			
Oil, 1½ barrels	1	13	3			
Verjuice (crabapple juice) 90 gallons	1	2	6			
Mustard, 180 gallons	1	14	4			
Vinegar, 40 gallons ('from myne owne lags')		13	4			
Foreign Spices (ginger, turnsole, liquorice, saffron, etc., etc., 23 varieties)	26	12	11			
				33	9	4

7. *Lights*						
Wax, 327 lbs. (for devotional candles)	12	5	7			
Resin, 39 lbs. (for torches)		4	10			
Tallow, 1,094 lbs. (for candles)	4	11	2			
Cotton wick, 51 lbs.		8	6			
				17	10	1

8. *Fuel*						
Coal, 200 tons	19	3	4			
Charcoal, 5 tons	1	0	0			
Kindling wood (64 loads, plus carriage)	3	4	0			
Faggots, 3,500 (Brewery and Bakehouse)	4	12	2			
				27	19	6

9. *Equipment*						
Stone jars, 240		10	0			
Rough pewter vessels hired for feasts	2	0	0			
— — — bought for feast days	2	0	0			
Two silver-plated vessels (for feast days)	3	10	0			
Two brass pots	1	6	4			
Linen (for tables and kitchen) 70 yards	2	6	8			
Armoury (buckles, leather, nails, emery and oil)	1	0	0			
Fletcher (feathers, wax, glue, silk, etc.)	1	0	0			
Bowyer (horne, glue, etc.)	1	0	0			
				14	13	0

Carried forward

10. *Horses*	£	s.	d.	£	s.	d.
Oats, 25 ton	10	0	0			
Shoeing	3	12	0			
Pasture rent	16	6	0			
				29	18	0

11. *Wages*						
Laundry (household, not personal)	2	6	8			
Haymaking for horse fodder	11	0	0			
Priests, etc. in private chapel	35	15	0			
Household staff	153	6	7			
Allowances to feed servants' horses	32	0	0			
				234	8	3

12. *Extras*						
Poultry and wild birds (26 varieties) for High Table and Feast Days only				105	15	4

13. *From My Lord's own Estates*						
Fresh-water fish				—	—	—
20 Swans				—	—	—
20 Bucks				—	—	—
29 Does				—	—	—
Total				938	3	9

QUEEN ELIZABETH TO QUEEN ANNE

III

◇◇◇◇◇◇◇◇◇◇◇◇◇◇◇◇◇◇◇◇◇◇◇◇◇◇◇◇◇◇◇◇◇◇◇◇◇

New Beginnings in Retail Distribution

◇◇◇◇◇◇◇◇◇◇◇◇◇◇◇◇◇◇◇◇◇◇◇◇◇◇◇◇◇◇◇◇◇◇◇◇◇

> There is such a calling for fardingales, kirtles, busk-points, shoe-ties, etc. that seven pedlar's shops—nay all Stourbridge Fair—will scarce furnish her.
>
> <div align="right">Peter Stubbes, <i>Anatomie of Abuses</i>, 1583</div>

I F a critical point can be discerned in the slow evolution of retail trade, then its date is the epoch of Elizabeth I and the early Stuarts; its place, London. It is here that we get the first glimpses of consumers feeling a new authority in their purses, a new confidence in the exercise of choice. Hitherto, the scarcities and local shortages and the general inefficiency of everything connected with distribution had resulted, generally speaking, in a seller's market and the buyer was accustomed to scant respect in the market-place. But now, retailing began to come of age and to take seriously the business of wooing the consumer. Something that we nowadays recognize as shopping had begun. It did not, of course, happen overnight and even in this era of rapid change many Londoners did not realize that anything especially new was happening, but looking back it is clear that decisive developments were taking place.

Why at this particular time and in this particular city did the slow process of change suddenly accelerate? The answer in brief is, because there was a conjunction of three important circumstances: there were more people, there were more wealthy people, and there were more luxury goods available from abroad. These three profound changes, all happening together,

55

worked a transformation in London's retail trade in a couple of generations. But before we come to consider it in the next two chapters and to see how the new shopping patterns that emerged affected the consumer, it will be as well to pause and look more closely at these three causes of change and at the immediate effect they had on retailers and their suppliers as well as on the attitude of the authorities to retail trading.

Among all the social changes of this era, none is more striking than the five- or six-fold increase in London's population, from perhaps 60 thousand in 1540 to 300–400 thousand a century later, and the great extension of London's built-up area that went with it. London's nearest rival, Norwich, was no more than a fifth of the size in 1540 and it stood still while London was going ahead. Contemporaries were not particularly happy about the enlargement of the capital; then as now, the authorities that administered it found that its problems grew even faster than its size, while other cities feared that 'London is going to eat up all England'. Nevertheless, for the first time England had a great city and as a market for consumer goods it was unique. Much of the change and innovation in retailing that took place there is simply due to this fact.

But not all. For population size is not the only factor in creating consumer demand; equally important is purchasing power. London during this time began to contain not only many more customers, but many more rich customers than had been gathered in one spot before. The provinces increasingly felt the pull of the capital's progress. Not only were more of their products drawn up to London for export, and more of their farmers being stimulated by the opportunities of the London market to specialize in supplying it with food, but more people of substance were being attracted from the countryside into the capital, either as visitors or as permanent residents, and bringing money and their custom with them. Court life became more competitive, more ostentatious and more extravagant, while the practice of visiting London to transact business at the centre of affairs or to taste the pleasures of London society was causing more and more country gentlemen and their wives to spend on a spree in London the extra purchasing powers that they accumulated from plain living in the country.

Experience teacheth that the residence of noblemen in cities makes them to be more glorious and more populous . . . by cause a nobleman spendeth much more largely through the accesse of friends unto him and through the emulation of others in a City where he is abiding and visited continually by honourable personages than he spendeth in the country where he liveth among the brute beasts of the field and converseth with plain country people and goes apparrelled among them in plain and simple garments.[1]

The attraction of London for the well-to-do was not, of course, wholly new, but in the last two decades of the sixteenth century, increasing prosperity enabled more people to respond to it.

However, the new prosperity was not for everyone for it was accompanied by renewed attacks of the strange economic disease that first appeared in the mid-sixteenth century and for which the Elizabethans had no name and no cure; prices had nearly doubled between 1543 and 1551, and then, after two decades of stability and before people were thoroughly reconciled to the higher levels, they started up again in 1570, doubling again by 1620. When the process finally worked itself out in the 1620s and 30s the value of money stabilized at a level roughly one-tenth of present-day prices and stayed that way until the stresses of the Napoleonic Wars. The upheavals of such a prolonged rise in prices, uneven and unsettling as they were, played their part in creating a new social climate in London, by putting money into new hands. 'I grew to consider,' wrote Nashe in 1592, 'how many base men had wealth at command. I called to minde a Cobler that was worth five hundred pounds, an Hostler that had built a goodly Inne and might dispende forty pound yearly at his hand, a Carre-man [carter] in a leather pilche [leather trousers] that had whipped out a thousand pound out of his horse tail.'[2] On a different level, opportunities for land speculation or business ventures were hopeful; fortunes were being lost and made. All this encouraged people to spend freely, either to display new wealth or sometimes, even more recklessly, to bolster a waning credit.

Most of the gentry who now came permanently or for the

---

[1] G. Botero, *A treatise Concerning the Causes of Magnificence and Greatness in Cities*, quoted in F. J. Fisher 'The Development of London as a Centre of Conspicuous Consumption', *Trans. Roy. Hist. Soc.*, 4th ser., XXX (1948), p. 63.

[2] Thomas Nashe, *Works* (ed. R. McKerrow, 1910), I, 158.

winter months to London had seen their own fathers keep state in the country all the year round, supporting large households with plentiful provisions and the poor at the gate with bread and the generous leavings of the table. This sort of expenditure stopped when the wealthy landowner came to London; the large establishments dispersed and the houses were shut down. 'Mock-beggar Hall' was the ballad-singers' gibe against the country mansion shut up for the winter.[3] Queen Elizabeth, in 1596, ordered home all those who had come 'with covetous minds to live in London and about the Citie privately . . . without charge of company'. But neither the claims of old-fashioned charity at home, nor the frowns of the government in London, could stop the nobility and gentry coming and spending extravagantly and competitively on food, entertainment and clothes. And in their train came new, permanent migrants to the capital; the impoverished hangers-on, the fortune hunters and younger sons, the displaced peasants and ambitious craftsmen, the alien refugees from the Continent. And all these newcomers, in their hundreds a year, poor as well as rich, temporary or permanent, helped in their various ways to transform the retail trade of London; the rich, by the impetus that their new tastes gave to the provision of luxury goods; the poor by transforming with their labour the supply of manufactures; and rich and poor alike by the reforms that sheer numbers forced upon the organization of the food supply.

Compared with any town that had been known hitherto, Elizabethan London was socially top-heavy, and it is not altogether surprising that the demands of this new society for luxury goods, particularly for everything connected with dress and personal adornment, should have been very great. A man moving among strangers in a striving, competitive age needed to proclaim his status in the most obvious manner possible. 'To be an accomplished gentleman—that is a gentleman of the time—' says one of the characters in Ben Jonson's *Every Man Out of His Humour*, 'you must give over housekeeping in the country and live altogether in the City among gallants, where at your first appearance t'were good you turned four or five acres of your best land into two or three trunks of apparell.'[4] This was not dramatic hyperbole

---

[3] W. Chappell, ed., *Roxburghe Ballads* (1871), pp. 155–7.
[4] Ben Jonson, *Every Man Out of His Humour*, Act I, Scene i.

but wholly sound advice. Clothes were, as he implied, an investment rather than a charge on current income; they would be sold, in due course, and re-sold many times thereafter, repaired, re-trimmed, unpicked and turned until worn to extinction. To spend the equivalent of a modern seven or eight hundred pounds on a wardrobe and to renew it at frequent intervals was an outlay which, if few could truly afford, fewer still if they had any claim to gentility could afford to neglect. The current literature is full of stories on the theme of the many who 'have broke their backs with laying houses on 'em', or 'beggared his belly to make his back a gentleman'.[5] The Earl of Leicester paid —or was charged—£543 for seven doublets and two cloaks; he died a bankrupt.[6]

This passion for fancy dress did not merely create more work for native weavers and tailors. It created a demand, highly concentrated within the city's square mile, for manufactures of all kinds, from swords and daggers to felt hats and dyed feathers, from gold and silver lace to starch and embroidery, from fans and masks to buckles and jewellery. And as is always the case, the more frivolous the demand, the more exacting the buyers and the more profitable the role of the distributor. While Elizabethan houses and furniture and public buildings were characterized by solid comfort and sober good sense, there was a wild exuberance about their dress and its accessories that expressed the buoyant spirits and soaring optimism of the times. If there was a higher compliment to be paid to an article of dress than 'Pray, what did you pay for it?' it was 'Pray, where did you get it?' And the highest praise was 'far-fetched', meaning—literally—just that. People demanded goods with the stamp of Italy or Spain or Flanders about them.[7]

Merchants were not slow to exploit such an undiscriminating passion for the exotic. Not all foreign goods were first-class; not all first-class goods were foreign. When the alien refugee craftsmen came to England in the sixteenth and seventeenth centuries, they began producing fine fabrics, lace, goldsmiths' work and leather-work in England, and much of their output

---

[5] Nashe, *op. cit.*, I, 170.
[6] L. Stone, 'The Anatomy of the Elizabethan Aristocracy', *Econ. Hist. Rev.*, XVIII (1948), p. 5.
[7] P. Stubbes, *Anatomie of Abuses* (ed. F. J. Furnivall, 1877), pt. I, pp. 49–62.

was marketed as foreign, and claimed by its proud purchasers to be 'from beyond the sea, far-fetched and dear-bought'.

All this new wine would not go into the old bottles of commerce. By this time, merchants were beginning to abandon their old function of being buyers and sellers of all things to all men, and beginning to deal in larger quantities of a narrower range of goods. Now that goods were becoming more plentiful, the business of stocking and serving a retail shop was becoming an increasingly profitable specialization. We begin to hear about 'the rich retailers'. Stow, in 1603, describing the city's business men says, 'In wealth, merchants and some of the chief retailers have first place.'[8] It was possible now to stock more specialized shops and to claim that a retail shop demanded 'a full stock and a full attendance', and although we may not entirely believe the writer who claimed 'A merchant cannot be a retailer for want of skill and acquaintance with customers, which requires an apprenticeship to bring them into it',[9] still, there is no doubt that shopkeeping, as distinct from random trading and the keeping of a miscellaneous warehouse, was becoming an important occupation.

By the early seventeenth century, the smaller of these shopkeepers had become 'petty tradesmen', or true retailers in the modern sense, while the more substantial ones still made little distinction between wholesale and retail selling since the selling of goods to traders in the provinces remained an important part of their business. The change from medieval times was not that the new retailers always dealt in smaller quantities than their predecessors, but that they had become—and were called— 'shopmen', with their shops the scene of their chief activities. 'The merchant to his accounts and the shopman to "What lack you?"'[10]

But shopkeepers were appearing in other ways too. Besides those who had divided off from the merchant class, selling by retail the kind of goods brought from overseas (though often in fact made in London) other retailers arose from among the craftsmen class, and in the long run this was the more important development. There had always been some handicraft workers

[8] J. Stow, *Survey of London* (Everyman edition), p. 492.
[9] *Calendar of State Papers, Domestic, Addenda 1566–79*, p. 344.
[10] Nicholas Breton, *Fantastickes*, quoted in J. W. Dover Wilson, *Life in Shakespeare's England* (1926), p. 277.

who could not afford to rent a City house and shop, and merchant haberdashers had, from very early times, been the salesmen for the working capmakers, pin- and needlemakers, girdlers and so forth. In the major crafts, too, there had always been some working pewterers, for example, or goldsmiths or leatherworkers who sold, besides their own and their apprentices' handiwork, the output of a few poorer colleagues who were not householders—that is, did not have their own shops. . . . But the majority of skilled craftsmen had been their own salesmen.

However, in the century before the Civil War, the proportion of artisan craftsmen working for wages increased very sharply; a sign of this was the many charitable endowments which were made to 'set up' young journeymen in trade by granting them loans to buy stock. But though charity could help a few individuals to set up shop in the time-honoured way, it could not alter the general trend. As the number of artisans increased, they overflowed into the suburbs, into the overcrowded cottages that sprang up in a ring close round the City walls from Stepney and Shoreditch to Clerkenwell, Westminster and Southwark. Here they were joined by the migrant craftsmen from the provinces and the alien refugees who were also barred from selling retail in the City until they could afford to buy themselves the freedom of a company, or find (as many prosperous aliens did) a foothold in the free enclaves or 'Liberties' of St Martin le Grand, St Bartholomew or Blackfriars, which retained the sanctuary rights of the monasteries of former days.

As might be expected, more handicraftsmen without shops meant that those lucky or wealthy enough to have shops, especially in busy streets, gave more attention to trading and less to making their own goods. They supplied materials, often on credit, to workmen without resources and they bought back the finished products more or less on their own terms. This happened in many trades; bookselling is a well-known case in point. Caxton and his successors had taken orders for books directly from the public who called at their workshops. Now, bookselling ceased to be a mere side-line of the printer's craft, and became an important trade in its own right to which the printers were increasingly subordinated. In all such trades some working craftsmen managed to preserve their independence although they no longer dealt directly with the consumers; men who took apprentices and employed journeymen and found satisfactory outlets for their goods to honest shopkeeping colleagues. But many more were exploited, indebted, unorganized, debarred by poverty or deprived under technicalities from any voice in their guild or company, victims of the sweating system that was to disfigure London's industrial life for centuries.[11]

Even in the middle ages, as we have seen, it had never been the universal practice to buy manufactured goods from the actual maker on his own premises. Indeed, it is doubtful if even a majority of manufactures reached the consumer in this way. Now, in London, it was becoming even less common. Purely commercial interests—in other words, shopkeepers—were coming to stand between the makers and the buyers even in the same parish. More and more of the so-called brass-founders and hatters and joiners and saddlers and so forth (the list could be extended through nearly all the traditional trades) were now simply retail traders who, whatever had been their early training as apprentices, never, as masters, handled a tool or performed any creative process whatsoever. These shopkeeping tradesmen in their role as middlemen can now be seen to have supplied the capital and the enterprise to increase the volume of goods being made and to have distributed them to the public more conveniently than their makers could do. That is the view of hindsight. At the time, they were reviled and satirized for being impostors or parasites, degrading the true craftsmen and exploiting the consumers.

The figure of the craftsman-retailer did not disappear, however. As he became rare in the old trades, he cropped up in new ones. For many products whose workmanship was highly skilled it was still necessary for the working craftsman to keep his own shop. No retailer could yet hope to act as intermediary between the customer and, for example, the gunsmith who began to appear in the sixteenth century, for firearms long remained individual works of art, custom-built for gentlemen who wanted to discuss their personal requirements with the expert. And the same applies to the makers of musical instruments, spectacles, watches and clocks who became fairly common in the seventeenth century. These craftsmen made costly goods and dealt only with the customers themselves. (As, presumably, did the man who

[11] G. Unwin, *Studies in Economic History* (1927), p. 308.

stated that he made lead coffins to measure and put them by until required, at the sign of 'the Four Coffins' in Fleet Street.) And finally, at the other end of the scale, rather different specialist traders were appearing in new, purely commercial lines such as tobacco, and glass, and later in tea and coffee and china.

Here, then, were no fewer than four new kinds of shop-keeper brought into existence in London by the changing social climate of this remarkable century; the importing merchant who began to specialize on the selling side of his business and to con-centrate on particular kinds of goods; the master-craftsman living in a busy street who found it paid better to sell other men's products than to make his own; the man of new skills who could make clocks or guns or instruments; and finally the trader who helped to introduce and develop a taste for some entirely new commodity. Novelty and diversity were appearing on every hand to tempt the shopper in London, and the capital became to an increasing extent the shop-window for the whole country to gaze in.

Meanwhile, equally great but quite different changes were taking place on the other side of distribution, the selling of food. As a commodity, food was in a class by itself, for its trade was supervised with anxious care by the civic authorities, who dreaded, with almost superstitious intensity, any departure from traditional methods. The new beginnings in the food trades that took place in this period in London were related chiefly to the way that authority was forced to loosen its grip on the market.

The simple market system of the middle ages could not just be expanded as London expanded; it had to be reorganized on new lines. But although the public street markets were becoming 'unmeasureably pestred with the unimaginable increase and multiplicity of market folkes' the authorities were determined to allow commercial interests no freedom in so vital a matter. Not only were they habitually suspicious of large-scale food trans-actions but only with the greatest reluctance would they allow any food to change hands other than in the authorized markets. There were many reasons why the City's rulers often saw London's growth and enrichment as an abnormal, a morbid phenomenon, but the chief anxiety was that such growth would probably exact a fearful price from its inhabitants if food supplies should fail in a year of dearth.

And this was not a fanciful idea. Though the diet of the rich was liberal—indeed, gluttonous by modern standards—the community as a whole lived from hand to mouth. The yields of harvest and livestock were erratic. There was no food preservative except salt or more rarely vinegar, while even storage of grain was an uncertain gamble against damp. And now the City authorities saw with dismay thousands upon growing thousands of Londoners, with only small reserve in their houses—or no reserve at all—utterly dependent for food on what they bought for cash, week by week, in the markets.

London's meat consumption alone was the marvel of foreigners; droves of cattle from the Midlands and Wales, their hooves shod for the journey, were brought by road to the market towns near London where local graziers bought them, lean from their travels, to fatten for the London butchers. Fruit and poultry and dairy products were drawn from all over the home counties to feed London. Corn came regularly from all the adjoining counties as well as down the Thames Valley from as far as the South Midlands, and by ship from the coasts of Kent and Essex and as the seventeenth century advanced from places farther and farther along the north-east and south-west coasts.[12]

The quantity of foodstuffs that poured increasingly into London by land and water was impressive, but the responsibility for supervising its distribution in the public interest was becoming more alarming every year. Freemen of various food trades were constantly complaining about their privileges being infringed by 'foreigners' in selling food in the City in unauthorized ways, yet increasingly the Council had to allow the outsiders more scope. Citizens, appalled by rising prices which they noticed particularly in foodstuffs, cried out on food traders for profiteering and hoarding. The authorities tried harder than ever to enforce the time-honoured regulations about trade. They fought a losing battle against hawkers buying a packful of food at one end of the market and reselling it in small quantities farther along the street, or in the lanes of the outer suburbs; they also fought (and until the Civil War, nearly always with success) any application for new markets outside the City boundaries which would encourage the population to spread.

[12] F. J. Fisher, 'The Development of the London Food Market, 1540–1640', *Econ. Hist. Rev.*, V (1935).

They found food being retailed in inns and taverns, often by the proprietors, sometimes by the customers, and imposed heavy penalties on such underground transactions.

But their main concern was the novel and dangerous and seemingly irresistible rise of middlemen. The food tradesmen who themselves had a job to do on the food before passing it on to the consumer, such as butchers, brewers, bakers and cooks, had in London long since outgrown the capacity of the street markets to supply all their needs for meat, corn and poultry direct from the producer on the same retail basis as the ordinary householder. They needed large amounts, and in spite of all the laws about forestalling the market and 'regrating' the price and making 'secret' bargains, their needs attracted a class of wholesale dealers who would not and could not be put down. They first appeared outside the control of London itself, in small towns in the home counties that were growing rich as entrepôts for London's food. Leighton Buzzard market and Barnet market, for example, became great sales depots for livestock where the rich graziers who fattened cattle by the hundred found it more convenient to sell to dealers than to bring cattle into London.

Many towns in Middlesex, Hertfordshire, the Thames Valley and Surrey, likewise grew rich as the collecting places for the corn and barley flowing towards London from farther afield. And then because they had the fuel, the water-power, the space for malting and milling, which London was finding increasingly difficult, it was inevitable that the local malsters and millers should soon become rich dealers, buying barley and wheat from the countryside in large quantities and selling malt and meal wholesale to the London brewers and bakers who were of course forbidden to go forth themselves and 'forestall' the London markets by buying up large quantities in the nearby countryside. Some country maltmen engrossed 'into their handes . . . verie greate quantities of Malte which they send to London daylie eyther out of their houses or els from their private shopps in market townes'.[13] And since the prosperity of these small market towns was being so dramatically increased during this period by such activities it is hardly surprising that the dealers, while openly breaking the laws against forestalling (that is, buying privately on the farms) and engrossing (or

[13] N. S. B. Gras, *The Evolution of the English Corn Market* (1915), pp. 184–7.

hoarding), were able to 'invente quirks and quiddities, shiftes and put-offes ynough to blinde the eies of the local magistrates'.[14] While at the London end, much as the Council would have liked to make them sell all their stocks by retail in the open market, it could never quite control private wholesale bargains and was never quite sure that it could afford to do so.

Instead, the City Council was worrying about a different side of the problem; if, as they well knew, London brewers and bakers had in the past broken the City's laws by buying more than they needed for their trade and making a quiet penny by secretly retailing malt and meal from the stocks in their houses at enhanced prices for the convenience of citizens, even this seemed preferable to the new state of affairs in which increasing numbers of brewers, bakers and millers no longer held any stocks at all. So powerful were the wholesalers in the country towns becoming, since they were free to raise their prices as they wished, that more and more of the London victualling craftsmen were getting into their debt and depending, week by week, on small deliveries. In view of the chronic dread of scarcity this tendency was ominous and the authorities revived old ideas of making municipal provision for corn. Using the organization of the livery companies, they required each of them to raise funds to buy stipulated quantities of grain in the early months of each harvest, purchasing it at a distance, or even abroad, and to store it against a rise in price. This practice, begun at first in years of real scarcity, helped to tap more distant sources of supply, and when the companies' grain or meal was released, bit by bit, in the street markets, either at or below the market price, it had the effect of restraining panic prices, while making a comfortable profit for the companies concerned.

Other towns took similar steps in years of dearth, but the London of Elizabeth tried to make this stockpiling a permanent Company responsibility. Unfortunately it was not always easy to judge the market accurately, and in some years of plenty various companies lost money and lost, along with it, their enthusiasm for this form of public benefaction. The City Council was in earnest, however, about the need for keeping up these emergency stocks, and for nearly all this period held the livery companies to the task, even, on one occasion, committing to

[14] E. M. Leonard, *The Early History of English Poor Relief* (1900), p. 193.

Newgate prison no less a person than the Warden of the great Fishmongers' Company for disobeying a direct injunction. In famine years something of the order of one-seventh of all the City's consumption of flour was supplied in this way.[15]

When prices rose very high, different methods were used, sometimes the public supplies were sold only to the poor at a special price, using a system of tickets supplied by the church wardens to the poor of each parish, while in 1608 the Lord Mayor told each company 'to cause the quantity of [so many] quarters, parcel of your own store and provision, to be ground into meal and baked into white and wheaten bread . . . and to sell the same in Cheapside or Leadenhall or elsewhere within the City to such as will buy the same. And you do, notwithstanding this order, still continue serving the markets with such quantity of meal as by order of me you were formerly required.'[16]

Meanwhile, however, the City's food supply was reorganizing itself in spite of the authorities. The pressure of demand, the chances of making money, were forces too strong to be resisted, and the food trades, one after the other, were bursting out of the strait-jacket of the retail street markets and of municipal control. Let us take corn once more as an example, for it was by far the most important commodity since it furnished both bread and drink and fed horse as well as man. As supplies came from farther afield, more of them came by ship up the Thames and landed, not into the hands of country dealers but straight on to Billingsgate (which was then a general wharf) and when that got too small for them, on to Queenhythe Wharfe. Coastwise supplies grew from about one-third of the total in Elizabeth's reign to nearly a half in the years just before the Civil War.[17] There, all comers could buy as much as they liked, often cheaper than it was grown in the home counties, and without any pretence of pushing trans-actions through the bottleneck of the retail street markets. This was the chance for the London corn dealers.

There had always been some dealers in London (called regrators in the middle ages) who had been allowed to buy any corn left unsold on the City markets at the end of the day and have it ground into meal for retailing on the same market

15 Gras, *op. cit.*, p. 450.
16 *ibid.*, p. 91.
17 Fisher, *op. cit.*, Table I.

to poor consumers who only wanted small amounts. Hitherto they had never become very important in the trade because general mistrust of their somewhat speculative activities had prevented them from being free to buy up or store large quantities, or to sell from their own premises. These corn-chandlers or mealmen, as they came to be called, found their customers multiplying as London grew; more people wanted frequent small quantities of ready-ground meal, not only the poor as of old, but hundreds of small households in 'rents' or apartments with little storage space, as well as small bakers and cookshops that were springing up everywhere. Eager to cash in on this growing demand, the corn-chandlers started wriggling in the grip of medieval laws, and in the century we are considering they wriggled round them and through them and finally out of them altogether.

Forbidden to sell from his house the corn or meal he bought on the open market, the chandler, foreseeing the great advantages of retailing from fixed premises, started buying at the quayside. For instance, in 1586 we hear of 'a chandler who dothe sell by retayle in his shoppe weekelie four quarters of rye meal, which he gets from Billingsgate and other marketts, as he saithe'.[18] Forbidden to 'haunt all the Marketts neare unto London and sweepe the Marketts of all the corne that comes . . .' they arranged for farmers to bring corn outside the forbidden 35-mile circuit so that they could meet them there to buy it—and were promptly ordered to do their buying still farther afield. It was often complained, as in 1616, that they did 'sell meal within their shops and other obscure places within this Cittie, to the great decay of the common meal marketts within this Cittie'; whether this meant that stricter efforts were made to force them into the public markets, or whether, as seems more likely, they were simply more active everywhere, they were next blamed for outselling the country mealmen in the markets, and 'forcinge them out of their accustomed standings', and they were all ordered to get out of the public markets and leave these to the country folk, and to 'utter by retayle in their shopps as formerly they have been accustomed'. Even then the jealousy of the country mealmen were not appeased; they soon convinced a committee of the Council that it was 'not fitt . . . being noe part of the

18 Gras, *op. cit.*, p. 185.

Trade of Corn Chaundlers' that London freemen should 'sell the Meal and Flower of Wheate in their houses or shopps', and the chandlers were ordered back into the markets once more.

And through all this persecution the chandlers flourished. Time and the growing urban demand and the increasing remoteness of the supplies were all on their side. Middlemen of some sort were bound sooner or later to come between the farmer and the City consumer, and in the competition to fill that role, the chandlers, as freemen of London, were bound to win, in spite of artificial handicaps. They were better placed at the centre of communications by land and sea than their rivals in the country towns; they had premises for storing and retail selling which no doubt many of them went on using, in season and out of season, whatever the law said. And they could mix meal from various corns and regions and have it boulted into flour in their own boulting houses, and this was not only found to improve the quality of all but the very finest grains, but it also provided the chandler with an indistinguishable product, and so obscured the true extent of his profit margin.

Reviled as hoarders and monopolists, the chandlers were tolerated until they became indispensable, and eventually took the whole corn trade into their hands, some becoming wholesale merchants, some having mills and factories in the provinces, most becoming retail shopkeepers, 'buying cheap and selling dear', adding to their stock 'almost all manner things, as namelie butter, cheese, faggots, pots, pans, candles, and a thousand other trinkets besides'.[19] This was the start of the chandler's shop which remained a regular and important household supplier until quite recent times.

A similar story, different in detail but the same in spirit, could be told about all the chief victualling trades in this period. London fruiterers, butchers, poulterers, fishmongers, cheese and dairy-produce sellers no longer waited in the City for supplies to be brought in by the producers, in order to buy their stock, under various handicaps, at the tail end of the City markets. They started to ignore, or circumvent, the law against forestalling principally by means of by buying direct from producers well beyond the vicinity of London. Retailing food traders prospered and multiplied, some gaining, others merely

[19] Stubbes, *op. cit.*, pt. II, p. 49.

assuming, the privilege of keeping fixed shops; some reselling to smaller colleagues and eventually turning wholesalers; others stocking, and no doubt exploiting, the army of hagglers, hucksters, fishwives or costermongers.

There is, to modern eyes, a certain contradiction in the part played by authority in fighting against the establishment of retail food shops while allowing or even encouraging the purely retail shop in other trades. In the non-food trades, the relative leniency of the City government in the past had enabled the guild organizations to grow into powerful liveried companies. Now, those of them concerned most with trading, the Haberdashers, the Drapers, the Mercers, and the ruling castes within many others such as Goldsmiths, Pewterers, Ironmongers, Cordwainers, were misusing their very considerable powers to favour commercial over manufacturing interests, to subordinate the craftsman to the dealer. On the other hand, these same individuals as leaders of some of the richest City companies, had another role as councillors and aldermen of the City government, and in this capacity they experienced traditional anxieties about food shortage and reacted with the traditional restrictions on the food trades. Men who were growing rich by supplying shops or keeping shops for apparel or household goods were exerting all their influence to stop the victualling trades from following their example. No doubt it was experience of their own businesses which gave an edge to their voices when they pleaded, in the name of fair dealing and the consumer's interests, against any move to advance the food trades beyond the medieval street market.

Fortunately, the forces of economic growth were too strong to be held back indefinitely. Retail food shops and the wholesale organizations to supply them grew up in spite of public policy. The fears so often expressed that any concessions to *laissez faire* in the food trades would mean high prices for consumers and private fortunes for commercial interests proved, of course, perfectly justified. As N.H. remarked in a pamphlet published in 1684 when the struggle for a free, wholesale food-market had been virtually won:

In your buying provisions you'll find it best to go to their Fountains, for the further from thence the so much the dearer, there being no second-hand but so licks his own fingers that, while he hath his gains, the commodity is enhanced. . . .[20]

The even greater fears, however, that any freedom would mean disorganization, hoarding and scarcity could not have been more mistaken.

In all these ways, then, the hundred years that lay between the accession of Elizabeth and the restoration of the Stuarts saw a transformation in the supply of consumer goods of all kinds to the London market. This is not a book about wholesale merchanting but about retailing as it affected the consumer, and so this sketch of the forces at work in the background must be left here, but it may help to explain why seventeenth-century London, and gradually the other cities of England, were able to turn their backs on the medieval shopping pattern of market and fair.

[20] N. H., *The Compleat Tradesman* (1684).

IV

❖◇❖◇❖◇❖◇❖◇❖◇❖◇❖◇❖◇❖◇❖◇❖◇❖◇❖

Buying Food in London

❖◇❖◇❖◇❖◇❖◇❖◇❖◇❖◇❖◇❖◇❖◇❖◇❖

The Markets being most principally intended for the Benefit and Advantage of Housekeepers and others who buy for their own Use to be spent in their Families, and may provide for themselves in the Morning at the best hand and pay moderate Rates for their Provisions.

Act of the Common Council of London, 17 Sept., 1674

THE England of Elizabeth was famous on the Continent for the richness and plenty of its diet and especially of its meat. 'Other nations esteem us gluttonous', Fynes Moryson remarked with satisfaction, but the fact was that foreign travellers judged England by London, and London by the lavish diet of the wealthier classes. The London markets displayed a quantity and variety of food that impressed visitors from abroad, and during the seventeenth century the markets went on growing as London grew, attracting ever more specialized products from the provinces while at the same time taking the place of Antwerp as the great European market for exotic luxuries.

Consider the following meal. In February 1601, the Earl of Rutland on a visit to his town house gave a dinner to fifteen guests for which his steward bought the following things. All of them, it is pretty clear, were bought on the London markets.[1]

2 Caponnes, 5s.; 6 hens, 10s.; 6 mallard, 6s.; 2 heron, 8s.; 6 rabits, 6s.; 4 woodcock, 4s. 8d.; 10 tame pigeons, 10s.; 4 partridge, 8s.; a pheasant 20s.; 12 snipe, 11s.; 6 knot, 3s.; 12 blackbirds,

[1] *Hist. MSS. Comm., Rutland Manuscripts, Vol. IV* (1905), p. 433.

2s. 6d.; a turkey, 3s. 6d.; 2 doz. larks, 3s.; 10 lbs. lard, 10s.; anchovies, 1s. 6d.; bacon, 1s. 5d.; eggs, 5s.; 24 lbs. butter, 10s.; 4 joints veal, 8s.; 6 joints mutton, 13s.; half a lamb, 5s.; 100 apples, 2s. 8d.; 200 chestnuts, 8d.; oranges and lemons, 7s. 4d.; vegetables, 8s.; ½ pint capers, 1s.; ½ pint oil, 4d.; onions, 4d.; verjuice, 4d.; mustard, 3d.; 16 marrowbones, 8s.; 2 lbs. suet, 1s.; 16 lbs. fat, 9s. 4d.; quart vinegar, 8d.; a bushel of oysters, 2s.; 2 gallons 1 pint Rhenish wine, 6s. 8d.; 6 quarts Canary, 5s.; a pot white wine, 10d.; ale, 4d. Total £10 9s. 4d.

Obviously money was no object here, but even so this is an impressively varied shopping list, and a similar one occurred every few days for weeks on end. (The absence of fish, of course, was not due to any scarcity but was a matter of courtesy on a non-fasting day.) At this date, such a shopping list would be strictly *ex post facto*; many of these items the steward could not have been sure of finding, or finding in the right quantity, so there was no point in drawing up a menu in advance. He or his assistants would go round the markets with open minds and draw up a list of what they actually brought back.

At the other end of the scale, the labouring poor relied heavily on the three basic articles of ale and bread and cheese, with the cheaper sorts of meat or fish as extras when they could be afforded. Indeed, throughout the seventeenth century, the amount a family spent on meat was a close indication of its prosperity. It was not, as nowadays, a question of taste, for meat was everybody's taste; it was simply a question of how much the family could afford. Nevertheless, many of the poorer sort of workmen ate it only occasionally for the Elizabethan price rise carried meat out of their everyday reach.

There is an interesting passage in Defoe's *Journal of the Plague Year* which since it relates to a great event in his own lifetime may be taken as authentic in this respect. He describes how a well-to-do London saddler decided, as did many others in 1665, to shut up himself and his family in the house and avoid all contact with the outside world, and for this siege he provided only five articles of food, namely flour, malt, salt, butter and cheese. He explains that he was fortunate in having three domestic appliances that were far from being universal, a well, an oven and a brewing copper, so that they lived on ale, bread and butter and cheese. Meat, he feared, might be already contaminated with plague, so that he 'made shift' to do without it. What he leaves out is more eloquent than what he puts in. Not a word of regret for fresh fruit or vegetables or eggs or milk or even drinking water in a siege of about two months. Yet the meticulous nature of Defoe's reporting leaves no room for doubt that this is exactly what many such families did in the Plague year with no great sense of hardship or privation. The satisfied way he refers to this arrangement when all the other hardships of confinement are stressed shows that even middle-class families recognized this as a good plain diet under necessity. After all, only cranks as yet connected diet with health; ordinary people were content to believe that a minimum quantity of any sort of food kept them strong, and anything beyond that was merely a matter of taste or fancy.

Meanwhile, what was the prospect that faced the ordinary housewife in setting out to buy supplies for her family in the seventeenth century? The most important difference from today was that food buying was 'marketing', not 'shopping'. For although there were some food shops and more as time went by, it was not until well into the eighteenth century that the big open markets ceased to be the normal place to buy food. The City authorities, who drew handsome revenues from the markets, had plenty of reasons—quite apart from their horror of food speculators—for trying to keep it that way. But in the course of the seventeenth century the suburbs grew out of the City's grasp, and while the Council was fighting a bitter rear-guard action against rival markets on its doorstep,[2] the suburbs in lieu of convenient markets became 'infested' with private food shops, as well as street hawkers of all sorts of food. For 'they could ill-afford to take time off from their work to go to the London markets'. The suburbs got their markets at last, in the course of the seventeenth century, but permanent food shops already had a good start there.

To begin, however, with the markets of Elizabethan London which continued almost unchanged until the Great Fire, except in the important respect that they grew bigger and busier and 'unmeasureably pestred with the unimaginable increase and multiplicity of market-folkes' year by year and progressively

---

[2] T. F. Reddaway, *The Rebuilding of London after the Great Fire* (1940), pp. 296–7.

less able to cope with the swelling volume of trade.[3] Not counting the livestock market at Smithfield, there were twelve old-established retail markets, most of them in busy streets. On the eastern side there was a group which filled the main route going south to London Bridge. First Leadenhall, where it still stands today, a crowded, square building with stalls overflowing into all the surrounding streets. It was the market especially reserved for outsiders, country people, provincials or even aliens, to come and sell their produce and was famous then as now for poultry (in the street), as well as meat and dairy produce and inside for hardware, leather, and some kinds of cloth. Where Leadenhall market-people spread down Gracechurch Street they almost joined up with a general market held all along that street, while across the foot of Gracechurch Street the London butchers kept their own meat market of Eastcheap, many of them living there and selling from the fronts of permanent shops.[4]

Gracechurch Street was the highroad out of London to the south, and beyond the butchers' stalls in Eastcheap it became New Fish Street, the home of London fishmongers and another busy street market this time in fish, before narrowing between the shops that lined London Bridge and emerging on the other side straight into the great Southwark street-market which served all the south bank and was 'much resorted to by them on this side of the river for cheapness'.

The centre and west of the City were served by another group of markets, equally obstructive, along the main east-west thoroughfare. Cornhill, once it was free of the country poulterers straggling out from Leadenhall, was soon encumbered by hawkers at the South Gate of the Royal Exchange, while beyond this lay the great meat and fish market of the Stocks, its original stone house jutting into the crossroads at the present Bank corner, the actual market crowd milling about in the big open space round the foot of a well-used pair of stocks. Past this crossroads, Cheapside broadened out to hold the biggest and most varied market of them all—again, a 'foreigners' market—with hundreds of trestles filling the wide street and hundreds more sellers standing over a sack or basket on the ground or

[3] J. Stow, *Survey of London* (Howes edition, 1631), p. 1023.
[4] J. Stow, *Survey of London* (Everyman edition), p. 194.

carrying their offerings in their hands. Meat, fish, poultry, tripe, trotters, pies, fruit, vegetables, cheese, butter, eggs, loaves, flowers, gingerbread, milk from the ass, bread for horses, corn or meal in some years from the granaries of the City companies— the list of things on sale, legally or illegally, was endless.

Where the highway narrowed into Newgate Street it divided to either side of St Nicholas' flesh shambles where the City butchers, encroaching from the side streets to the north, occupied permanent stalls in the middle of the road and even started to spread up Newgate Street itself into the Market House of Newgate Meal Market. This was the next obstruction in the road, and the prosperous City butchers bribed their way to stalls inside it and pushed the corn and meal sellers, and on alternate days the fruit and vegetable sellers, out onto the steps and into the narrow roadway on either side, 'to the damage of their goods and the danger of their persons by the coaches, carts, horses and cattle that pass through the street'. Just before the Great Fire, Pepys was 'driving through the backside of the Shambles in Newgate Market when my coach plucked down two pieces of beef into the dirt upon which the butchers stopped the horses and a great rout of people in the street . . .!' etc.

These were the main retail markets in the century before the Great Fire. The rest consisted of a small fish market in the present Queen Victoria Street and three big quayside markets at Queenhythe, Bear Key and Billingsgate for the sale of miscellaneous incoming goods. These quays too were traditionally 'open markets' where all comers could buy, but as the volume of goods arriving by water increased over the years they were gradually given over to wholesale trade. But the law did not acknowledge this until late in the seventeenth century and meanwhile the consumer could—and did—insist upon his right to be served with a gallon of butter or a dozen sprats by a seller who was really looking for someone to buy a boatload. In general, however, the only consumers who patronized these quays after Elizabeth's time were the stewards of big households.

Westminster, a separate city, had its own market in King Street and as the intervening spaces along the Strand and Holborn were gradually built up into fashionable suburbs, aristocratic speculators like the Earl of Clare and the Duke of Bedford pressed for royal permission to set up private markets on their own property. And they acquired these gold-mines readily enough, particularly after the Restoration. The names still mark the sites; Clare Market (1650), Covent Garden (1661), Southampton Market (1662), St James' Market (1664), Hungerford Market (1680) and so on. In the industrial suburbs to the east and north some small private markets eventually won a more grudging royal assent at Spitalfields, Stepney, Rotherhithe and Hoxton. Less is known about these industrial suburbs than about the City and the West End, but clearly both their shops and markets were busy places. 'In several out-parts of London there were within the compass of two or three small streets, lanes and alleys two or three thousand people, working tradesmen and their families . . . and most of their money was spent every week in the neighbourhood on strong drink, several sorts of flesh, bread, butter, cheese, sugar, spices, Spanish fruit and cloathing.'[5] This was written in 1694 about conditions around the time of the Restoration.

To outward appearances, all these markets, even the official City ones, were no more than the casual mingling together of buyers and sellers in the streets. But in fact they were far from that. As in the middle ages, a close network of regulation surrounded them and although the increasing volume of business threatened to burst out of the old bounds, this age had its own characteristic methods of law-enforcement. For one thing, informers were active, being well paid for their tales whenever their evidence led to a trader's conviction. The common informer found marketing offences his main support.[6] For another thing, the administration of the markets was farmed out for a large fee for the concessionaires to make what they could, not only from stall rents but also from fines for minor offences. In 1699 the Farmers of the Markets were said to get £2,000 a year from fines alone in the City's markets, an astonishing figure if only approximately true.[7]

From the consumer's point of view, the rules that probably mattered most were those relating to hours of opening. London markets operated six days a week, and only continual pressure

<hr />

[5] Anon, *General Considerations Relating to Trade* (1694).

[6] M. W. Beresford, 'The Common Informer, the Penal Statutes, and Economic Regulation', *Econ. Hist. Rev.*, X (1958), pp. 221–37.

[7] *Petition to the Lord Mayor* (1699), Brit. Museum 816.1.43.

from the authorities ('Let no butcher be seen with his aprone aboute him!') prevented open business on the sabbath. Fish alternated with flesh on Wednesdays and Fridays, and some commercial products, hides, tallow, wool and so on seem to have favoured certain days in certain markets. Tuesdays and Thursdays were traditionally the slack days until fruit and vegetable sellers began to make these days as busy as any others. But so far as one can judge, although different days and markets had their special emphases, it was possible to buy all things at all times somewhere in the City. Even the Long Fast was not completely inviolate; 'What's a joint or two,' asks Mistress Quickly with a wink at her audience, 'in a whole Lent?'[8]

At six in the morning in summer, or at sunrise in winter, the market-bell declared the start of business and for the first hour or two, according to the particular market, sales were confined to true retailing 'because the markets are principally intended for housekeepers who buy for their own behoof'. This was the time when the markets were busiest, the goods freshest and cheapest, before the city tradesmen, the hawkers, or the suburban shopkeepers were allowed to buy their stocks. In 1663 when Pepys gave a dinner party 'My poor wife had to rise at five in the morning to buy the provisions'. At four-thirty in the afternoon or at two-thirty in winter the bell tolled again and this time it went on tolling for a solid half-hour to warn everyone of the 'raising of the market'. While its clamour lasted the country folk were making a last hoarse effort to get rid of their remainders —so as not to have to carry them back home or throw them away—before ringing stopped, the trestles and chopping blocks were swept aside and the rakers moved in to cart away the rubbish.

By the time of the Commonwealth, London markets must have been at their very worst, choked in their narrow streets by several centuries of growth, near to panic at the shortages and threatened famine of the Civil War. It was in this period that the City companies finally abandoned the stock-piling of corn because the usual steadying effect of their sales was now quite lost in the hysterical confusion of the scramble for food. To steady things down after the Commonwealth was established the City Council passed an act to the effect that 'No victualler of

8 W. Shakespeare, *King Henry the Fourth, Part II*, Act ii, scene 4.

the City shall give any rude or unfitting language, or make any clamour on any man or woman in the open market for cheapening of victual, under pain of three shillings fine'. Cromwell took a more realistic line; he virtually excluded all City tradesmen in food from buying their stocks in the markets, whether they clamoured or not, thus driving them to seek their supplies farther afield and relieve the general shortage by their own efforts (a courageous reversal of the old restrictionist policies that were never to be fully restored). Observing, moreover, that Cheapside market was a nuisance to traffic, he bundled the lot without ceremony into the churchyard of nearby St Paul's—a gesture most happily characteristic of the man.

For effective reform the City markets had to wait until the Great Fire, after which four new sets of buildings were put up big enough to take them all off the streets—a testimony to the City's soaring wealth at that time.[9] The biggest of them, said to be the biggest market in Europe, was Leadenhall, which absorbed into four spacious courtyards all the street sellers from Gracechurch Street, Cornhill and the Poultry, much of the fish and butchery from New Fish Street and Eastcheap and all that of the old Stocks Market. Pattern and order replaced the old free-for-all mixtures of goods; in one court, beef only on 100 stalls; in another, 140 more stalls for all remaining kinds of meat; here, rows of fish; there, rows of butter; round the corner, rows of cheese; and so on. It was a monster market, the object of civic pride and one of the showpieces of the town.[10] But one wonders what the simple farmers' wives, with their few hens and a cheese and odd sack of apples from their cottages beyond the suburbs, thought about being thus regimented alongside their commercial successors who had perhaps driven a flock of turkeys from a specialist farm in Norfolk or brought a score of cheeses from distant Cheshire. One wonders what the consumers thought about this new, spacious, orderly and almost certainly more expensive way of selling food.

Other new markets, though smaller, followed the same pattern as Leadenhall. They were all rectangular courtyards open to the sky, since as yet the roofing of wide spaces was too costly to be practical for market houses. The market which had given

[9] Reddaway, op. cit., p. 297.
[10] H. B. Wheatley & W. Cunningham, *London Past and Present* (1891), II, p. 375 ff.

its old Saxon name to Cheapside could not be moved too far from its ancient site and was installed in nearby buildings off Milk Street, called Honey Lane Market where all classes of food continued to be sold. The Shambles and Newgate Market took joint premises close by near Paternoster Row, usurping, so rumour said, by a bit of quick building, the site that Wren was seeking for his new St Paul's. The remaining open markets of the City itself were now recognized as officially wholesale; Queenhythe for corn, Billingsgate for fish and the Stocks for fruit and vegetables (including, presumably, gilliflowers to which it gave its own unlovely name of stocks). For by the 1670s the pressure of customers in the central London markets was as great as ever in spite of the new building and the growth of suburban shops and markets, and the anxious authorities were at last compelled to realize that they must allow food wholesaling to come of age as the only way to get enough supplies from far afield.

The reform of the physical conditions of the markets after the Fire was apparently enough to be going on with so far as the authorities were concerned, without interfering with any of the private rackets which the farming out of their administration involved. There were still many lucrative offices connected with most of the markets, offices like that of the 'Keeper-Clean', 'Weigher', and 'Porter', with exclusive rights and payment geared to the volume of business, offices which had grown out of charity jobs for the poor in medieval times into fat sinecures with their nominal duties neglected or abandoned and their inflated revenues a heavy tax on the market trade. The 'Keeper-Clean' of Newgate for instance, received 'a brazen dish of meal' (or its value) for every quarter of meal sold in the market, yet the mealmen's stocks went bad through having to set their sacks on top of the rotting fruit left behind by the vegetable women of the previous day.

Or again, as late as 1699, 'Most provisions are not sold by weight and those that are people are forced to get weighed at the scales of the neighbouring inhabitants, the Farmers [of the markets] not providing any weights and scales at convenient places'.[11] In a petition to the Lord Mayor that year about conditions in Newgate Market it was also said that whereas

[11] *Petition to the Lord Mayor* (1699), Brit. Museum 816.1.43.

fixed, covered stalls had been provided when it was built, these had disappeared, and 2s. 6d. for two days was being charged for 'moveable boards' so that the sellers were 'sheltering under the penthouses of neighbouring inhabitants and paying the householders for so doing', which sounds as though the markets were creeping back into the street once more—no doubt because of 'the further oppressions not complained of for fear of further extortion'. The petitioners in this instance described themselves as eight women 'being all poor people who sell small provisions in Newgate Market, viz. lamb, pork, butter, eggs, oat-cakes, hoggs' puddings, sausages, etc. in small quantities, none of them ever bringing more than a horse-load into the market on any one day . . . for which they aught not to pay more than twopence a day'.[12] Not until the very last years of the century did the City authorities interfere in the administration of the markets, fix the stall rents and put an end to private extortions.

So much for the markets. What of the food itself? The first food everybody thought about was bread, and it was on sale everywhere, fresh from the midnight's baking. In every market the bakers' wives or apprentices stood with baskets over their arms crying 'Hot Bread', and it was still here rather than in the bakers' shops that bread was bought. In Elizabethan times there were about a hundred bakers in London; before the Civil War there were about twice as many; and in the early eighteenth century they were said—on doubtful authority—to number 2,000.[13] The numbers grew because they were all small businesses, typically a master-baker with one or two journeymen and two apprentices. About a third of them specialized in coarse brown bread for poorer customers and in horse-bread, while the more prosperous majority confined themselves to the dearer white loaves. All cakes and fancy bread were the monopoly of the so-called 'ginger-bread cooks' except at Christmas and Easter when bakers could bake what they liked.

Every loaf had to be stamped with either an H to represent housewives', that is brown, bread, or a W for white or wheaten, so presumably the difference was not always obvious. It also

[12] *ibid.*

[13] N. S. B. Gras, *The Evolution of the English Corn Market* (1915), p. 450 (quoting report of the Lord Mayor to the Privy Council, 1573); S. Thrupp, *Short History of the Worshipful Company of Bakers* (1933), p. 69.

bore the baker's seal, usually an initial with some arrangement of dots.

> Pat a cake, pat a cake, baker's man.
> Bake me a cake [i.e. loaf] as quick as you can.
> Nick it and prick it and mark it with T
> And put in the oven for Tommy and me.

These seals, which were all carefully registered at the Halls of the two bakers' companies, applied not to the baker but to his bakery and they enabled any loaf that was defective to be traced at once to its manufacturer. Suburban bakers, however, were another matter. Few of them were freemen, or had been apprenticed to freemen, and the bakers' companies had no control over them.[14] In the City itself there were other ways of getting bread. The poor still took their own dough to certain bakers and waited while it cooked but this practice was dying out. Taverns, cookshops and inns which baked for their own use often sold the surplus, illegally, at the back door. Or there was country bread. There was a long tradition in London of country bakers (particularly from Stratford, once full of windmills) bringing loaves to sell in the City markets. Their 'long carts' had been a feature of Cheapside for centuries, and although in Elizabeth's reign they began to find easier sales in the new industrial suburbs, a few still continued to come. Their loaves were supposed to be 'a penny in the shilling' heavier than city loaves to compensate for their not paying scot and lot (i.e. local rates) like city bakers, but they seem to have taken the rules fairly lightly in the seventeenth century. They were said to make a habit of sending only their wives or servants to sell their bread in the City, so that even if these were unlucky enough to have some lightweight loaves confiscated they could escape 'playing bo-peep through the pillory' by pleading that the law said 'baking light loaves' not 'selling' them.

The Assize of Bread still fixed the weights of the halfpenny, penny and twopenny loaf of every kind of bread as it had done without fail ever since the thirteenth century and as it continued to do until it was abolished in the nineteenth. The London Assize had never allowed the bakers much profit margin

[14] S. Thrupp. *op. cit.*

between the price of corn and the price of loaves, but during the
century of the price rise it squeezed their livelihood very
seriously indeed in spite of several adjustments in the basis of
calculation. And in the seventeenth century a new hazard arose
for the poor City baker; the staple of trade became meal rather
than corn, but the Assize still continued to be based on the price
of unground corn on which the mealman had to make his profit
too. Many bakers became so desperately mortgaged to mealmen
that they pleaded they were obliged to bake whatever rubbish
the mealmen chose to send them or risk being jailed for debt,
while only by now and then dodging the Assize and baking some
light loaves could they make ends meet. But the authorities were
deaf to their grievances. Some bakers had tried to make money
retailing meal to the public and all were damned as secret
hoarders and regrators. More fundamentally, the bakers were a
poor handicraft; bread, by its nature, offered no opportunity for
a rich trading class to arise who could wear the company's livery
and influence policy in high places as did the fishmongers or
vintners.

Nothing can now recall for us the taste and texture of seventeenth-century bread; one deeply suspects that it was very poor
stuff. The great ovens were built thick enough for the bricks to
remain hot on all sides when they were heated, not by a fire
underneath—this had to wait for metal ovens—but by burning
wood actually inside them and then hastily raking out the
embers and thrusting in the dough to bake as the oven slowly
cooled. Ovens were therefore both massive and more or less
specialized to bread. They also baked pastry and 'baked meats'
which were meat cut or minced small enough to cook while the
oven cooled, but oven-roasting had to wait for a continuously
heated oven. The schoolmaster in the Elizabethan 'French
Lyttleton' by Claud Hollybande begins school dinners with the
ominous words 'Let every man draw his knife and chip his bread
if there be any ashes or coles in the cruste'.[15]

Meat was the next most important food. To the very poor
this meant—if they could afford it at all—tripe, offal, trotters
and hoggs' puddings from the country women in the markets.
To everyone else it meant principally beef, with mutton, pork
and veal as generally less popular alternatives. Hens of a sort,

[15] Claude Hollybande, *The French Lyttelton* (1593).

fed on the sweepings of the corn-tub, were still in most back-yards even in London but choice poultry and wildfowl were rich men's dainties. The city butchers specialized in being either mutton butchers or beef butchers, and the beef butchers, the aristocracy of the trade, had practically no competition from outside the city. As in Elizabeth's reign, on Wednesdays and Fridays (fast days), they shut up shop or stall and went to Smithfield to buy live cattle and drive them home, 'not' as the law said 'at a trot in the streets, but peaceably. And if any ox happen to be let go when he is prepared for slaughter, the butcher shall forfeit two shillings besides recompense to any person hurt thereby'.[16] Slaughtering was done in any con-venient shed or backyard mostly around Eastcheap or St Nicholas Shambles, but as time went on, increasingly outside the walls at Whitechapel- Holborn- and Temple-Bars. Here the wholesale meat trade began to take root, linking the grazier with the retail butcher. But the term 'wholesale' should not conjure up any picture of big operators dealing in large quan-tities; it was rather that the job of slaughtering for resale to the trade became a separate occupation from retailing, a modest one on the whole, though a few carcass butchers grew rich and dealt in large quantities and others were stallholders on suburban markets or sold meat to hawkers.

Defoe in his *Journal of the Plague Year* describes the White-chapel Shambles as they were then. The carcass butchers and their families lived behind Whitechapel in a warren of courts and alleyways so narrow that the dead-cart could not get in to reach the house doors. The meat must have gone in on the hoof and come out in horse-panniers or on the heads and shoulders of porters. The disposal of blood and offal became an increasingly unsavoury problem. The smell of St Nicholas Shambles was said to upset Sunday churchgoers passing on their way to St Paul's; its daily effect on the aliens just over the wall in St Martin le Grand must have been unbearable, while the neigh-bours of the live-poultry houses were also said to be 'almost weary of their habitations'. Stinking Lane in the middle of the Shambles was re-christened Butchers' Hall Lane just before Shakespeareans had a chance to point out that the road by any other name would smell of meat.

[16] Act of the Common Council of London, for the Reforming of Markets, 1646.

But the smell and the offal, the flies in the summer and the mud in winter were small inconvenience to set against the all-important buying of beef. The consumer before the Fire could choose whether to go to the shops or stalls in Eastcheap and Gracechurch Street, to the stalls in the Stocks Market, to the 'foreigners' inside Leadenhall or to one of the many shops or stalls in St Nicholas Shambles. In the suburbs there were many butchers' shops and meat of a sort was hawked illegally in bags and baskets all round the houses or offered in clandestine bargains in inns and wine-taverns. But in spite of all these outlets, contemporary accounts give an impression of constant shortage of beef. This, after all, is reasonable in view of the article's brief span between death and putrefaction; no butcher would fell what he could not pretty certainly sell and no grazier wanted unsold steers eating out of his pocket in the capital, so to get good meat at a reasonable price the housewife went early to market. Even then it was likely to be tough, stringy flesh from little runts that had hardened their muscles on the long trek from the north. Fat flesh was at a premium and the buyer had to watch that the fat was not just pinned on for appearance. 'All fats were much dearer than meat,' says Thorold Rogers of this period. 'The seventeenth-century farmer rarely had the wherewithal to put flesh, still less to put fat, on his stock, and I believe that in later, as in earlier times, every particle of fat, the skimmings of the pan as well as the trimmings of the meat, was carefully preserved, the best for the kitchen, the coarser kinds, after having been refined as best they could be, for the home manufacture of the commoner candles.'[17]

The buyer also had to see that the flesh had been properly drained of blood to a pallid shade of pink as well as thoroughly cold from the night's slaughtering, because otherwise, when she carried it home to thrust it, not into a refrigerator but into a brine tub, it might 'not take salt or long continue sweet and be very unprofitable to the buyer'.[18] For butchers were a deceitful race; when the price rise began and attempts were vainly made to peg the price of meat, the idea had been introduced of selling joints not by their appearance but by weight, and as the practice of

[17] J. E. Thorold Rogers, *History of Agriculture and Prices in England* (1866), V, 360.
[18] A. Pearce, *History of the Butchers' Company* (1929), quoting the Company's ordinance of 1607.

G

weighing slowly grew, the butchers started leaving some blood in the carcasses to 'incorporate itself in the flesh and so thereby the flesh may not only be the weightier but also seem both fresher, fairer, newer, tenderer and younger'. What a comment on the 'properly' drained merchandise.[19]

But sale by weight gained ground very slowly, for in the seventeenth century scales were dear things. In 1607, the Butchers' Company ordinances, while referring to the need for the Wardens to check regularly the weights used by the beef butchers ('They do weare greatlye') also stated that lamb must not be quartered 'deceitfully' but must have ten ribs in the forequarter and three in the hind, and any piece cut off in between was liable to forfeit. So people were still buying lamb by the eye at that date. Other foods were even later in being weighed out for sale. In a pamphlet *What England Wants* in 1667, one demand was 'That most, if not all, eatable things exposed for sale in markets as well as in shops may be sold by weight as is done in Spain'. (Three centuries later consumers are still agitating for prepackaged goods to be obliged to declare their weight.)

Joints were obviously much bigger then than they commonly are nowadays. Stow's remarks about meat prices in Elizabeth's reign are interesting not so much for the money prices mentioned as for the terms in which he, writing as a consumer, describes them:

Pieces of beef weighing two pounds and a half at the least, yea, three pounds or better, for a penny on every butcher's stall in the City, and of those pieces of beef, thirteen or fourteen for twelve pence, fat mutton for eightpence the quarter and one hundredweight of beef for four shillings and eightpence at the dearest.[20]

The luxury meats were choice poultry and small game. Venison was rarely on sale in London, though poached deer could be had in many a tavern. 'When my master got his wealth, his family fed on roots and livers, and necks of beef on Sundays. But now I fear it will be spent on pultry. Butcher's meat will not

[19] P. Stubbes, *Anatomie of Abuses* (ed. F. J. Furnivall, 1877), pt. II, p. 26.
[20] Stow, Everyman edition, *op cit.*, p. 168.

go down!'[21] In the course of the seventeenth century, poulterers became prosperous and important tradesmen, and the more stringent Game Laws of the Restoration barely checked their stride. They bought their stocks, often under annual contract, from breeders all over the home counties who specialized in supplying the growing London market with domestic birds,[22] as well as of old from the catchers of wild ones. Many birds were brought alive to London. Turkeys, as they became popular in the second half of the century, were bred in Norfolk and Suffolk and walked to the capital in droves of up to a thousand. (Imagine meeting that on horseback!) The poulterers who then fattened these birds artificially in London storehouses were taking over on a commercial scale the long-established practice of big households who had fattened dainty poultry in their own houses—especially, in the previous century, quail from the Low Countries and heron from the east coast. The battery system is not essentially new.

The bulk of the sales of the commoner poultry, however, was not from the poulterers but from the farmers' wives in the general markets who would usually have a pair of rabbits or geese or hens along with whatever other 'country drugges' they brought. City butchers and poulterers had their own markets and were not allowed to set up an extra stall among the country sellers in Stocks or Leadenhall, but in fact they were always trying to squeeze in there, passing themselves off as farmers selling their own produce straight off the farm. In Cromwell's time, for instance, 'No poulter shall deceivably occupy the market . . . or stand in strange clothing so to do. . . . The Stranger market people have the Preheminence of the market.'[23]

It was said in the late seventeenth century that as much money was spent on fish in London as on meat.[24] Such a claim could not have been made at any time since, and it is doubtful if it was true

---

[21] *The City Madam, A Comedy* (1658), quoted in J. Drummond & A. Wilbraham, *The Englishman's Food* (1939), p. 131.

[22] F. J. Fisher, 'The Development of the London Food Market, 1540–1640', *Econ. Hist. Rev.*, V (1935).

[23] The Lawes of the Market, 1653, quoted in A. B. Robertson 'The Open Market in the City of London', *East London Papers* (1958).

[24] John Sellers, *A Moderate Computation of the Expenses of Provisioning the City of London*, quoted in P. V. McGrath 'The Marketing of Food in London in the 17th Century' (unpublished London M.A. thesis, 1948).

even then, but certainly fish was a much more important food then than we now remember. The legal obligation to observe the Friday and Lenten fasts did not survive the civil war, but the fish-eating habit lingered well into the eighteenth century. London fishmongers as a class were wealthy and important citizens, for it was not an easy trade for the authorities to control. Much of the sea-fish came ready dried and salted from ports far up the east coast; many luxury fish were imported, like anchovies from Italy, sturgeon from Germany or oysters from France; and some of the inland stewpond cultivation of fish, as well as some east-coast fishery, was actually financed by London fishmongers. It was therefore a trade that used a considerable capital, and as London's appetite grew, these far-reaching connections of the fishmongers became indispensable to maintain supplies, so that they were allowed to commit the sins of forestalling, regrating and engrossing with impunity. The result was that although London's fish supply in this period was not cheap it was certainly plentiful and, especially as regards freshwater fish, immensely varied.

First, and cheapest, there was the old familiar stockfish, dried ling, or cod or haddock now known as poorjohn and sold, as a rule, by the long hundred of a hundred and twenty. Bought this way, haberdon (cod) worked out at about 6d. each, the bigger foreign ling at anything from 1s. to 2s. 6d., but bought in small quantities of one or two fish at a time, the price could be doubled. It also cost more to buy it seasoned or old than to buy it 'green' from the current year's catch. These fish, along with the herring dried, pickled or smoked in innumerable ways, were the common household stores.[25] By comparison, there was only a small volume of fresh fish eaten, but whether from sea, river or stewpond it was always several times dearer than the same fish in preserved form because of the great expense and trouble of keeping it alive in tanks and water-carts. In earlier times, a fishmonger standing over his tank of live fresh fish would pull one out and slit it open to show the customer how nice and fat it was inside, and then, if the customer still didn't want it, would put in a few stitches with a needle and thread and throw it back into the water where it would continue to live.[26] This

---

[25] Rogers, *op. cit.*, V, 422 ff.

[26] Thomas Platter, *Travels in England* (1599), (trans. C. Williams, 1937), p. 175.

leisurely way of doing business seems to have died out by the seventeenth century. It remained true, however, that 'a fish' was the least one could buy—such things as fillets or steaks are never mentioned as saleable quantities.

Whether he was the servant of a wealthy establishment going with a long purse to seek out fresh fish, or the spender of a more modest budget content to buy the ordinary barrels of the dried and pickled varieties, the shopper had a choice of markets. Before the Fire, there were the City fishmongers in New and Old Fish Streets (now Fish Street Hill and Queen Victoria Street), where the best all-round selection of fish was to be had. And there were the markets where for two days a week fish entirely replaced meat; and after the Fire permanent fish stalls in all the new markets. And always and everywhere there were the fishwives, those 'disorderly lewd women and maids fitted for painful and laborious service' who from very early times had hawked fish about the town. 'New fresh herrings! Quick-a-lye. Quick-a-lye!' and 'New Oysters, New Oysters, New-new-cockells!' These tough characters seem to have been numbered—at least sometimes—in their hundreds, the roughest of female professions with a large casual element. Reviled though they were for everything from their smell to their morals, they could always, at the last resort, count on popular support against their traditional enemies, the high and mighty fishmongers, who were perpetually trying 'to persecute and prosecute, to weary out and utterly discourage them from following their Imployments'. Here is how Donald Lupton saw them in 1632:

These crying, wandering and travelling creatures carry their shops on their heads and their storehouse is ordinarily Billingsgate or the Bridge-foot. They set up every morning their trade afresh. They are easily set up and furnished, get something and spend it jovially and merrily. Five shillings, a basket and a good cry, is a large stock for one of them. . . . They are free of all places and pay no shop-rent, but only find repairs to it. If they drink out their whole stock, its but pawning a petticoat in Long Lane or themselves in Turnbull Street for to set up again. When they have done their fair they meet in mirth, singing and dancing and, in the middle, scolding. When in any evening they are not merry in a drinking-house it is suspected they have had bad return or else have paid some old score or else are bankrupts. They are creatures soon up and soon down. . . . [27]

The fishwives were an old London institution, but in this period their numbers and activities were greatly increased with the arrival on the scene of a virtually new food trade in which they could take a hand. Fruit and vegetables were in the course of emerging as major articles of diet. Hitherto, English apples, pears, gooseberries and nuts, together with some rather poor cabbages, beetroot, celery, turnips and onions had been brought into the market by farmers' wives and found, on the whole, an indifferent sale. But the Dutch had shown what could be done to improve this kind of food, and as their methods of market gardening crossed the North Sea a mounting volume of bulky perishable merchandise began to demand more and more room in the crowded markets. A new class of tradesmen, the fruiterers, appeared and itinerant street hawkers took a fresh lease of life. Frederick Hackwood in his book *Good Cheer* mentions the appearance at this time of better apples, strawberries, gooseberries and cherries; new strains from America of raspberries and walnuts and later of currants and apples; and more plentiful oranges and lemons, plums, apricots, peaches and quinces. Among 'edible roots and herbs' (the term vegetable had not yet arrived) there were cauliflowers, broccoli, kale, French beans and artichokes, all novelties introduced to English gardeners from abroad, as well as greatly improved carrots, turnips, onions and cabbage from the Dutch gardeners. Potatoes, however, were extremely rare, except in Lancashire, until about 1700.

All fruit and vegetables were very dear by present-day standards, and prices varied erratically with the irregularity of supplies. Even the cheapest home-grown apples and pears cost several pence a pound. The oranges and lemons from Spain commonly cost a penny or twopence each, and cabbages and cauliflowers up to about fourpence. The only really cheap vegetables were peas and beans, traditionally regarded as fodder for the stable, the sty and the pigeon-loft, but coming increasingly into the diets of the poor under pressure of the price-rise. [28] In

[27] Donald Lupton, 'London and the Countrey Carbonadoed', *Harleian Miscellany* (1812), IX, 300 ff.

[28] Rogers, *op. cit.*, V, 50–3.

spite of its price, the new fruit was such an improvement on the bitter and stunted medieval commodity that it started a new fashion in casual eating. 'Cherries ripe-ripe-ripe' and 'Pippins-fine! Pippins-fine!' must have made splendid ringing cries, rhythmical and distinctive, to tempt young appetites to greedy indulgence. As early as 1546 the growing sales of fruit by street hawkers were causing concern to the City Fathers—no doubt because they could not bear to see any sort of food, even inessential luxuries, sold indiscriminately. The Mayor issued a proclamation confining all fruit selling to the public markets. After mentioning 'the gredy appetyte that youthe hathe to frute' this proclamation asserts that in order to obtain the money for this delicacy apprentices and children 'do oftentymes by sundry means and wayes brybe, ymbesill, pyck and steale from the seid maisters, fathers and mothers, greate substance of goodes, wares and readye money and so therebye first vyciate and corrupte and do proceed many tymes (the more is the pytie) to open thefte and felony, and oftentymes do make . . . great affrayes, murders and manslaughter . . .'[29]

The proclamation against hawkers was quite ineffective, and in spite of this dreadful warning these youthful cravings soon became the popular taste of the whole city. The sales of fruit as well as vegetables expanded enormously; they occupied an important place in the new suburban markets and were among the first foods to be awarded an official wholesale market of their own.

Dairy produce, like green vegetables, was still at this time a means of ekeing out meat or fish. Milk for cooking was brought into the town by milk women from the nearby farms, walking long distances with a pair of churns on a shoulder yolk and crying 'Milk-maids Below!' as they went about the streets. For a long time it was considered unwholesome to drink raw milk (and perhaps rightly so) but by Pepys' time there was a Milk House in St James' Park where the passer-by could drink a glass of freshly-drawn milk in clean and attractive surroundings. For the use of infants and those with disordered digestions, milch-asses were walked from door to door, their product drawn directly into the customers' jugs. On May Morning, the milk-maids traditionally came round to their customers in parties to

[29] A. W. Gould, *History of the Fruiterers' Company* (1912), p. 78.

dance with music and flower-garlands for their annual tip. Pepys, for example, wrote on May-day, 1667:

> To Westminster, on the way meeting with many milk-maids with garlands upon their pails, dancing, with a fiddler before them. And saw pretty Nellie (Gwynne) standing at her lodging door in Drury Lane in her smock-sleeves and bodice looking at them.

Butter, like milk, was used as a rule for cooking, and was bought, heavily salted, in barrels. In smaller quantities, it was bought by the gallon, not as a liquid but moulded on the farm into a gallon pot, for convenient measure. Eggs, too, were mostly local farm produce, very cheap and little esteemed. 'To take eggs for your money' was a catch phrase meaning to be swindled. The one dairy product that was really important was cheese; it was eaten in large quantities by all classes, by the poor for cheapness and by the wealthy for enhancing the taste of wine. Cheeses seem generally to have been bought whole. There is never any reference to anyone buying anything less than 'a cheese', although each one varied a good deal in size and shape, not only according to its district but also to the whims of the farmer's wife who made it.

Essex used to supply nearly all London's cheese before the seventeenth century, but then they began to come increasingly from counties much farther afield, from Gloucester and Wiltshire, and especially from Cheshire. Cheesemongering in the capital became a full-time occupation and shops were opened to sell nothing but cheeses. But they were articles that would keep well and were easy to store, and all sorts of tradesmen dealt in them as a useful sideline; grocers and chandlers in particular, but many other tradesmen as well, had a cheese or two put by to sell when they could.

Cheese, in fact, leads us out of the realm of markets into that of shops. It has been said that food shopping was virtually synonymous with marketing in spite of the rise of the corn-chandler and of a handful of other traders in various lines who were edging into wholesale dealing from fixed premises. But there was one important and much older exception. One of the famous shoppers of literature, the shepherd in *A Winter's Tale*, was not off to market at all:

Let me see, what am I to buy for our sheep shearing feast? Three pounds of sugar. Five pounds of currants. Rice. (What will this sister of mine do with rice?) I must have saffron to colour the warden [pear] pies. Mace. Dates, none—that is out of my note. Nutmegs, seven. A race [root] or two of ginger (but that I may beg). Four pounds of prunes and as many raisins of the sun.

These were all grocers' goods, and the list could have been extended ten times over without exhausting all the available varieties, many of them now forgotten, of dried herbs, dried fruit and colourings. Most of them were imported, from the Mediterranean and Far-East; a few were from home, like mustard from Tewkesbury (although it was finer from Dijon) or saffron from Essex.

London grocers had specialized to some extent since the middle ages. In the fifteenth century they had been general merchants dealing in pretty nearly everything except fresh food and things connected with dress. But now, at least in London, retail grocers, while still stocking miscellaneous household materials like firewood, paper, paints, wax, canvas, arsenic, tar and so forth, were beginning to lose their former marine-store character and to concentrate on the non-perishable food items available in ever-increasing quantities from the Mediterranean, the Far-East and the New World.

One of the most important of these was sugar. In the middle ages, sugar-loaves from India and Arabia had cost up to two shillings a pound, but first Canary, and in the seventeenth century Caribbean sugar, brought the price tumbling down so that it was selling around fourpence a pound by the 1680s. The English had always been partial to sugar and as the falling price brought it within reach of the whole population it caused quite a big change in diet. Above all it accounts for the continually growing popularity of fruit. As a writer remarked in 1684, '. . . apples, pears, plums, gooseberries, currants, none of which would be made food and so advantageous to us if they were not mixed with such sweets'.[30] Another recently cheapened food which the English ate greedily and the grocers did well out of was currants and raisins, the consumption of which quadrupled in the century up to the Civil War. 'The very Greeks that sell them

[30] Anon., *General Considerations Relating to Trade* (1694).

wonder what we do with such great quantities thereof, and know not how we should spend them except we use them for dyeing or to feed hogges.'[31]

Consider the very important role of the grocer in supplying the ingredients for this very modern-sounding recipe published in 1667:

> Take half a peck of flower, two pounds and a half of currants, three or four nutmegs, one pound of Almond paste (i.e. ground almonds) two pound of butter and one pint of cream, three spoonfuls of rosewater, three quarters of a pound of sugar, half a pint of sack, a quarter of a pint of yeast and six eggs. So, make it and bake it.[32]

Grocers' shops were scattered all over the city, with a concentration of the most important in Bucklesbury and the Poultry. In Bucklesbury, too, were the apothecaries, which Stubbes declared sold 'But druggie baggage and such counterfeit stuff as is stark nought'.[33] But he underestimated them. For instance, 'Skirvie grasses for My Ladie, iis.' says the household book of Lord William Howard in 1612. 'Skurvy grass or gittings to put in the children's ale' say the Earl of Bedford's accounts in 1653. Vegetable decoctions could certainly cure mild scurvy which was very prevalent owing to defective diet, although its exact operation was not scientifically understood. Similarly, ginger and honey would ease a cough, and several other medicines were far from useless.[34] We may have less confidence, however, about the order to 'run into Bucklesburie for two ounces of dragon water'. A medical treatise of 1639 throws light on the stock of an apothecaries' shop with '*A Catalogue of those Medicaments which the Rich aught to have in their Houses*'.[35] It contains 65 items, prominent among which are 'Foure pound good common honey. A pound honey of roses. A pound honey of violets. Half a pound red rose leaves, as many violets. Foure ounces white poppy seeds. A pound of good sena of Levant. A quantity of pills of three or foure sorts'.

As the grocers' stock overlapped with the apothecaries' at one

---

[31] Fynes Morison, *Itinerary Containing Ten Years' Travels* (1907), IV, p. 176.
[32] Anon., *The Ladies' Cabinet* (1667).
[33] Stubbes, *op. cit.*, pt. II, p. 55.
[34] Drummond & Wilbraham, *op. cit.*, p. 174.
[35] Anon., *The Charitable Physician* (1639).

end of the scale, it did the same with the chandlers' at the other.
'Chandler' meant simply a retail dealer. The tallow-chandlers
proper sold in their shops chiefly soap, vinegar, butter, hops
and seville oil (olive oil), all by the barrel or the sack. The
emerging corn-chandlers, however, also dealt in these things
as a side-line to their corn or meal. One commodity they all sold
was soap, and it was the subject of a notorious monopoly granted
by Charles I as a money-raising device. Foreign soap was
excluded from the country for a while, shopkeepers were forbidden to deal in any but the patent soap and consumers were
forbidden any longer to make their own coarse soap for household use as they had often done before. Coarse soap had been
2½d. a pound and sweet or best soap, 3d., and the monopoly
nearly doubled these prices in the 'thirties for a new and inferior
variety. A sort of black-market soap, made privately, fetched up
to a shilling a pound, but two of the makers died in prison for it.[36]
This monopoly, together with several other patents in commodities as divers as salt, wine, glass and playing-cards, which
mulcted the consumers to provide a small revenue for the
crown and a larger income for the patentees, lasted until the
Civil War.

Two more items of household provision lay outside the
sphere of the markets, namely beer and coal. 'The malt liquors'
as a later writer described them 'that are in a considerable degree
our Nourishment and the common Diluters of our Food' were
bought by the cask from one of the bigger ale-houses that still
brewed their own beer, or else from a 'common brewer' down by
the Thames who brewed and sold in quantity.

There were two chief sorts: 'double' beer, now the weakest
and sometimes called 'small' at about 1½d. a gallon, and 'best'
or strongest at twice the price, as well as various illicit, stronger
brews like 'Huffcap' or 'Stingo' sold in ale-houses. All good
housekeepers kept a 15-gallon kilderkin or at least an 8-gallon
firkin of beer in the house, constantly renewed, but the poorer
sort in their rooms or 'rents' and the bad managers who ran
short could send a boy round to the ale-house for a quart pot.
There was forever trouble about the return of the pewter
tankards that the ale-houses sent out. There was never any
question of charging a deposit on tankards—probably the chronic

[36] G. Unwin, *Gilds and Companies of London* (1908), pp. 321–2.

shortage of halfpence would have made this impracticable. But it was often alleged that thousands of them were lost or stolen every year from the house-railings where they were left, like present-day milk-bottles, for the pot-boy to collect. They went to the coiners to make false shillings or to the illegal but highly profitable export trade in melted-down pewter. This went on right up to the Napoleonic wars, when *The Times* indignantly reported that all the publicans in London had agreed to stop lending out pewter pots, or, as *The Times* put it, 'to estimate the loss of a few pots above that of their customers!' There must have been an ale-house or a victualling house (that is, an ale-house that served meals) on nearly every street corner. In the City itself in 1614 the Lord Mayor had them counted and found there were over a thousand in the square mile, with a stock of beer of 40,000 barrels.[37]

Considering that beer was a basic necessity of life, its provision in the London of this period seems to have given rise to surprisingly little trouble. The government kept an eye on all brewers because beer was subject to excise duty from the Commonwealth onwards, but more important to the peace and good order of the trade in liquor was the fact that it was bought direct from the manufacturer, locally (for though it was now practically all made with hops, and was far stronger than the medieval liquor, it still would not keep long in store or bear the shaking—or cost—of long transport), and so its sale in London was highly competitive, and middlemen had no part to play. Coal on the other hand, although an equally important basic necessity both for heating and for cooking, was the subject of more fraud, extortion, official corruption and bitter recrimination than all other items of household provision put together, a condition related not merely to its continuous scarcity throughout this period, but to the number of times it changed hands between the leaving the pits in Durham or Scotland and reaching the London consumer.

Before ever it reached the retailers, the whole trade in sea coal was violently erratic, subject to the interruptions of weather and the depredations of privateers and monopolists. But it was the evils they could see nearer home that incensed the con-

[37] W. H. Overall, ed., *Analytical Index to the Remembrancia of the City of London, 1579–1664* (1878), p. 159.

sumers; the false rumours of wars and storms deliberately put about to panic the market; the false measures and small sacks; the 'winking money' paid to the City coal inspectors who grew rich by shutting their eyes to fraud; the artificial shortages created by hiding coal until the winter season; the exacting of cash payment from customers months in advance of delivery. Coal, in fact, exhibited all the evils of a sellers' market run riot. It was one that had sprung to life fairly recently since London, in her sudden expansion, had consumed all the burnable wood within easy reach. But sellers' markets were nothing new in London and the authorities had had plenty of experience in cracking down heavily, even on honest traders, when they thought the interests of the consumers demanded it. Indeed, in the early seventeenth century, the corn shortage was exercising the Common Council to its wits' end, while the growing scandal of the coal trade went almost unheeded.

It is not altogether clear why the coal trade was allowed so much freedom. The answer must be, in part, that it did not share in the almost mystical importance that traditionally attached to even the least of the food trades; and, in part, that even when it had risen to be an important commodity, it was still, for a long time, not important to the right people. It started as the poor man's fuel, a dirty, smoky, smelly substitute for honest wood and charcoal, containing a good deal of stone and black earth. ('Oh, husband, we shall never bee well, we nor our Children, whilst we live in the smell of this Citie's seacole smoke.') In the 1590s, sea coal was already 'the chiefest fuel of the poor'. As late as 1644, the House of Lords could still pass a measure, admittedly an abortive one, to create a smokeless zone in the fashionable end of the town by banning sea coal west of London Bridge. Whatever the reason, the cries of the wronged consumers went unheeded until it was too late and the evils that had fastened themselves on the trade plagued rich and poor alike until the reforms of the eighteenth century.

There were two ways of buying coal, according to whether the purchaser wanted big quantities from big dealers or little quantities from little ones. Instead of the present tons and hundredweights it was sold, in the absence of enough big scales, by volume; in chaldrons (1.1/3 tons) and bushels (a little over a hundredweight). The bushel measure has left its mark on the city of Hull, where coal is retailed to this day in 140 lb. sacks. The poor 'daily buy their provision by the peck or bushel, not having means to make any store beforehand'. They bought their meagre ration from one of the many shopkeepers—mainly corn or tallow chandlers—who kept coal in their backyard as a side-line to their main business, and they carried the sacks home on their backs. What they paid for it is hard to determine, because prices swung up and down so erratically. During the Civil War for example the price was officially fixed at 13s. 6d. a ton retail, but J. U. Nef says that at times of crisis in this period, the poor of London were asked to buy coal at prices approaching 80s. or even 100s. a ton, while even at the lowest prices (which the poor seldom enjoyed, since coal was not a perishable com-modity), it would cost about one-tenth of a labouring man's wages to light a fire once a day to cook some food. It was said, and it may well have been true, that during the Civil War 'Many poor have perished, being unable to buy fuel'. This was one respect in which the poor of the metropolis were worse off than their counterparts in the country who could nearly always gather some sort of firing by their own efforts.

The better-off Londoner who could buy and store a chaldron and upwards, went or sent to the Billingsgate district to a wood-monger's yard (the old name survived for a long time), and struck the best bargain he could, having regard to the state of supplies and the state of his own cellar. At this period coal was always sold for cash, if not actually paid for in advance. That, however, was not the end of the transaction, for the coal dealers for a long time enjoyed a monopoly of all the coal carts allowed on the streets, so that too good a bargain made in buying coal was almost certain to be followed by a correspondingly bad one for the hire of a cart to carry it away. The cartage monopoly was only broken at the Restoration. Something of the anxiety attending the buying of coal is reflected in Pepys's diary, in the great trouble he took to enlarge his coal cellar, and in such entries as 'Got some coals at 23s. a chaldron. A good hearing I thank God'.

Prices never fell again after they shot up in the famine years of the Civil War. By that time coal had become virtually all London's fuel. Price enforcement only dried up the supply and was timidly abandoned, and 'private villanies inflamed and increased Public Misfortunes'. Anyone with a few pounds to spare could speculate in coal dealing, could charge what he could get and deliver as short measure as he could bribe officials and customers' servants to overlook. The motto of the coal merchant was said to be 'It is a Cheat, to be Just, and Just to Cheat'.

Throughout this period and long after it, food and fuel were the bulk of the expenditure of all but the very rich. Today these things take only one-third of the average income, which is why the prices of necessities always sound so high in relation to wages before the industrial revolution. Allowing for differences in the value of money, food and fuel *were* exceedingly dear, so dear that they left very little room in most family budgets for anything else, and the buying of them was a correspondingly anxious and important job. Moreover, they had all to be bought the hard way; the housewife or her servant (or surprisingly often, her husband) had to go out and bargain hard for them, item by item, with the patience to conduct lengthy battles of words while standing in the cold and wet and shouting over the noise of the crowd. She had to guess at weights, watch for deceit, pay cash, accept all goods loose without wrappings or containers of any kind and get them home with no help from the seller. Yet none of these things is complained of by the writers of those days. They were content to rejoice that in London, as nowhere else, so many goods were there for the buying.

> Strangers have admired at the prodigous plenty of all sorts that are to be seen in the great and well-furnished Markets . . . where any sort of goods may be purchased at a convenient and reasonable Rate. Nor is there any Place in the Kingdom where Poor People (or such as would be very Frugal) may live *Cheaper*, or the Splendid Liver, *gallanter* . . .[38]

[38] N. H., *The Compleat Tradesman* (1684).

V

⟡⟡⟡⟡⟡⟡⟡⟡⟡⟡⟡⟡⟡⟡⟡⟡⟡⟡⟡⟡⟡⟡⟡⟡⟡⟡⟡⟡⟡⟡⟡⟡

Shopping for Pleasure in London

⟡⟡⟡⟡⟡⟡⟡⟡⟡⟡⟡⟡⟡⟡⟡⟡⟡⟡⟡⟡⟡⟡⟡⟡⟡⟡⟡⟡⟡⟡⟡⟡

> That which hath been the bane of almost all trades is the too great
> number of Shopkeepers in this Kingdom . . . because the Shop-
> keeping trade is an easy life and thence many are induced to run
> into it and there hath been no law to prevent it, which maketh
> very many (like a Mighty Torrent) to fall into it, which hath been
> verified for several years past by the many Husbandmen, Labourers
> and Artificers who have left off their working trades and turned
> Shopkeepers.
>
> N.H., *The Compleat Tradesman, 1684*

W H E N we turn from the food markets of London to the places
where people bought other kinds of goods it is hard to believe
that we are still looking at the same period and the same
customers, for the growth of genuine retail shops in this era
was so rapid that there is almost a modern ring about some
contemporary references to shopping. Then, as now, clothes
and personal accessories constituted the chief bait for the
strolling shopper, and groups of little establishments for the sale
of these things grew up in several fashionable spots; in Cheapside and London Bridge and the Royal Exchange; in Paternoster
Row which was filled with mercers and lace-men; in Cannon
Street which was famous for linen as was Cordwainer Street for
hosiery. And gradually, as the seventeenth century progressed,
ever newer and more fashionable shops spread westwards along
Fleet Street and the Strand.

These early retail shops, although they were far removed
from the world of the middle ages, were not all of them quite

shops in the modern sense. To begin with, there was still some ambiguity about the very word 'shop'. As used then it meant anywhere where selling took place, from a mere tray round the neck of a hawker, or a market stall, to a merchant's warehouse. 'Stall' too, though generally used in the modern sense was occasionally applied to the display or shop-window of an ordinary shop. The usual term for what we would call an ordinary shop was 'standing shop', while an 'open' shop seems usually to have meant a shed built out on the front of a house, perhaps rented from the house-owner or even owned quite independently. Some of these sheds had wooden sides, but more often they had only a penthouse or roof supported by posts. But the commonest kind of retail shop occupied the ground floor of a house and by the end of the seventeenth century this was what the word had come to mean; by then, too, many of them had had their open windows glazed with small panes, and the counter and the business dealings taken inside.

Meanwhile, six o'clock in the morning was the time to begin the day's business (or in the depths of winter, eight) when the market people were taking up their stands in the street and the apprentices came out to 'unbutton' their masters' shops, let down the boards and set out the goods. Two and a half feet was the most that a board might project into any street or alleyway within the City of London, and if the upper half of the shutter, as was often the case, was swung up on hinges to form a little roof or penthouse to protect the board, it must be at least nine feet above the ground (as with tavern posts and signboards) to allow the passage of people on horseback. By nine o'clock the shopkeepers were at the 'heat of the market', and they kept at it until eight or nine o'clock at night, or in winter until it was too dark to see. 'The modest hour of nine being just proclaimed by Time's oracle from every steeple, the joyful alarm of Bow Bell called the weary apprentices from their work to unhitch their folded shutters and button up their shops till the next morning.'[1]

But this long day did not produce a great deal of business; it merely spread it out. Barnaby Rich in *The Honestie of the Age* in 1614 tried to estimate a shopkeeper's turnover:

[1] E. Ward, *The London Spy* (1698), p. 25.

H

It may well be supposed to be but an ill-customed shop that taketh not five shillings a day, one day with another throughout the whole year, or if one doth take lesse, two other may take more. But let us make our account but after two shillings six-pence a day, for he that taketh lesse than that would be ill able to pay his rent or to keepe open his shop-windows. . . .

Rich may have been wrong in this guesswork; obviously silk-mercers or goldsmiths, for instance, took far more than five shillings if they made a sale at all. But the guess itself is illuminating; who would suggest that a modern shopkeeper could make a living on takings of, say, twenty-five shillings a day? And in fact all the evidence on seventeenth-century London retailers points to a general acceptance of very slow turnover, very high profit margins, and, with a few notable exceptions, to a poor and precarious livelihood.

For much of the day the shopkeeper, or his apprentice, stood beside the board, or out in the street, shouting his wares and accosting the passers-by. The incessant bawl 'What lack ye? What lack ye?' was not the mark of the cheap jack only. 'Madam, will you buy?' was an appeal that attracted the attention of many a fine lady and could lead her to quite expensive purchases. And when a possible customer was attracted the shopkeeper did not grudge the time or the dignity to bargain endlessly over every item he showed the customer in an effort to force a sale. 'If any chance to step in, he hath hocus tricks enough to delude them, and rarely shall they stir out (like sheep engaged in briars) but they shall leave some fleece behind them.'[2]

Some of the shopkeepers' 'vent', however, depended on a newer and less strenuous kind of salesmanship: the growing practice of making an attractive display of goods on the shop-board, so that the fashionable throng strolling at leisure should be tempted to buy on impulse. Several writers in the seventeenth century commented on this habit of making a show, the more puritan of them strongly disapproving of the inducement to extravagance that a well-stocked shop window provided. But a visiting Frenchman, in 1663, was full of praise:

There is no City in the World that has so many and such fine shops. For they are large and their decorations are as valuable

[2] N.H., *The Compleat Tradesman* (1684).

as those of the stage. The scene is new everywhere which exceedingly pleases and attracts the eye as we go along . . . [3]

The typical retail shopkeeper at this time, whether his shop was big or little, was a man with anything from one apprentice to half a dozen; as many as he could get and his Company's regulations would allow him to take. Each apprentice was hopefully on the road to membership of his master's Company and so to civic freedom. All the donkey-work of the house and shop was performed by the youngest boy; the meanest maid-servant could generally order him about, set him sweeping and cleaning, fetching water and carrying slops, and he did not escape until a more junior boy succeeded him. But the status of the older apprentices was directly geared to that of their master. As shopkeeping in London became increasingly profitable and respectable during the course of the seventeenth century, so the best shops attracted recruits from better-class families—younger sons who, a hundred years before, might have been apprenticed to substantial merchants but have thought a 'mere retailing shopkeeper' beneath their station. Such apprentices were paying premiums of forty or fifty pounds in mid-century, eighty to a hundred towards the end of it, for their indentures. Goldsmiths or rich silk mercers sometimes charged several hundred pounds. Youths whose fathers could pay these sums often enjoyed generous private pocket-money, and good clothes and, as was inevitable, were often accused of being lazy, insolent, and 'above their business'. Class distinctions were widening between shop-apprentices as between their masters. Consider the implications of this extract from *The English Rogue*, written in Charles II's reign.

My master was not only a tailor but kept a broker's shop wherein he sold all sorts of clothes, new and old. He lived in one of the principallest streets in the City and was in good esteem with his neighbours, who were all persons of some quality, not of the meaner sort but substantial tradesmen, as goldsmiths, grocers, drugsters, scriveners, stationers, etc. And I, being now well fitted with clothes and having my pockets well lined with money which I had still kept by me, was a fit and welcome companion to the best sort of apprentices, into whose society I was soon to insinuate myself . . . [4]

[3] *The Antiquary*, XIII (1886), p. 35.
[4] Meriton Latroon, *The English Rogue* (1668-9), II, 163.

Retail shopkeeping was thought of as a man's trade, and a man took only boys as apprentices. In the City, women were not yet allowed to enter men's trades, except in the case of the widow of a freeman who could take over her husband's business. But there was one spot where the dykes of the City's privileges had been breached and non-freemen—and women—had begun to keep standing shops. This spot was the Royal Exchange in the very heart of the City, and the shops there were rather special. Sir Thomas Gresham, the famous Elizabethan financier whose mind was far above haberdashery, dreamed of modelling London on the glories of Antwerp as an international financial centre, and he decided that in order to attract foreign merchants to his city it would be a good idea to start by bringing the existing ones in out of the rain. Hitherto they had been conducting their business in the open in the middle of Lombard Street. For them he built the first Royal Exchange at his own expense, in 1568. Except that its courtyard was not roofed, the building was very like the present one, very foreign and classical. Like its model in Antwerp it had a 'pawne' or gallery, and here and round the courtyard there were about a hundred small booths or shops whose rent was intended to provide the upkeep of the building.

The merchants took to their new quarters at once with appropriate gratitude, but the foreign idea of detached—what we should nowadays call 'lock-up'—shops all massed together inside a building was treated by tradesmen with considerable suspicion, and after three years many of the lettings still had no takers and the whole project was threatened with failure. As Howe described it, writing in 1631:

After the Royal Exchange which is now called the Eye of London had been builded two or three years it stood in a manner empty. And a little before Her Majesty was to come thither to view the beauty thereof and to give it a name, Sir Thomas Gresham, in his own person, went twice or thrice in one day round and about the upper pawne and besaught those few shopkeepers then present that they would furnish and adorn with wares and wax lights as many shops as they either could or would, and they should have all those shops so furnished rent free for a year, which otherwise at that time was 40 shillings a shop by the year. And within two years after he raised that rent to 4 marks (£2. 13. 4d.) and within a while after that to £4. 10s. a year. And then all shops were well furnished according to that time, for then the milliners and haberdashers in that place sold mousetraps, bird-cages, shoeing-horns, lanthorns, jew's trumps, etc. There was also at that time kept shops in the upper pawne of the Royal Exchange, armourers that sold both old and new armour, apothecaries, booksellers, goldsmiths, and glass-sellers, although now it is as plenteously stored with all kinds of rich wares and fine commodities as any particular place in Europe, into which place many foreign princes daily send to be served of the best sort. [5]

The shops, as Howe reminds us, were so placed as to need artificial light all day, in spite of the fact that the practice of passing off shoddy goods by candlelight had long been a notorious abuse and was, indeed, something of a stock joke of the times. Nevertheless, once the new idea of a shopping precinct was well launched it became a great social, and therefore commercial, success. The shopkeepers seem to have been so busy that they had to attend to their stocks on Sundays, for we find 'The Keepers of the Pawne in the Royall Exchange presented [prosecuted] for that they suffer those that have shops therein to have recourse thither on Sabbath days for setting up of their wayres'. [6] Something of the flavour of this new kind of shopping can be gathered from this excerpt from a book published in 1605, which depicts a scene in the Royal Exchange.

Shop Assistant:
Madame, what doth it please you to have? Would ye have any faire linnen cloath? Mistresse, see what I have and I will showe you the fairest linnen cloath in London. If you do not like it you may leave it. You shall bestowe nothing but the looking on. The payne shall be ours to showe you . . .
Lady:
Into what shop shall we go?
Gentleman:
Madame, will it please you to enter into this shop? This mayde doth invite us to it by her tongue, which she hath as free as any that I ever heard.

---

[5] H. B. Wheatley & W. Cunningham, *London Past and Present* (1891), p. 182.
[6] Kenneth Rogers, *Old London; Cornhill and Around* (1935), p. 42, quoting the Wardmote Inquests of Cornhill Ward, 1577.

Lady:

Yet she is scarce worthy of your love, though she be reasonable
fine and pretty. But seeing that you affect her, we will see what
she will furnish us for your sake. Now my friend, have you
any fair holland?

Shop Assistant:

Yes forsooth Madame. The fairest lawne that ever you handled.

Lady:

Thou speakest a proud word! What knowest thou what
lawne I have handled? It may be that I have had better than any
that is in all thy shop.

Shop Assistant:

I do not say to the contrary Madame. But so it is, notwithstanding that I have as good and faire as ever was made.

Lady:

Well, well. You do but your duetie, but God knoweth how
largely you will speake when you shall be for yourselfe, seeing
that you praise so highly your master's merchandise . . . But you
learne your trade for to live thereby heerafter. How sell you
the Elle [1¼ yds.] of this cambricke?

Shop Assistant:

I know you have such good judgement in linnen cloath that
I dare not show you anything for good unless it were so.
There needes no reply to such a lady as you are. You may
say, your pleasure, the cambricke will cost you twentie shillings
the elle.

Lady:

Truly it lacketh no price. And if things be so much worth as
those that sell them make them out to be, your cambricke is
very good, for you holde it at a good price. But yet I will not
give so much though.

Shop Assistant:

How much will it please you to give then, Madame, to the end
that I may have your custom?

Lady:

I will give you fifteene shillings. If you will take my money,
make short, for I have other business than to tarye heere.

Shop Assistant:

Truly, Madame, I would be verye sorie to denie you if I could
give it at that price. But in truth I cannot unless I should lose
by it.

Lady:

I will give you sixteene and not one hafepenny more. Mistress
Dupont Galliard, is it not enough?

106

2nd. Lady:
>Methinketh it, Madame, that you offer too much. As for me, I would not give so much.

Lady:
>Let us go then, to the shop on the other side.

Shop Assistant (*to her employer*):
>Shall we give it her at that price, Mistris?

Proprietress:
>Show me the mark of it. Yes. Call them backe.

Shop Assistant:
>Madame, if you finde any better, I am content to give you mine for nothing.

Lady:
>Let it be as good as it will, you shall not have of me a penny more for it, for I have offred too much alreadye.

Proprietress:
>Madame, I am content to lose in it of the price that I sell it to others, in hope that you will buye of us when you shall have need. How many elles will it please you to have?

Lady:
>Halfe a dossen elles.

Proprietress:
>Go to. . . . Where is the Elle?

Lady:
>Make good measure.
>
>Master DuVaultl'amour, I pray you to buy for me yonder wastcote that I see in that other shop, for if I cheapen it they will over-price me by the halfe. As for you, they know that you have better skill in it. Joley, (*to her maid*) pay for this cloath. Now, are you paid and contented?

Proprietress:
>Yes, Madame, I most humbly thanke you. Beleeve me, you have bestowed your money very well and you have good cheap. Will you buye no skirts, ruffes, falling bands, handkerchers, night coyfes, falls, sockes, edged-lace, boot-hosen wrought, or any other thing that we have. All is at your commaundement.

Lady:
>Not for this time I thanke you.

Proprietress:
>Madame, God have you in his keeping.[7]

The principal shopping street in the City in the seventeenth century was Cheapside, 'worthily called the Beauty of London'.

[7] Peter Erondell, *The French Garden* (1605).

It was very wide, as streets were reckoned then, and very busy, being packed every day with the throngs and stalls and paraphernalia of the great food market as well as with a good deal of passing traffic. It was the setting for all the great civic gatherings and processions and it was lined continuously with fine houses over the richest shops at the highest rents in the kingdom. By the seventeenth century there were all kinds of shops and many taverns in Cheapside, but in Elizabeth's reign, it had been almost monopolized by goldsmiths and silk mercers, the two richest retail trades. Robert Herrick, who wrote *Cherry Ripe*, must have grown up with the sound of that cry under his window on many a summer's morning, for he was the son of one Cheapside goldsmith and apprenticed to another. Maitland, looking back to the London of 1600 which was a century before his time, says, 'Then it was beautiful to behold the glorious appearance of goldsmiths' shops in the South Row of Cheapside, which in a continuous course reached from the Old Change to Bucklersbury, exclusive of four shops only of other trades in all that space.'[8]

The sight of so much precious metal and jewellery gathered in one spot impressed contemporaries in different ways. Visitors regarded it as one of the sights of London. The underworld saw it as an open challenge and not only did shop-lifting teams 'heave many a booth' there but the more subtle confidence tricksters reaped a good harvest, for it was part of the goldsmith's trade to lend money on valuables. The melancholy writer, Stubbes, saw Goldsmiths' Row as a nest of extortioners. 'If you buy a chain of gold or a ring or any kind of plate . . . you shall pay almost halfe in halfe more than it is worth, for they will persuade you that the workmanship of it comes to so much, the fashion of it so much, and I cannot tell you what . . .'[9] But it was the impression it made on the tax assessors that was finally fatal. Seeing so many golden eggs, they could not resist the temptation to kill off many of the geese that laid them, and at last they scared many of the goldsmiths off to less conspicuous situations or else to follow their customers into the growing suburbs in Holborn, Fleet Street and the Strand.[10] 'It was

---

[8] W. Maitland, *A History and Survey of London* (1756), p. 301.

[9] P. Stubbes, *Anatomie of Abuses* (ed. F. J. Furnivall, 1877), pt. II, p. 25.

[10] N. J. Brett-James, *The Growth of Stuart London* (1935), p. 390.

remembered how impoverished the City is since the last [royal] loan,' wrote a member of King James's court in a letter in 1622, 'and it is a strange sight to see the meaner trades creep into Goldsmiths' Row, the glory and beauty of Cheapside.[11]

The supposed ruin of the famous street struck many observers, including Howe, who remarked that 'goldsmiths' shops were turned into Milliners, Booksellers, Linendrapers and others'. It was the first, but far from the last, example of a street of shops 'going down'; streets that 'go up' have never attracted particular attention. In 1629, Charles I ordered the goldsmiths to return and told the Lord Mayor to close every shop in Cheapside that was not a goldsmith's. And a fine mixture they were, stationers, milliners, band-sellers, drugsters, a cook, a girdler, and so forth, some twenty-four in all.[12] This was evidently the street's new character which royal interference did nothing to alter, a mixed shopping street distinguished chiefly by the prosperity of its tradesmen, those able to 'undergo the great fyne and yearly rent of a house in Cheapside'.

It was in the smart shops of Cheapside that the practice grew up of having the tradesmen's wives sitting in seats 'built-a-purpose' at the doors of the shops to engage passers-by in conversation and entice them into making purchases. 'You are full of pretty answers,' says Jaques in *As You Like It*. 'Have you not been acquainted with goldsmiths' wives and conned them out of rings?' These talkative ladies developed a famous line in badinage with the men-about-town who idled up and down that length of street and showed off to their friends by allowing themselves to be teased into making extravagant bargains. The wit and beauty of these Cheapside wives became something of a legend. 'In truth, a fine-faced lady in a wainscot carve'd seat is a worthy ornament to a tradesman's shop, and an attractive, I'll warrant. Her husband shall find it in the custom of his ware, I'll assure him!'[13] The fashion seems to have been practically confined to Cheapside, where no doubt the wit was sharpened by constant practice and mutual consent as well as stimulated by an

[11] *Calendar of State Papers, Domestic, 1619–1623*, p. 457.
[12] W. H. Overall, ed., *Analytical Index to the Remembrancia of the City of London, 1579–1664* (1878), p. 106.
[13] Stubbes, *op. cit.*, pt. II, p. 276n., quoting Marston, *The Dutch Courtesan* (1607).

expectant audience, but there are some seventeenth-century
ballads that speak as though it was not unknown elsewhere:

> But if thy wife be fair and thou be poor
> Let her stand like a picture at thy door . . .

It sounds a chilly occupation for the wives, but the people of
that time seem to have been nearly impervious to cold and wet;
certainly they lived far more out of doors than we do, fore-
gathering with their friends in the street, taking their
pleasures in public gardens and in open-air theatres and cockpits,
doing their marketing and shopping all in the open. So it is not
entirely surprising that the shopkeepers and their wives should
also have felt at home in the street among their customers.

Another fashionable group of shops, but of a rather different
character, appeared on London Bridge. This was still the only
bridge over the Thames and it was lined on both sides with tall
houses, so that except for an occasional glimpse between the
buildings of the river below, it was like any other London street.
It was very narrow and choked with traffic entering London
from the south, but it also had a busy pedestrian traffic of
Londoners walking over to Bankside to enjoy all the amuse-
ments—bull- and bear-baiting and theatres—that were banned
from the City. The bridge was far too crowded a place to become
a fashionable rendezvous like the Exchange or Cheapside, but
there were enough rich customers passing to and fro over it to
provide a brisk trade in fashion goods and nearly every house
was a retail shop. Its ballad-sellers were famous, and later on its
bookshops; and several painters, following Hans Holbein in
Henry VIIIth's reign, had their workshops there. In 1633 a
fire destroyed the first forty-one of its ninety houses, and a contemporary record of it gives us a list of the shops on the northern
half of the bridge. The houses were not numbered, of course, so
the order in this list is probably arbitrary. Nevertheless, it gives
a striking picture of how largely dress and its accessories were
responsible for the development of retail shops; apart from one
private house and two empty ones, only six of these forty-one
shops are not concerned with some form of wearing apparel.

SHOPS ON THE NORTHERN HALF OF LONDON BRIDGE
IN 1633[14]

1. Haberdasher of Small Wares
2. Hosier
3. Haberdasher of Small Wares
4. Hosier
5. Shewmaker
6. Haberdasher of Hattes
7. Hosier
8. Silkman
9. Milliner
10. Hosier
11. Haberdasher of Small Wares
12. Glover
13. Mercer
14. Private House
15. Silkman
16. Empty
17. Stiller of Strong Waters
18. Girdler
19. Silkman
20. Lyning Draper
21. Mercer
22. Wolling (woollen) Draper
23. Salter
24. Haberdasher of Small Wares
25. Haberdasher of Hattes
26. Haberdasher of Hattes
27. Glover
28. Hosier
29. Grocer
30. Empty
31. Haberdasher of Small Wares
32. Haberdasher of Small Wares
33. Haberdasher of Hattes
34. Haberdasher of Hattes
35. Haberdasher of Small Wares
36. Haberdasher of Small Wares
37. Grocer
38. Woolling Draper
39. Needle Maker
40. Scrivener
41. Hosier

The ubiquitous 'haberdasher of small wares' is probably the hardest of all these early retail dealers to envisage. His was a kind of all-sorts shop whose stock overlapped with that of the glover and hosier and needlemaker and so forth but included every kind of small manufacture too unimportant to have a specialist shop of its own. He even sold books occasionally until specifically forbidden to do so in 1637. Here is an Elizabethan woman getting ready to go out; all these knick-knacks and a great many more she would normally have bought at a haberdasher's shop:

> Give me my girdle and see that all the furniture be at it. Look if my cizers, the pincers, the penknife, the knife to close letter with, the bodkin, the ear-picker and my seal be in the case. Where is my purse to wear upon my gowne? And see that my silver comfet box be full of comfets. Have I a cleane hankercher? I will have no muffe for it is not cold, but shall I have no gloves? Bring me my mask and my fanne . . .[15]

[14] Richard Thomson, *Chronicles of Old London Bridge* (1839), p. 294.
[15] Peter Erondell, *op. cit.*

One of their paying lines was 'estrich' feathers dyed in bright colours, so popular that 'every child hath them in his cap'. Improvements in felt manufacture in Elizabeth's reign made big felt hats very popular in place of the knitted or woven cap, and a fine hat-band and feather were needed to set off a hat to advantage and were more expensive than the hat itself. The *Gull's Hornbook* warns the innocent that although he may bestow forty shillings on the latest shaped hat and a feather he may see someone at the playhouse wearing 'the very same block . . . when the haberdasher swore to you that the impression was extent that very morning'.[16] Plumes were also necessary for ceremonial occasions, for armour and escutcheons and hearses. The Duke of Rutland's steward bought some from a foreigner trading in one of the liberties: '29th March, 1613. Paid to Mrs Gascard, a frenchwoman in Black Friars, for the plume of my Lord's caske, for the fetheres for his Lordship's horse, for the fetheres for the two spare horses, for fetheres for 2 pages and thirteen yeomen, £24.'[17] (Multiply that by ten!) But the normal way for a private citizen to buy his hat feathers was from the haberdasher.

Points were another of the haberdasher's regular lines. They were constantly in demand by everyone at 2d. or 3d. a dozen. They wore out quickly, so they were not sewn onto clothes but simply looped through holes (known as O's), and these loose strips of soft leather or linen tape were always getting lost. (Schoolboys, who were not normally blessed with pocket-money, used them to gamble with.) Buttons came in in the seventeenth century, in pewter, brass or silver and cost from a few pence to a few shillings a dozen, and by their relative durability spoiled a good market. Points survived only in shoe-lacing.

Ruffs and bands were sometimes bought at the haberdasher's, but more often, like shirts, if they were not made at home they were ordered to be made to measure by a seamstress who was supplied with the necessary amount of lawn—again, very often bought at the haberdasher's. Fine sewing and embroidery was an acknowledged occupation in London of 'pure maids' or 'puritans' in the suburbs, some of whom, we are told, took the opportunity to embroider their clients' underwear with scriptural

16 Thomas Dekker, *The Gull's Hornbook* (1609), (ed. Chas. Hindley, 1872), p. 62.
17 *Hist. Manuscripts Comm., Rutland Manuscripts, Vol. IV* (1905), p. 493.

texts in place of the more conventional floral patterns.[18] Another respectable womanly occupation was starching, which was a skilled trade and several degrees above laundering. Until the sober days of the Commonwealth put an end to the fashion, the making and starching of ruffs was almost an industry in itself. The setting was done with various sorts of metal cone, called 'poking sticks', which were heated in the fire and held in place until the heavily starched linen dried in frills. But the English climate made nonsense of this Italian style. 'If it happens that a shower of rain catch them . . . they go flip flap in the wind like rags flying abroad, and lie upon their shoulders like the dishe-clout of a slut.'[19] So poking sticks of different kinds and sizes were part of everyone's equipment, either to attempt launder-ing at home or even more to effect running repairs, and, of course, these too were obtained at the haberdasher's.

It is no accident that among all the fashion shops on the northern half of London Bridge we find only one shoemaker. Boot and shoemakers were all over the city, making goods to the customers' orders, but the ones patronized by fashionable people were the aliens, who had whole rows of shops in St Martin's and Blackfriars. For foreigners in the liberties enjoyed a position of some advantage in the shoemaking trade, being outside the war which the Cordwainers' (that is, the shoe-makers') Company was waging at the time with the suppliers of leather and which led to an endless series of restrictive and even contradictory regulations about the way that leather for shoes could be tanned and the way that shoes could be cut out and punched and sewn. London shoemakers, and even many in the suburbs, found themselves entangled in red tape; the regula-tions masqueraded as safeguards against faulty workmanship and were sharply enforced by periodic inspections and fines, although they were really only weapons in the battles between the richer shoemakers and the rich leather-sellers over the right to sell leather ready-cut or in small quantities to the working shoemakers.[20] Hampered by these out-of-date rules, in a period when styles and tastes were changing rapidly, the English shoe-makers found it hard to compete in the expanding market for

[18] Stubbes, *op. cit.*, pt. II, p. 53.
[19] *ibid.*, pt. II, p. 51.
[20] G. Unwin, *Gilds and Companies of London* (1908), pp. 252–3.

novel footwear. Theirs was, however, one of the few crafts that fought the 'putting out' system which in so many other trades was dividing the makers from the shopkeepers. They were not allowed to sell any shoes that had not been made on their own premises, or to evade this rule by keeping more than one shop, and shoemakers too poor to rent a shop of their own were not allowed to sell to the trade but had to do mending or 'cobbling'. This was a feature of the cordwainers' rules in many towns, and one that lasted into the eighteenth century; and indeed, the craftsman-retailer remained prominent in the shoe industry until the days of mass-production and machine manufacture.

Meanwhile, in the seventeenth century, the man or woman of fashion was looking for the new light-weight footwear, the slippers of velvet or soft white or red Spanish leather, or the heel-less shoes for men known as pantoffles which they kept kicking against the house walls to keep on their feet. These and many other up-to-date kinds of shoes and boots were almost a monopoly of the foreigners. 'If thy quicksilver can run so far on thy errand as to fetch these boots out of St Martin's, let it be thy prudence to have them.'[21] At the beginning of the century, it was usual to give about the same price for shoes as for the knee-length stockings to go with them. A servant or apprentice, for example, wore hand-knitted woollen or grey worsted stockings at from 2s. to 3s. a pair with plain shoes whose price was tending to rise as the years went by. A prosperous tradesman or plain gentleman wore machine-knitted stockings of wool or thread costing about 10s. (but getting cheaper as machine knitting improved) with a pair of good quality English-made 'Spanish' or Spanish leather shoes for anything up to about five shillings. And the dandy wore nothing but silk on his legs for which 16s. was a cheap price and which sometimes cost up to 37s. in James I reign; 'and how could they be less when as the very knitting of them is worth a noble or a royal'[22] (15s. or 16s.). And these stockings would be matched with an equally expensive pair of exquisite but impractical pumps from one of the foreign shoemakers.

'Riding' boots and 'riding' stockings were both heavier and dearer than everyday ones, just as 'riding cloaks' were thicker,

[21] Dekker, *op. cit.*, p. 26.
[22] Stubbes, *op. cit.*, pt. II, p. 57.

'riding hats' more waterproof, and even 'riding swords' were more businesslike. Arms were part of every gentleman's wardrobe and the usual equipment was a duelling rapier, a dagger and a riding sword which, at least until the middle of the century, were not kept solely for ornament. Spanish arms were still strongly favoured, although English craftsmanship was improving fast about this time and many a home-made product passed for Spanish in the shops. The armourer, now beginning to call himself a cutler, sold both arms and knives, and Fleet Street was his favourite home. Here is a dramatist's idea of a fool buying his first sword, not from a cutler but from a confidence trickster.

> Brainworm: Gentlemen, please you change a few crowns for this excellent good blade here? I am a poor gentleman, a soldier. . . .
> I assure you the blade may become the side or thigh of the best prince in Europe.
> Knowall: Aye, with a velvet scabbard, I think.
> Stephen: Nay, an't be mine, it shall have a velvet scabbard, cos, that's flat. I'll not wear it as it is, an' you give me an angel.
> Brainworm: At your worship's pleasure, sir. 'Tis a most pure Toledo.
> Stephen: I had rather it were a Spaniard![23]

No account of buying clothes in the London of this period would be complete without some reference to Houndsditch and Long Lane. This is how Donald Lupton described them in the year 1632.

> A man that comes here as a stranger would think there had been some great death of men and women hereabouts, he sees so many suits and no men for them. Here are suits for all the lawyers of London to deal withal. The inhabitants are beholden to the hangman for he furnishes their shops. The jailer and broker are birds of a feather; the one imprisons the body and the other the clothes and both make men pay dear for their lodging. . . . [The second-hand clothes dealer] loves birds best that so often shed their feathers. In short, he is no tradesman; if you weighed the whole bunch of them you shall not find an ounce of honesty for a pound of craft.[24]

[23] Ben Jonson, *Every Man in His Humour*, Act II, scene iii.
[24] Donald Lupton, 'London and the Countrey Carbonadoed' *Harleian Miscellany* (1812) IX, 320.

Now that clothes were getting so elaborate and expensive the second-hand-clothes market flourished accordingly. The shop-keepers called themselves brokers on the excuse that they advanced loans on clothes, but there were brokers in several more respectable trades who resented this misuse of their name. In Elizabeth's reign, pawnbrokers were said to charge exhor-bitant interest rates, 50 per cent or even 80 per cent, and goods were forfeited at once if the monthly interest was not paid on the due day.[25] One broker in Long Lane in 1635 took no less than 360 cloaks to pawn in the short space of twelve days, and this not in the spring but in the chilly days of October. But the main part of a Houndsditch broker's business was to buy and sell clothes outright, and to ask no awkward questions about their origin. Fancy clothes were all so costly to buy new that there was a flourishing industry in stealing them, especially in 'angling' them with hook and line through the open window while their owners slept. 'This dunghill trade of brokery, newly sprung up . . . the shop of all mischief, hath made many a thief.'[26] An Act against the Abuses of Brokers in 1603 seems to have been a dead letter, as there were technical difficulties about prosecuting receivers of stolen goods although their activities were illegal.

Not all their stock was stolen property, of course. They bought from impoverished owners and from public hangmen, from jailers and from heirs of deceased persons. In one of Thomas Nashe's books, when a rich man is dying: 'I know a broker in a spruce leather jerkin with a great number of gold rings on his fingers . . . shall give you thirty shillings for the doublet alone, if you can help him to it.'[27] Even in the year of the plague, this trade flourished, although there was some objection to clothes being hung out where they might blow in people's faces. An Order in Council forbade brokers 'to make any outward shew, or hang forth on their Stalls, Shop-boards or Windows towards any Street . . . any of the Apparel to be sold'. The brokers of Houndsditch and Long Lane (and later in the century, of Monmouth Street off Shaftesbury Avenue which

25 Robt. Greene, *A Quip for an Upstart Courtier* (1592), p. 33; *The Old Book Collector's Miscellany* (ed. Chas. Hindley, 1871), I.

26 Stubbes, *op. cit.*, pt. II, p. 38.

27 Thomas Nashe, 'Strange Newes of the Intercepting Certaine Letters', *Works* (ed. R. B. McKerrow, 1903), I, 288.

came to be known as 'Rag Fair') were famous all over the kingdom. They were the first outfitters to many a hopeful lad and lass newly come up from the country in search of the gold-paved streets, as they were also the last hope of many a beggarly lady and gentleman in need of the price of a meal.

But although at this time expenditure on dress and its accessories was the favourite extravagance, there was a growing interest in spending money on houses. New building was difficult in the City itself, but under the Stuarts fashionable suburbs arose along Holborn and the Strand, while many fine new manor houses were going up in the country. And in all houses, both new and old, a great deal more attention was paid to comfort and working efficiency than hitherto. Sir Henry Wotton, who wrote a book on domestic building and the importance of the home, described it as 'a kind of private prince-dom' which deserved to be 'delightfully adorned'. Some items of this 'adornment' were bought in shops but most of them were the creation—and often the personal taste—of craftsmen working on the spot. Furniture was still scarce and the chief ornaments in a gentleman's house were fixtures, such as carved staircases and chimney-pieces and panelled walls and window embrasures, while other items such as cupboards, tables and beds, although not actually built into the fabric of the house were often made on the spot and too large ever to be removed from the rooms.

A lot of this work was no longer wainscot, that is made of solid planks split in the old way down the grain of the wood; the new style was for jointed or 'joyned' furniture, that is, built on a framework and panelled over with thinner sheets sawn across the grain. People of means asked merchants trading to Flanders or France to bring them cupboards or chests from abroad, while others had similar things made at home by English workmen and then decorated by foreign carvers with up-to-date French or Italian designs. Miss Barbara Winchester describes in *A Tudor Family Portrait* how the newly married couple sought for a bed by looking for a long time at the beds of all their friends and acquaintances in London and elsewhere until eventually they found one they liked and commissioned the same joiner to design one for them. Their home was in the Midlands and the bed was sent down from London on the carrier's cart, or presumably (since it was what we nowadays call a four-poster) the main carved posts and tester were sent, to be assembled on the spot by a local carpenter.

In the course of the seventeenth century, as clothes became less well-padded, so upholstery began to be attached to the wooden furniture, chairs took the place of stools, wall-hangings became commoner, and new items called 'nests of boxes' (no odder name, surely, than our 'chests of drawers') began to be used. But still the prevailing taste was for a few large, essential items and a dignified, uncluttered appearance which gave little encouragement to the spread of small shops offering miscellaneous household trivia. The floors were still covered, until well into the seventeenth century, with rushes bought in the market; the walls were hung with plain woven woollen cloth. The Earl of Rutland in 1601 gave £71 for a 'suyte of hangings for the great chamber at London, of 8 pieces conteyning 225 elles of 11 foot deipe'; yet his father's furnishings at Belvoir Castle, the family home, had been valued fifty years earlier at 43 pieces of tapestry worth only £35 15s. 4d. for the whole place.[28] Even after allowing that prices had doubled in this interval, this means that the son was now spending as much on hanging one room of his Savoy lodgings with cloth as his father (also a very wealthy man) had owned in picture tapestries for the whole castle.

Of course there were cheaper materials than fine woollen for hanging on walls. One of the cheapest substitutes was a coarse canvas or linen, undyed, and probably unbleached too, painted in tempera or water-colour with decorative scenes and patterns often mixed with texts and proverbs. Such were the 'painted cloths' which were popular for clothing naked walls. For some reason they became in the seventeenth century especially associated with taverns and ale-houses, where their particular brand of humour was proverbial. 'Glasses, glasses is the only drinking. And for thy walls, a pretty light drollery . . . in water-work is worth a thousand of these bed-hangings and these fly-bitten tapestries,' said Falstaff to the hostess of the Boar's Head, giving her up-to-the-minute advice which no doubt Shakespeare's audience found uproariously funny in a play supposed to be about the time of Henry IV.[29]

[28] Rutland Manuscripts, *op. cit.*, IV, 345, 438.
[29] W. Shakespeare, *King Henry the Fourth, Part II*, Act II, scene i.

Most housewives of moderate means probably made their own soft furnishings themselves with the help of the servants. There were hangings for beds and walls (though seldom, as yet, for windows), carpets or 'blanquets' for beds and benches, as well as the stuffing of cushions and beds with flocks or feathers. Twenty to twenty-five pounds of feathers at about 4d. or 6d. a pound was a typical start towards making a bed. For those better-off, there were craftsmen called upholders who would do all this work. 'There are not more than half a dozen well-to-do tradesmen in our craft,' said a London upholder in 1585, while in 1615 a court case decided that theirs was not a skilled craft, but one which 'one that hath been an apprentice unto it but seven days is able to perform'. Upholsterers would bring their own stuffings of wool-combings or feathers to the job, but it was said they commonly obtained these from merchants who supplied them with 'cow-hair, thistledown, naughty flocks that would breed worms . . . lime, dirt, dust, stones and other rubbish'.[30] Fortunate was the householder who managed to save plenty in his own feather-tub or could obtain reliable wool or feathers direct from the country.

But if there was little shopping to be done for household goods generally, when it came to equipping the table and the kitchen there was increasing resort to such tradesmen as the retailers in ironmongery, brass-sellers, pewterers, goldsmiths and later glass-sellers. Tableware was mostly metal, and still fairly simple. A plate and standing cup, a basin and spoon for each person, with serving dishes and salt cellar and candlestick in the middle, with perhaps a bigger basin for washing the hands and some smaller ones (saucers) for sauce or gravy. Some or all of these might be silver or plate, bought from the goldsmith and valued principally by weight. A good deal of silver must have been wafer thin; in 1597, Magdalen College, Oxford paid £7 17s. 4d. for 20 silver bowls weighing only 29½ ounces all together.[31]

The common ware was of course still pewter, and pewter shops were well stocked with ready-made articles. Although, as surviving pieces testify, much that they sold was ill-shaped and clumsy, it was a metal that could lend itself to fine ornamental

[30] Unwin, *op. cit.*, p. 249.
[31] J. E. Thorold Rogers, *History of Agriculture and Prices in England* (1866), VI, 464.

workmanship and some of it must have been very handsome before it was battered by hard usage. Pewterers took back old and battered articles in part-exchange for new; for example, All Souls College traded in some old pewter in 1611 at 2½d. a pound in exchange for new 'wrought vessels' valued at 1s. 4d. a pound, and again soon after, they turned in old at 2½d. and bought new at 1s. 0d.[32] In fact, all metal vessels at this time, not only pewter, but also gold and silver, and even copper, iron and brass, were bought by weight with an allowance added for workmanship; it is a practice that survives today only in the description of silver articles for sale, although nowadays the high cost of modern workmanship or a high antiquarian value usually overshadows the value of the metal itself. Pewter in simple shapes like plates or basins was cheaper per pound than in kettles or flagons, but servants and inferiors in big houses, as well as people of modest means, still often ate off common trenchers or square boards of beechwood and shared their beer out of one big leather 'black jack'.

Before the time of the Civil War, cutlery was still scarce. Knives were things that people were expected to provide for themselves at table. 'He that hath two knives let him lend me one,'[33] a dinner guest is represented as saying, as he seats himself at a sumptuous banquet at a merchant's house. Kitchen knives, on the other hand, were needed in large numbers to do much of the trimming to flesh, fish and fowl that is now performed by the tradesman; the mincers, the carvers, the choppers, the cleavers could cost, on occasion, up to five shillings each. English cutlers managed to get a ban placed on foreign imports in the sixteenth century and by James I's reign 'a right Sheffield knife' was becoming known even in London, and asked for in the Fleet Street cutlers' shops.

Immigrants began making glass in England in Elizabeth's reign, and as it got suddenly cheaper in the seventeenth century, what had once been a foreign luxury became popular both for drinking vessels and for windows. Glass-sellers opened shops in London to sell nothing else. Venetian and crystal glasses still cost around three shillings a piece, but common ones could now be had for twopence.

[32] ibid.
[33] Erondell, op. cit.

It is a world to see in these our days wherein gold and silver most aboundeth, how that our gentility, as loathing those metals because of the plenty, chose rather the Venetian glasses . . . but such is the nature of man generally that it most coveteth things difficult to be obtained . . .

The poorest also will have glass if they may, but with the Venetian is somewhat too dear for them, they content themselves with such as are made at home. But in fine, all go one way—that is, to shards at the end.[34]

In kitchen and buttery and dairy all large households processed their own food and drink and the equipment was correspondingly elaborate and expensive. Much of it was bought from the ironmongers congregated in Lothbury, Laurence Lane and Thames Street. Iron fire-bars and fire-backs, spits and broaches of every length and thickness for roasting operations, and iron pans and skillets and chafing dishes, meat-hooks and door locks and iron-shod wooden buckets and shovels, would all be available in an ironmonger's shop; many of the smaller items, such as nails and chains, were sold in Leadenhall market. Some better quality goods came from the brazier's: brass pots and kettles, brass taps and cocks for tubs, brass jacks or wheel-and-chain arrangements for turning the spits, brass mortars and pestles. In the saddler's shop would be leather jacks or jugs, leather buckets, harness for a dog to turn the spits, while the turner kept a multitude of wooden objects indispensable to any household, such as chopping blocks, wooden spoons and shovels and peels (long-handled bread shovels), trays and pails and tubs for all kinds of storage from the tiny barm pails for making yeast to the big corn- and meal- and flour-tubs, cheap wainscot chests and cupboards and stools, woven baskets for storing hops and beef and loaves, birch brooms and fire-bellows and all the different sized barrels from the little firkin to the great pipe and sets of spare hoops for each of them.

These, then, were the most popular kinds of shops in seventeenth-century London, the drapers and mercers and haberdashers, the shoemakers and the cutlers, the goldsmiths and pewterers, turners, ironmongers and saddlers. But while these were the most numerous, there were many other kinds

[34] J. Dover Wilson, *Life in Shakespeare's England* (1926), p. 219.

as well. For example, there was a variety of new shops, generally run by the craftsmen themselves, selling watches and clocks, spectacles, books, harps, viols and recorders, pistols and sporting guns, dogs and dice, to well-to-do visitors. (The best place in London to buy loaded dice was from the jailer of one of the prisons, but not all provincial visitors knew this.)

One characteristic, however, of all seventeenth-century London shops that sold more than bare necessities was this. In summer-time, when the courts had their long vacation, trade fell away to nothing for many weeks. The students (some two thousand of them) departed from the Inns of Court, the litigants disappeared, the country gentlemen were busy with their harvests and social life was dead; in the long vacation tailors starved, it was said, and shopkeepers 'broke'. This seasonal doldrums, very marked at the beginning of the seventeenth century, became less noticeable as the permanent population grew bigger and the total of trade increased over the years, but its effect was still being felt, especially in the fashion trades, well into the eighteenth century.

We have been considering, in this chapter, the shops at the end of Elizabeth's reign and in the first half of the seventeenth century, but conditions even during this short period were far from static; trade was increasing almost continuously, more shops and new trades were appearing, and above all the built-up area was spreading beyond the old city boundaries so that people of fashion and the shopkeepers that served them were beginning to move westwards. Something of the changing character of London's shops over these years can be illustrated by examining, in conclusion, the fortunes of one particular building, the Earl of Salisbury's New Exchange.

When Gresham's Royal Exchange had proved a success, Salisbury decided to build one of his own. He acquired a frontage in the Strand a little to the east of the present Charing Cross Station by buying some land next door to his own house. The Strand at this time was a street lined with the garden walls of the mansions of the nobility. On it, at great expense, he built a rather fine two-storied classical building which one of his friends predicted 'will far exceed the fair long shop in Cheapside, though it hold that form'. But although closely modelled on the Royal Exchange, it was never to equal, let alone to exceed, the 'fair long shop' either architecturally or commercially. When it was opened in 1609 it had a covered arcade at street level for merchants and others to meet in, but it was too far from the centre of business to become a rendezvous for men of affairs, and this hope was finally abandoned and the space built upon.

Lining the narrow corridors on the ground and first floors there were about a hundred shops.[35] Many of them were little more than booths $5\frac{1}{2}$ feet deep, and the tenants found 'a want of Stowage in their shopps for their wares, the shopps being, as it were, smale chests rather than shopps'. For these, eleven-year leases were offered for the high price of £30 and a rent of £10 a year (when the Royal Exchange shops were only £4 10s.). This was typical of the kind of boundless optimism that was felt about the possibilities for retail trading. Leases were only offered to those dealing in fashion- and fancy-goods, books and perfumery. Rules were prepared about hours of business, rowdy conduct, sanitation and so forth and a pair of stocks provided ready to receive shop-lifters. In short, no effort was spared to create a high-toned establishment where members of the upper classes would resort on their way between the Court at West-minster and their houses on the fringe of the City.

The Lord Mayor and Corporation were appalled by this whole undertaking. The frontiers of trade and population were already creeping out along Fleet Street and into Holborn; Westminster, too, was a growing city. And here was an attempt on an unpre-cedented scale to encourage the drift to the west by stealing trade, the City's life-blood. Even allowing for the fact that the City was jealous of every hawker who sold an apple outside its boundaries, the vehemence of the Lord Mayor's protest to the Earl of Salisbury shows how important a hundred little haber-dashery booths seems in this period. 'For a Pawne being there erected and put into a pryme course of Trade will take all resorts from this place and put by that recourse from the Cittie which occasions much profitt to all sorts of Retailors in other places leading to the Exchange and in tyme will drawe Mercers, Goldsmythes and all other chiefe Traders to settle themselves out of the Cittie in those parts for the Supplie of Termers [law

---

[35] L. Stone, 'Inigo Jones and the New Exchange', *Archeological Journal*, CXIV (1957).

students] and such as reside thereabouts to the greate decay of the Trade within the Cittie.'[36]

But the City Fathers, dazzled by fine architecture and good publicity, had misjudged the scale of events. Although the king himself performed the official opening and named it Britain's Burse, Salisbury's new venture burned his fingers. The City was right in thinking that London was not yet big enough in 1609 to support two Exchanges, but it was the new one, not the old, that stood half empty during the next two decades. Britain's Burse might be 'neere unto the Court of Whitehall in the middest of the Nobility and where much of the Gentery lodge', but this was not good enough, for the manager was soon talking about 'the small circuet of inhabitants for buying, about the place, being but one street', and even more significantly of 'the want of houses to dwell in for the shopkeepers'.[37]

In 1623 the rumour was that Lady Hatton had paid £6,000 for the whole of the first floor to convert into a town house. The rumour proved false, but it contained the essential truth that London's residential suburbs were at last reaching the west end of the Strand, and a few years later the upper floor was, in fact, converted into sixteen private apartments which were let much more easily than the shops. Lincoln's Inn Fields and Covent Garden were now rapidly filling with houses and in another ten years the area was at last ready to support a substantial retail centre. In 1638 it was possible to turn all the flats back into shops and get high rents and willing tenants for them and the New Exchange at last entered upon its long phase of prosperity and fame. Even then, the fears that it would draw custom away from the Royal Exchange were not justified. The older institution maintained a more sober but steady trade; after the Great Fire its shops were rebuilt and re-let very quickly and it continued prosperous until near the end of the century.

The New Exchange in the days of the Commonwealth was already a noted resort of ladies of the nobility 'whose recreation lies very much upon the New Exchange about six o'clock at night, where you may fit yourself with ware of all sorts and sizes'.[38] The peak of its popularity, however, was the years after

[36] *ibid.*
[37] *ibid.*
[38] H. Neville, *Newes from the New Exchange* (1650).

the Great Fire when so many of the City's shops were destroyed
and its tradesmen driven to seek temporary quarters, many of
them in and around Covent Garden, which became for a while
the chief fashionable shopping centre. Several famous booksellers had shops in the lower walk of the New Exchange, but
its claim to fame is of an altogether more frivolous nature, as a
resort of pleasure for Restoration dandies. Plays by Wycherley,
Dryden and many others have scenes laid in its corridors where
the characters carry on their intrigues in the intervals of bargaining over the shop counters or disappearing into the booths to
have the corsets fitted for a new gown. 'Gloves and ribbands,
Sir! Very good gloves and ribbands!' 'Choice of fine essences!'
'Silk stockings will you buy?' The shopkeepers, who were nearly
all young women and girls, were said to constitute 'a jilt's
academy where girls are admitted at nine years old and taught
by eleven to out-chatter a magpie and outwit their parents . . .'[39]

> Madam, what is't you want?
> Rich fans of India paint?
> Fine hoods or scarves my lady?
> Silk Stockings will you buy?
> In grain or other dye?
> Pray, madam, please your eye.
> I've good as e'ere were made ye.
>
> Fine lace or linen, sir?
> Good gloves or ribbons here.
> What is't you please to buy sir?
> Pray what d'you ask for this?
> Ten shillings is the price.
> It cost me sir, no less.
> I scorn to tell a lie, sir.[40]

In the 'seventies it attracted rivals: two imitators called the
Middle Exchange and the Exeter Exchange, both close by. In
the 'eighties, fashionable society was already moving still
farther west to live in St James's and other parts of Westminster
and leaving the three Exchanges behind, to compete for middle-
class trade with more orthodox shops. They soon languished,

[39] Ward, *op. cit.*, p. 213.
[40] *ibid.*

for these tiny booths packed into indoor bazaars were not suitable for commonplace retail trade as it was conducted towards the end of the seventeenth century. Modelled on the shopping centres of late Elizabethan days, heavily dependent on having a promenade of fashionable society before their doors which they all helped to cultivate by joining in the general conversation, and gossip and flirtation, selling haberdashery and knick-knacks rather than building up large stocks of specialized commodities the famous shopkeepers of the New Exchange were already in Restoration times a bit out of date, when the aftermath of the Great Fire extended their lease of life.

VI

◇◇◇◇◇◇◇◇◇◇◇◇◇◇◇◇◇◇◇◇◇◇◇◇◇◇◇◇◇◇◇◇◇◇◇◇◇

Country Shoppers and Shopkeepers

◇◇◇◇◇◇◇◇◇◇◇◇◇◇◇◇◇◇◇◇◇◇◇◇◇◇◇◇◇◇◇◇◇◇◇◇◇

Live not in the country without corn and cattle about thee, for he that putteth his hand to his purse for every expence of household is like him that keepeth water in a seive.

Lord Burleigh, Household Book

THERE is no clear pattern of rural and provincial shopping in this period. The bigger towns followed behind—far behind—London's spectacular development of retail shops and a re-organized food trade, but towns were few, and communications slow and expensive. Most people were still country dwellers and at all levels, from the poor cottager to the rich landowner, they were still obliged to be fairly self-sufficient. The tendency still was not simply to think that some things would have to be made because they could not easily be bought, but rather of having to resort to buying the things they could not make. On the other hand, the range of goods that all but the poorest thought of as necessities was expanding all the time, and so was the appetite for luxuries. The earlier trickle of retail trade through fairs and markets was increasing to a steady flow in the small towns.

As in all periods, the only complete and fairly detailed records of domestic purchasing have been left behind by the well-to-do. Unfortunately, the bigger the establishments, the greater was their tendency towards self-sufficiency, and therefore they are not altogether typical of more ordinary households. Neverthe-less, their experience does illustrate some of the fundamental

127

shopping problems of the seventeenth-century country dweller, and it is worth taking a look at how two wealthy families managed their affairs before turning to more commonplace experiences.

In 1612, the household treasurer of the Earl of Rutland at Belvoir Castle in Leicestershire made some rough notes for a colleague of where he bought certain supplies.[1] The markets he mentions cover no less than seven counties. Much of the basic food for the household was not included in this, because beef, mutton, rabbits, venison, poultry and rent-corn were the products of his lordship's own land, precise quantities of each being due to his bailiffs on fixed dates throughout the year. But even in these categories 'What more needs, is bought' and he sent to Yorkshire every May for fresh steers for the domestic herd, to Bingham Fair in Nottingham every October for brawn and bacon pigs, to Grantham for Easter porks. Fish was bought economically in large quantities. Dried lings and haberdines were bought in the autumn from Stourbridge Fair; he bought them 'green' or freshly dried and noted 'it must be carefully ayred in March and October and not spent till the third year'. Barrels of fish in brine, intended for Lent, came from Lynn fish-fair every February, while all the year round for fresh fish the treasurer patronized one Paul Robinson, a fisherman who caught fish in the rivers of the Holland district of Lincolnshire. He sold his fish in two sizes, large for eating right away, and small for maturing in the domestic stewpond:

Pikes for store	20″, 2s.	the fish.	Pikes for present service	24″, 2s. 6d.
Breames — —	20″, 2s.	— —	Breames— —	— 24″, 2s. 8d.
Tenches — —	14″, 6d.	— —	Tenches— —	— 16″, 9d.
Carp — —	10″, 12d.	— —	Carp — —	— 18″, 2s.

Whatever these precise measurements really meant, at least they imply an abundance of fish in the rivers if one fisherman could supply large or small fish on demand.

The common wine at Belvoir as supplied to the gentlemen officers of the household was French claret, for which the Earl enjoyed at this time some royal exemption from customs duty. The treasurer bought it at the port of Boston, thirty-five miles away and a busy centre of the French trade, and tenants of some

---

[1] *Hist. MSS. Comm., Rutland Manuscripts*, IV (1905), p. 433.

of his lordship's land were conveniently placed to help to cart it home, the service counting as part of their rent. Vinegar and salt and Baltic iron for the smith all came the same way. (Salt was still made by evaporating sea water at places round the coast, and at this time was the subject of a notorious monopoly granted to patentees on the north-east coast, which was said to double its price to the consumer.)

Stourbridge Fair, in October, was some seventy miles away, a long journey for bulky goods in rough carts, but many household necessities besides fish were bought there. 'Baysalte for the dovecoat and stables is provided at Sturbridge Faire.' A stone of this expensive French salt was thought good for the stock. Reed mats to store fish in, corn sacks, barrels of pitch and tar, shovels, starch, mustard, all were thought worth fetching from Stourbridge, and about this time 660 pounds of 'cleane soape' was added to the list. No reason is given for this change in the long-standing habit of making their own soap (the patent soap monopoly was still twenty years off), but it was perhaps connected with an equally mysterious decision at that time to begin making their own lights at Belvoir instead of buying them twenty-nine miles away at Loughborough. True, the candle-maker there had formerly had 'all the rough tallow from the slaughterhouse, good and bad, at 3s. the ston' so it is hard to see what had been left over for soap-making except kitchen fat, but the tallow had been allowed to the candle-maker at a very low price and the candles bought back were far from cheap, so the change to making candles from making soap may have been an economy. Examples of this kind of juggling abound in seventeenth-century household accounts, making puzzles that are likely to remain insoluble; the housekeepers of those days faced more complexities and more tortuous and laborious alternatives in supplying their needs than we can well imagine in this simple money-for-goods age, but they seldom bothered to explain such things on paper.

Loughborough Market, however, was not abandoned entirely by the stewards of Belvoir Castle. 'Mats for to lay under feather bedds, being rough and shaggie, costs at Loughborough 18d. and 7s. the mat.' (He probably meant 7d.) Mats for chambers, on the other hand, called for a journey of twenty miles in the other direction to Folkingham in Lincolnshire where they were made. The last recorded occasion on which the main rooms of the castle were strewn with loose rushes was in the year Queen Elizabeth died; the Earl stepped into the new era on woven rush matting. It cost 4d. a square yard and was renewed every year, eight rolls of four-score yards apiece. His Lordship was well ahead of his time in this; indeed, it would be hard to exaggerate the height of sybaritic luxury implied in those rolls of matting bought in 1603 simply to be trodden underfoot. Other singular messages include journeys to Nottingham town to renew the well ropes, to Newark for birch brooms, to Stoke for ash trees and to Stamford in Lincolnshire to hire—not to buy—pewter for a feast.

Many purchases were not precisely described. Fuel consisted mainly of coal from Nottingham with a little charcoal from Lincolnshire, and it seems likely that brass, copper and pewter vessels were bought, and when battered, exchanged, near at hand. Craftsmen of several kinds were paid standing wages to make and repair articles about the house, such as the plumber, the cooper, the brazier and so on. The brazier, for instance, lived twenty-five miles away in Lincoln, and he was paid by the year to maintain the big brewing copper and 'to have sufficient warning to come'. Raw material for these men's work was a prominent part of the regular purchasing.

London was only a hundred miles away and the Earl himself visited his town house regularly. But the only household provisions bought there for Belvoir were imported goods; wax torches, 'frutt and spice' in generous quantities, table glasses and the long-distance wines like sack, muscadine and rhenish. For housekeeping supplies, only the immediate vicinity of the capital looked to it as an important distributing centre. The groceries, wine and wax bought there for Belvoir would all have been on sale at Stourbridge by the London importers, and it is open to speculation what advantages of price or quality made the treasurer go direct to London for them when he already bought so much at Stourbridge. Soon after the date of these notes, the old Earl died and his successor had more epicurian tastes; things the old Earl would never have thought of were added to the London shopping list: a keg of sturgeon, a barrel of oysters, dried neates' tongues, Westphalian ham and 'divers other necessarie provisions'.

Personal shopping for his lordship and the family centred far more, but still not exclusively, on London. It is not always clear where the material for clothes and servants' liveries came from, but the occasions on which it is mentioned seem equally divided between London and the local towns and fairs, and the same thing applies to hangings and bed-tapestries and upholstery generally. The biggest London purchases, by far, were from the gold- and silversmiths, for the fifth Earl was active and ambitious in public life, and exchanged New-Year (but never Christmas) presents with the leading men at court. The invariable present to the king, standardized almost like a tax, was a purse of £20, but gold and silver bowls, ewers, fruit-dishes and candle-sticks worth many times that sum were ordered to be made every year from different London goldsmiths, along with wedding and christening gifts on the same lavish scale. Part of the Earl's enormous goldsmiths' bills were paid by trading back old gifts to him, and one glimpses through these prosaic accounts an endless chain of ceremonial gift-exchange among men striving to hold their places in seats of power. But when the sixth Earl died in 1641, his successor turned his back on such ambitions, and thereafter the chief expenses for plate were for prizes at horse races, and the dealings with London goldsmiths gradually declined into the pawning of family jewels.

Another luxury bought regularly in London was tobacco, first mentioned as early as 1597 when the fifth Earl, soon after coming of age, ordered a pound for 35s.; a century later, his grandson's steward was bringing special little parcels of it back from the capital, now 6 pounds for 12s. There were also clocks and watches bought by the Earl himself in London with significant frequency and sent for repair to craftsmen in local towns; we may imagine the puzzled frown of the town blacksmith, brought from his ploughshares and stable-locks to peer into the intricate mechanisms brought hopefully for the exercise of his remedial skill. Musical instruments too, including virginals, viols, lutes and later 'a cithern' and harps, were bought in London and repaired locally. The occasional book was bought in the capital. 'Item, paied for Hollybands booke of 4 languages, 12d.' (This was *The French Garden* in which occurred the scene in the Royal Exchange quoted earlier.) And in 1613 the famous team from the Globe theatre known as Burbage and Shakespeare were paid 44s. apiece to design and paint an 'impreso' for a tournament.

It is interesting to set these glimpses of a wealthy household in the Midlands alongside what can be gleaned of a comparable, though rather smaller one in the wild country of the northern border at the same date. The Household Book of Lord William Howard of Naworth Castle[2] for the year 1612 relates to the prosaic domestic background of that picturesque tyrant Belted Will, glamourized by Sir Walter Scott in the *Lay of the Last Minstrel*. Legend asserts that he pacified that lawless region by hanging suspected thieves, preferably the tenants of his enemies, from his own battlements, but in fact he took the more arduous course of prosecuting them at the assizes, and the considerable expenses incurred in seeing that a long list of felons were duly 'suspen' (i.e. hanged) at Durham, Carlisle and Newcastle are scattered casually through the housekeeping accounts among the soap and eggs and children's bonnets.

Life was rough and poor for most border people and social development lagged far behind that of the prosperous south. Lord William's domain, 'amid nothing but hideous hanging hills and great pools and the murmuring noise of great waters was like a solitary wilderness' according to contemporary accounts, and Lord William was neither so wealthy nor so intimate with the court as the owner of Belvoir, but with his establishment of about fifty servants he managed to organize a fair degree of comfort in Naworth Castle itself. No general plan of routine purchasing appears among the voluminous household papers, and the accounts themselves suggest that the buying was not particularly systematic. Nevertheless, the general outline of shopping was surprisingly similar to that at Belvoir and, indeed, to that of other substantial households whose accounts for this period have survived.

Like all great landowners, Lord William got his beef and mutton from his own herds and flocks; he paid £41 in 1613 for the care of them. For rabbits, he employed a full-time warriner, and for venison 'I verilie think', wrote a visitor several years later, 'that his Honour may commaund venison there as oure southern gentlemen doe sheep heere, for I heard his lordship

<hr>

[2] *Household Books of Lord William Howard* (ed. G. Ornsby, Surtees Society, 1877).

say that his sonnes had then killed out of his owne parkes 120 buckes of this season.' To a local fisherman (who oddly enough was named Robinson like the one at Belvoir), Lord William paid a retainer of 1s. a week and paid by the piece for all the fresh fish brought to the castle from the nearby rivers. In one year this included as many as thirty-seven different varieties. Similarly, 6d. a week was paid to the fowler for the first option on all he bought, shot or snared, and he produced forty-nine varieties of wildfowl in the same period.

Naworth differed from Belvoir more radically, however, in having to buy nearly all its grain in the market. Among these northern hills the relations of landlords and tenants had never been founded on the produce of cornlands as they were in the Midlands, so that whereas the Earl of Rutland in Leicestershire, that same year of 1612, long after the full feudal system had disappeared, was still receiving large dues of wheat and oats and barley and peas, to say nothing of poultry and cartage services, from tenants scattered over a wide area, his colleague in Cumberland had little such tribute, but was paid rent in money by tenants of greater traditional independence. Only a few trifling rent-eggs and rent-hens occur. In the same way, it will be remembered, the Earl of Northumberland mentioned in Chapter II received little in kind from his tenants in Northumberland and Durham; some compulsory services seemed to be hinted at, but certainly no corn-rents were collected, although at that time in the Midlands and south of England, receipts in kind were a big part of the income of many great landowners.

The markets patronized for the supply of Naworth Castle were all a long way off, for Naworth lay just north of the Roman Wall, eighteen 'mountainous and rocky miles' north-east of Carlisle, and thirty-six miles from Newcastle. Grain and fresh food were bought as opportunity offered, sometimes seven miles away at Brampton, or twenty at Hexham, or even thirty-five at Morpeth. But large individual purchases are rare, and as often as not, it is a person, not a place, that is named against food items suggesting that much of the fresh food, especially eggs, hens, milk, and small game did not come through the ordinary market channels at all but was bought direct, in many small quantities, from isolated farms or offered at the castle itself by local farmers.

Half a samon, 14d., eggs 10d., Robinson 3s. 2d., 2 Moorcocks 6d., 2 Mallards 12d., a black cock 6d., 2 stockdoves 3d., Fowle 9s. 6d., Eggs 22d., 3 hares 18d., 2 woodcock 3d., Sum 20s. 6d.

This is a typical week's supply of fresh stores in January when there was little to be had. In the first week of Lent, however, the bill for 'fresh acates' jumped from 20s. to 30s. a week up to 54s. 6d., because Robinson was sending off the gloomy season to a good start. But he could not keep it up and by the end of Lent they were reduced to sending all the way to the east coast for eighteen lobsters, three crabs and some whelks, 4s. 4d. worth in all (but the bill for carriage was not paid until the following December). And finally, here was a week of good living at a family reunion in May:

Fish sent from Morpeth, 9s. Bringing it 4s. 31 chickens 5s., Eggs 4s. 1d., Fowle 8s. 9d., Shallots 10d., A hare 6d., Robinson twice 31s. 10d., For a seale 20d., Bringing it 3s. 4d., A sturgeon 3s. 4d., Bringing it 2s., Shrimps 8d., Bringing it 7d., Crozier 3d., 3 Kidds 4s., Sum £3 9s. 10d.

The seal sounds very cheap; perhaps the people who caught it were suspicious of eating it. Next month a porpoise was bought for only 20d.

It is strange at first sight that a household like this with a large family and about fifty servants should have laid out weekly sums for things like eggs, hens and shallots that they could easily have provided in the castle itself, but again we are led to infer a feeling of the responsibility for patronage, of *noblesse oblige* in these multifarious small purchases from named individuals. Occasionally food is bought 'at the gates', presumably from passing strangers. How different from the Earl of Northumberland who refused to patronize local people for fear they might take advantage of him; but he, of course, lived in a more settled and prosperous area.

Of course, Naworth Castle made its own beer, and when his lordship went to stay in the little house in Carlisle for the assizes he had his own beer and bedding sent ahead to make his stay comfortable. Once—but only once—a barrel of London beer was bought as an experiment, in Newcastle. London beer may have tasted splendid to the northerner in the capital, but another hundred years were to pass before it was made strong enough to travel so far. Furniture was often made and always repaired in the house. 'For 1000 tackets for stools and 6 sheep-skins, 4s. 4d.' Compare this with Belvoir: 'For 18 Brasile skynnes for chayres and stooles, 12s. 100 of great nayles 5s. 2,000 of small nayles 5s.'

Fuel was a matter of paying different workers to cut peat on the moors or faggots in the woods—many different workers for a few days at a time. Some candles were made at the castle and a few extra ones bought, a dozen from this market or that as required. Sixpennyworth of rushlights are once mentioned, perhaps bought at the gate. Bents and rushes to strew the floors were a constant item, but in 1624 two of the younger generation heard of the fashion for matting for their private chambers, and they sent all the way to Norfolk for it.

Newcastle was their door to the wide world, to the Continent, but even more important, to the capital. Here they bought haberdashery and grocery and occasionally wine, patronizing various tradesmen on no very clear principle and frequently buying all these kinds of goods from the same man. Newcastle was already a busy port with merchants trading abroad and keeping shops still stocked with the old jumble of mixed com-modities and wholesale and retail, but featuring many of the latest goods on sale in London, brought up by sea; later in the century it was one of the first provincial towns to specialize its retail trade in imitation of London. In 1699 a traveller said of it, 'Their shops are good and of distinct trades, not selling many things in one shop as is the custom in most country towns and cities.'[3] Carlisle was also a port, though of course a much smaller one, and in both these towns the annual fair was still a major trading event at which Naworth representatives thought it worth while to buy largely. Permanent shopping centres did not replace fairs for a long time to come; as the towns got bigger, the fairs got bigger too.

Wine was bought in all sorts of places for Naworth; by the butt or by the hogshead, from both towns, from neighbours, from 'a Scottish merchant'; only some years later did they start

[3] Celia Fiennes, *Through England on a Side-saddle* (1888), p. 177.

getting it from London. Lord William's apparent difficulties in getting wine, his willingness to buy it when and where he could, can be paralleled in other north-country households of the time. The explanation of this calls for a slight digression on the subject of buying this troublesome but indispensable commodity in the north. The distribution of wine was complicated by many factors, not least by its being perishable. It was still waiting—and went on waiting until the eighteenth century—for a means of airtight storage. The long-awaited invention was not bottles merely (these were already plentiful, though still dear), nor even corks (which were now being used in the bottles and tied down with pack-thread), but the humble corkscrew which would enable corks to be rammed in really tightly and yet retrieved again.[4] Sherry or Canary or the sweet dessert wines kept longer in the wood than the cheaper claret or rhenish, but all deteriorated in a twelvemonth.

Two-thirds of all the country's wine came into the port of London. What came directly across the North Sea to Boston, Hull and Newcastle was at once the cheapest, the most perishable, the most afflicted by heavy and variable taxation and, after mid-century, the most subject to the interruptions of war. For example, in 1666 the public sale on the north-east coast of the large cargoes of captured enemy wine ships brought claret down to less than a quarter of its normal price, yet in some other years it was almost unobtainable.[5] The best hope of getting reliable wine at reasonable prices was by personal connections. An understanding with a merchant in Hull helped many north-country houses as far away as Lancashire and Cumberland. A reliable friend in London was even better—always remembering that the dangers of damage and leaking in long transport were the customer's own. An obliging innkeeper in a large town would often help a gentleman to a butt of anything that was plentiful, but when wine was scarce he needed all he could get to serve his own inn.

There remained the wine-merchants who 'kept the fairs', most of them from London, but it needed considerable skill—or perhaps some degree of desperation—to lay out large sums on a pig in a poke.

[4] A. L. Simon, *Bottlescrew Days* (1926), pp. 252–5.
[5] A. L. Simon, *History of the Wine Trade in England* (1906), II, 100.

It is necessary that our English housewife be skillful in the (s)election, preserving and curing of all sorts of wines, because they be usual charges under her hands, and by the least neglect may turn the husband to much loss . . . Sacke, if it be Seres [i.e. sherry] as it should be, you shall know it by the marke of the corke burned on one side of the bung, and they be ever full gauged, and so are no other sackes . . . The wines that are made in Bordeaux are called Gascon wines, and you shall know them by their hazell hoopes . . . Galloway in pipes and hogsheads that be long, and that lack $2\frac{1}{2}$ sesterns in gauge . . . Angulle is quarter-bound and lacks little in gauge . . . etc.[6]

This is Gervase Markham in a book nominally addressed to the housewife, in 1638, in which the chapter on wine-buying leaves no doubt as to the enormous complexity of the subject but very considerable doubt as to how many housewives would ever master it. Besides knowing the characteristic colour and taste of different wines and how to tell if they were in their original barrels, the customer should not be prepared to take the seller's word for what those barrels contained. The official gauger at the Customs had left his marks, which she must recognize, to indicate whether, and by how much, the contents of a barrel fell short.

Then, having satisfied herself about the quantity and the quality of what was being offered, the customer must be able quickly to work out the price:

Now for Gascoigne, there goeth foure hogsheads to a tun, and so looke how many pence the gallons are, and so many pounds the tun is . . . *etc.*

All this theory was bad enough, but in practice, more complications ensued. Most wine came overseas in butts (from Canary called pipes) of about 126 gallons, but few private households wished to use over a quart of the same wine every day for a year. So it was repacked in smaller vessels, and the buyer was most often confronted, not with the reassuring hazel hoops, or quarter-bindings or burned-cork-marks and the authentic official gauge, but with a complete unknown. Did she

[6] Gervase Markham, *The English Housewife* (1637), pp. 155–66.

137

sometimes take her own gauging-rod to the fair? If not, she needed a quick eye to check the wet mark when the merchant plunged his rod through the little hole:

Every Terce (tierce i.e. 42 gal) is in depth the middle of the knot in the midst
The depth of every hogshead (63 gal) is the fourthe pricke above the knot
The depth of every puncheon (84 gal) is the fourthe pricke next to the puncheoner . . . *etc.*

There were of course many refinements for reading off short measure. Only then, having calculated what the bulk price worked out at per gallon, could the thrifty buyer begin the real business of the day, the bargaining, pretending that the wine was old, sour or pricking, against the seller's contention that it was a fine variety above the common run. 'Skilful' seems an understatement for the successful amateur wine-buyer.

But to return to Lord William at Naworth Castle. The personal expenditures and miscellaneous household purchases show even less methodical patterns than food-buying. Shopping for these was done mainly at Newcastle or Carlisle or at the fairs, and only occasionally in London where visits were rare. Hexham often figures for saddles and horse-furniture, Penrith for boots and shoes and small children's wear, Kendal for one pound's worth of wax candles for My Lady's devotions. There is linen 'brought from Yorkshire' and napkins 'brought from Lancashire', no doubt by the far-ranging elder sons who took their pleasures, particularly deer-hunting and horse-racing, all over the north. Pewter (we hear little of plate) was exchanged at fairs. There is a familiar note about the watches Lord William bought in London and was always getting repaired at Newcastle or even at York. The ladies seem hardly ever to have left the castle; even her ladyship's gowns were chosen for her by the steward. About half a dozen times a year she bought things from pedlars 'at the gate', mainly ribbon, bobbin-lace and pins, but occasionally glasses, or cheap Scotch cloth.

The buying of shoes was even more haphazard, two or three pairs being brought back by various servants when on business in nearby towns. Once '9 payre of children's shoes for 10s. 6d.'

were brought from London by one of the servants, followed next month by a note 'for takeing wooden heeles out of 4 payre of shoes of little Mr. Howarde 1s'. Before sizing was standardized, this buying by proxy must have meant ill-fitting shoes for most of the children; their poorer neighbours growing up barefoot or in home-made shoes were probably luckier. ('The common people walk barefoot and the children leap as if they had hooves, but it is almost the same all over the north,' said Roger North.)[7] As for quality, a nine-year-old girl, for example, wore out nine pairs of shoes in one year alone.

Clothes were nearly all made in the castle, chiefly by a tailor named Lancelot Hall and his man, who came for up to a month at a time and were paid by the day, 3d. and 2d. respectively with board and lodging. In 1612, they spent just under half the year altogether sitting in Naworth stitching away at petticoats and gowns, doublets and breeches, serge stockings and riding hose, 'boddies' for the children and 'cloaks' for the adults, all of them, no doubt, under her ladyship's direction. Hall brought his own thread, black and white, and was paid for as much as he used. In June one year, in the midst of his sewing, he was paid 4d. extra 'for his nag's meat at Penrith, going to buy the gent's cloathes', that is, cloth for the boys; but he did not normally take any hand in the buying of materials which went on all the year round, two or three yards of this or that, woollens, canvas, linens, silk, every few weeks. Points were bought by the dozen, and metal 'oes', or eyelets, for them by the ounce, whalebone by the yard, needles by the hundred, pins by the thousand, as well as buckram, lace, ribbon, embroidery silk, and buttons to wear on doublets where they would show.

But there was little extravagance. If one little girl had a silk 'body', she was also provided with a pair of leather ones for everyday. If a boy had a red satin doublet made, he also in due course had it 'let out' and was supplied with fustian breeches and serge stockings. The 4s. for a pearl head-wire and the 5s. tortoise-shell combs were offset by the 'translating' of old gowns, and even his lordship had his shirts re-cuffed and his cloaks mended. For at that time Lord William was building up his estates and the family lived frugally. Ten years after this, their style had expanded considerably; meanwhile they paid local

[7] Roger North, *Lives of the Norths* (1826), I, 290.

labour to 'mend all the old sheetes' and to re-foot knitted stockings, and to weave and bleach and dye home-spun yarn that had occupied the spare moments of the house-maids.

In later years there were more frequent visits to London; seven to ten days on horseback at a cost of £20 to £30 each way for his lordship and a couple of servants. Such trips were never undertaken for such trivial purposes as shopping, but Lord William often brought back several pairs of horn spectacles, numbers of books, clocks and garden plants, and occasionally a rich suit by a London tailor, a portrait, a dagger, a little silver-ware. In 1625, the eldest son, defying the Plague raging in the capital, made a visit there and thought to send back a second-hand gown for his young wife; it must have contained a louse for she died of the London infection on the evening of the first day she wore it. London shopping, roped up in canvas rolls and accompanied by a barrel of lemons or raisins, travelled cheaply in the dirty bottom of any empty collier returning to Newcastle, and a servant went with it to oversee the London porters, Thames boatmen, Newcastle warehousing, customs clearance, Tyne boatmen and final cartage. The coachman did this job in 1613 and was allowed an extra 5s. 'for byding long at sea'; although his 'passage and fright' cost only £1, the two wainloads of goods he brought totalled £4 7s. in transport costs.

Lord Howard's accounts for the year 1612 are detailed enough and complete enough—a rare combination—for us to see how one wealthy landowner laid out his income between various classes of expenditure. It was the budget of a thrifty and ambitious nobleman keeping down his expenses and building up his estates; a conscientious man resisting the lure of London life. Over half his income he invested in land and loans. The rest he spent as follows:

LORD WILLIAM HOWARD'S EXPENDITURE FOR THE YEAR 1612

	Consumables	Manufactures	Services and Raw material	Miscellaneous	Totals	
	£	£	£	£	£	
Lord Howard	—	3	—	28		
Lady Howard	—	46	4	4	85	8%
Food						
fresh	90	—	—	—		
salt	30	—	—	—		
herds	—	—	87	—		
grocery	44	—	—	—	432	43%
grain/baking	—	—	155	—		
„ /brewing	—	—	13	—		
wine	13	—	—	—		
House						
candles	—	1	2	—		
fuel	—	—	8	—		
utensils	10	9	5	—		
linen	—	9	5	—	146	14%
extras	3	3	20	25		
buildings	—	2	44	—		
Transport						
stables	11	6	14	—		
travelling	1	—	128	—	177	18%
freight	—	—	18	—		
Personal						
wages	—	—	111	—		
tips	—	—	64	—	175	17%
	£201	£79	£678	£57	£1,015	
	20%	8%	67%	5%		

This budget plainly reveals one aspect of the prevailing scarcity of shops and other retail outlets, and the backwardness of consumer industries. Only 8 per cent of Lord Howard's spending went to encourage industry—mainly the cottage industries of linen- and cloth-weaving—whereas no less than 67 per cent of it went on providing himself with raw materials and labour. Some of that labour, it is true, was rendering him personal services, but most of it was engaged, under his direction, on his premises and with his materials in making goods that would nowadays rank automatically as manufactured products. All the dress-making and upholstery and wool-spinning and soap-boiling and candle-dipping and countless similar activities in the houses of the well-to-do, while they were undertaken only because the relevant industries were small and few in the provinces, at the same time had the effect of discouraging the growth of such industries as there were. For the poor had little money to spare for manufactures and the rich, outside London, were only slowly abandoning the habit of making things, or having them made, at home. And between rich and poor there was a considerable gulf.

The remoteness of Lord William Howard's situation was not the reason why so many things were made at home, for the purchasing of the Rutlands at Belvoir was, as we have seen, very similar and so was that of nearly every wealthy household anywhere in the country. Bishop Cosin of Durham was a great landowner who resided mainly in a provincial town, at about the same date. He bought his bread from the baker and his candles from the chandler, but he brewed his own beer, and when he wanted a new reading desk, his treasurer's note began 'Pay'd Matthew Sheale for 20 Wainscott Boards . . .' etc., and when he wanted a new bed 'Pay'd Mary Wright for eight stone of feathers £3 4s. . . .'[8]

Where the middle class existed, however, its members seem to have spent a higher proportion of their incomes on manufactures than their wealthier country neighbours. They had less space and fewer servants to oversee the making of things on the premises. The Reverend Giles Moore, vicar of Horsted Keynes in Kent, when he wanted a bed, had no dealings with loose feathers, with cloth by the yard or with getting linen spun and woven and bleached and sewn:

> 7 *May 1656* For the parlour chamber I bought of Mr. Hely in London a bed with purple rug, curtains, etc. which cost me altogether £20 16s. 7d. and a pair of fine middle blankets, 15s. 2 flock beds and boulster tyckes, £1 1s. I bought of Thos. Booker 2 sheets for 9s. and of Widow Langley two more fine sheets for which I am to pay 18s.

[8] *Bishop Cosin's Correspondence* (ed. G. Ornsby, Surtees Society, 1870), pp. 340–1.

I bought of Wm. Clowson, upholster itinerant living over against the crosse at Chichester but who comes about the country with his packs on horseback,

A large fine coverlett with birds and bucks	£2	10s.	
A sett of striped curtaines and valance	1	8s.	
A coarse 8qr. coverlett	1	2s.	
2 middle blankets	1	13s.	6d.
One beasil or Holland tyke or bolster	1	4s.	[9]

This man kept only two servants to look after himself and his wife and bought all he could ready-made. But wives differed greatly, no less than now, in the amount of work they were prepared to do. Another parson, the Reverend Thomas Brockbank, living near Kendal in 1688 in very similar financial circumstances, had a wife more typical of her times, an industrious brewer and baker and sewer, perhaps a student of Gervase Markham's *The English Housewife*, which advised 'Let her diet proceed more from the provision of her own yard than the furniture of the markets'. The parson wrote regularly to his son at Oxford sending him money and home-made clothes.

The coat and breeches are of Keasar, of 4s. 6d. the yard, the best that was in Mr. Sympson's shop. The vest is of Searge. Youre deare mother hath sent you two shirts and two large pocket handkerchiefs and she desires to know who is your bedfellow and if you take care your linen be not changed [stolen]. In your breeches pocket we have put some silk, buttons and pieces of cloath which you may use when need requires . . .[10]

Both these parsons received a good deal in kind by way of tythes as well as gifts from their parishioners, and a good many of these items were food stuffs. But it was probably very common for middle-class professional households to do the same. Mr Burrel, a lawyer of Cuckfield in Sussex in the 1680s, who kept a staff of six for himself and his wife and farmed a small estate, records in his diary few payments for professional work, but quite incredible numbers of gifts—haunches of venison, twenty-four 'china' oranges, eighteen woodcocks, and so on, which must

[9] 'Diary of the Reverend Giles Moore', *Sussex Archeological Society Transactions*, I (1848), pp. 65–127.
[10] *Diary and Letter Books of Thomas Brockbank, 1671–1709* (ed. R. Trappes-Lomax, Chetham Society, 1930), p. 10.

surely have been fees for work done for his neighbours.[11] Currency was scarce, and well-to-do people were often slow in paying their debts for this reason alone; there was no particular shame in offering goods instead of money for a small debt, particularly if the creditor was not himself poor. The cathedral auditor of Canterbury did some legal work for a local merchant in 1609 for which he was paid in sugar loaves to the value of 45s. and returned 8d. change.[12]

Supplying any household was still a compromise between shopping and self-help. Even quite a modest house fit for a gentleman, unless it was actually in the middle of a busy city, would as a matter of course have 'fish in pond, conies in warren, pigeons in dovecote and fruit in garden', but for the minor gentry and upwards there was now so much more to be had in the county towns and in London that they often spent immense time and labour riding to and fro for what seem disproportionately small purchases, as well as lavishing money recklessly on the costs of carriage and rewards to messengers. Take a page at random from the diary of Adam Eyre, a small landowner in Yorkshire in 1647:[13]

This morne I came to Sheffield . . . and here I bought things which cost me 2s. and spent 1s. with the saddler on whom I bespoke a sadle, and received my bridle bit which I left with him and a gerth which I have not payd him for, and then went home. In all 18 myle.

Similarly, the daughter of Judge Fell who managed his estate near Ulverston in the 1670s sent for market goods to Ulverston's weekly market on Thursday or to Dalton's, five miles away, on Saturday, but when it came to manufactured goods or luxuries she had to go or send eighteen miles to Kendal or twenty-five miles over the sands of a tidal estuary to Lancaster, and so far from grudging these arduous journeys she did so every few weeks. From the former, in quick succession, came bellows, pans, soap, shoes and 'by money paid Danl Cooper for carrying 2 petticoats to Kendal and bringing them again and that he payd for dieing them ash colour, of sisters Susannah and Rachael,

11 'Household Accounts of a Country Gentleman, 1686–1715', *Sussex Archeological Collections*, XXXIV (1850), *passim*.

12 *The Diary of Thomas Cocks* (ed. J. M. Cowper, 1901), p. 58.

13 *Yorkshire Diaries* (ed. C. Jackson, Surtees Society, 1875), p. 69.

1s. 6d.'[14] From Lancaster she bought and had carried across the sands by the weekly carrier, bedsteads, garden tools, seeds, nails, bridles, salt fish, grocer's goods and many other things, while for salt she sent ten miles in another direction to Rampside near Barrow. It is hard to believe that wine was not to be had in Lancaster, but if so, it did not please Sarah Fell who commissioned the Kendal-Newcastle carrier to bring wine and Holland's cheese from Newcastle. London shopping seems to have been more difficult to arrange:

> By mony pd. for 3 neates tongues that I am to send to London to Will Towers for buying 2 cloaks. 1s.[15]

And when a member of the family visited London she wrote asking her to buy a cask of wine 'for we have none, only some old cider and March beer bottled up. Also anchovies, olives, two larding needles, lemons, oranges and what else you think fit'.[16]

One of the things one would most like to know about the provinces in this period is how many shopkeepers there were in different sized towns and villages. Unfortunately, although there is a good deal of incidental evidence about them, it is virtually impossible to guess at their numbers. For one thing, their nomenclature is so vague and so confused with that of other occupations. For example, although there are records of impressive looking numbers of 'mercers' and 'drapers' in the market towns of some cloth-producing areas like Gloucester, or of 'ironmongers' in Derby, we know that these men must have been more concerned with wholesaling the local product than with true retailing, although they may have retailed as well. Again, there was everywhere a growing habit of doing a little retailing as a sideline to other occupations. Particularly in small villages, the man who was described for some purposes as a retailer or shopkeeper was often many other things—and more important things—as well. He might be practising a craft, or, as often happened, be a wool-broker or a putter-out of materials to cottage weavers or nail-makers or knitters. Such men found

[14] *The Household Account Book of Sarah Fell, 1673-78* (ed. Norman Penney, 1921), p. 123.
[15] *ibid.*, p. 155.
[16] *ibid.*, p. xvii.

it easy to sell in their houses to the many people who called to collect or deliver work (they were the earliest kind of truck-masters, in some cases) and they picked up an assortment of small saleable goods in the city when they went to market the cloth or nails or stockings.[17] Mrs M. G. Davies, in her study of *The Enforcement of English Apprenticeship*, mentions many cases of part-time retailers and the difficulty of identifying their true occupations. In short, any attempt to measure seventeenth-century retailing by counting heads leads to absurdity.

But the general picture is clear enough. In the older, corporate towns, the mercers and grocers and drapers, the true retailers, traditionally apprenticed and duly elected freemen, tried hard, though with failing success, to go on monopolizing all retailing except for the craftsman's sale of his own work. Even those craftsmen who 'kept open shop' or 'sold divers kinds of wares', the tailor who sold cloth, the cloth-weaver who sold lace and thread, were liable to be informed upon and brought up before Quarter Sessions for doing so. The newcomer to an ancient borough, although in theory he could usually buy his freedom to set up in most trades, was likely to find that in practice entry to a trade which was pure retailing was barred. Not until the Municipal Corporations Act of 1835 over-riding all local restrictions, was it made specifically legal to open a shop anywhere in the kingdom. Not only commercial jealousy and out-dated laws about the need for apprenticeship stood in the way of new shopkeepers in towns; popular prejudice was still widespread. In 1636 a parson in Dorset wrote to a friend in New England as follows:

I heare shopkeeping begins to grow into request amongst you. In former ages all kinds of retailing wares (which I confess is necessary for man's more convenient supply) was but an appendixe to some handicraft, and to that I should reduce it if I were to advise in the government. Superfluity of shopkeepers, innholders, etc. are great burthens to any place. We in this towne are, of my knowledge at charge 1,000 li per annum in maintaining several families in that condition, which we might well spare for better employments, wherein their labours might produce something for the common good, which is not furthred by such as drawe

17 G. Unwin, *Studies in Economic History* (1927), p. 320.

only one from another and consequently live by the sweat of other men's brows . . .[18]

Nevertheless, in all towns, shopkeepers were increasing throughout the seventeenth century, and the barriers to retail trade were coming down fast by 1700. In the villages and the countryside, although retailing was often subsidiary to other occupations, it was undoubtedly growing fast in total. And not all country shopkeeping consisted only of spare-time dealings in a back room. Population and cottage industries were growing in many districts and providing a rural market for shopkeepers' wares. Moreover, new towns like Manchester and Birmingham and Leeds were growing fast, relatively unhampered by restrictive traditions, and in them, as in a hundred smaller communities, men were free to follow what occupations they pleased, and shopkeeping was one of them. 'It is true that custom formeth trades, and in some towns they are very well distinguished already. But in some they are not . . . and in these latter, many shopkeepers do not get as much by their trades as some workmen do by theirs.'[19] There were many wild allegations made in this period about the 'multitudes' of new shopkeepers, especially in the countryside, and they are not wholly to be believed, but there were enough outbursts like the following to indicate that some sorts of shops at least were rapidly gaining ground outside the old centres of trade:

For now in every country village, where is (it may be) not above ten houses, there is a shopkeeper, and one that never served any apprenticeship to any shopkeeping trade whatsoever. And many of those are not such that do deal only in pins and such small wares, but such that deal in as many substantial commodities as any that live in cities and market towns and who have no less than a thousand pounds worth of goods in their shops, for which they pay not one farthing of any tax at all, either parochial or national . . . If the cities and market towns be depopulated for want of trade then what will the countrey man do to have money for all his Commodities, as his butter, his cheese, his cattel, his wool, his corn and his fruit? The shopkeepers in countrey villages will yield but

[18] Bernard Bailyn, *New England Merchants of the 17th Century* (1955), p. 22, quoting a letter of the Rev. John White, 1636.
[19] Anon., *The Trade of England Revived and the Abuses Thereof Rectified* (1681), p. 34.

little help in this case and the pedlars much less. It is manifest that the people living in cities and market towns consume all these commodities of the farmers and do help them to ready money for the same.[20]

All these new shops outside the towns that are referred to as 'general' or 'open' shops should not call to mind a picture of the modern village store, for they were anything but food shops. No doubt their proprietors were only too willing to sell anything and everything that came their way, but perishable commodities demanded a quick turnover and a regular supply that was quite beyond them. Food still meant markets, as it had always done, and in the country as a whole the markets were getting bigger and busier and more frequent. The growing numbers of country shopkeepers in villages and small towns actually helped to swell the volume of business in the markets, for like the local craftsman-producer they often made a habit of taking a stall on market day, while the more enterprising ones would sometimes shut up shop once a week to shoulder a pack and tramp many miles in the early hours to seek a little trade in another town on another market-day.[21]

New, unauthorized 'free' markets were springing up spontaneously in response to demand. There was usually some town authority or local landowner who expected to have the tolls from any new market or feared that interests in an existing market would be damaged by competition, but free markets and small fairs spread nevertheless. The terms 'market' and 'fair' were becoming less distinct. The major annual fairs still flourished as important local events, and they were becoming increasingly identified with wholesale trade in the products of their particular region, although household accounts make it quite clear that they were indispensable to the consumer all through the seventeenth and most of the eighteenth centuries. But numerous, smaller, so-called fairs, monthly or even fortnightly, sprang up in new places and were in reality markets trying to slip into existence under another name.[22] It has been tentatively estimated that the number of markets in Essex

20 N.H., *The Compleat Tradesman* (1684), p. 26.
21 See the early chapters of W. Hutton, *The Life of William Hutton* (1816).
22 G. H. Tupling, 'Lancashire Fairs and Markets', *Trans. Lancs. & Cheshire Antiq. Soc.*, L & LI.

5. A page from a housewife's account book, 1699.

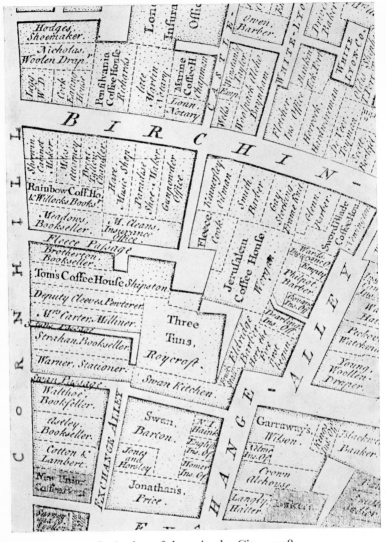

6. A plan of shops in the City, 1748.

increased from nineteen to twenty-eight in the course of the century.[23] Or again, at Blackburn where the townspeople instituted a new fortnightly market during the democratic days of the Protectorate, an attempt at the Restoration to collect tolls from it for the local lord resulted in a riot. 'In the end they drove their beasts in a tumultuous manner to the town's end and with a great shout and beating upon the beasts passed the toll-takers and would pay no toll. Something must be done against them before the next fortnight's fair.'[24] The next fair, the unhappy agent mustered twenty would-be collectors of toll, but they were beaten off by an angry mob, and the attempt was abandoned for good; one more free market had been established. It would be interesting to know how many of the new free markets were achieved in this revolutionary spirit, but the evidence is hard to come by.

Only rarely can we get a glimpse of retail trade in this century from the point of view of the shopkeeper. (Except when he was writing pamphlets telling lies about his rivals, he was not very articulate.) By coincidence, among the surviving diaries of the late seventeenth century are those of two shopkeepers, both from Lancashire. One of them had a village general shop in Leigh, the other was a grocer (in the very broadest sense of that word) in the sizeable town of Lancaster.

The first was Roger Lowe,[25] who seems to have been a penniless orphan, who apprenticed himself for nine years, probably for the sake of a home, to a small mercer in Leigh. His master, having one apprentice already, immediately opened a second shop for Lowe in a village six miles away. He paid for the boy's board and lodging, provided his clothes and stocked the shop. Probably it was a one-room cottage or shed, or else the apprentice would have been expected to sleep in it. Lowe was left, with very little guidance, to run it as best he could. 'I thought it sad for me to be engaged nine years to stay in Ashton and sell my master's wares off, and get no knowledge.' It says much for the soaring prosperity of Lancashire at that time that the boy eventually made a small profit, and when he was freed

---

[23] K. H. Burley, 'The Economic Development of Essex' (unpublished London Ph.D. thesis, 1957), p. 285.

[24] *Hist. MSS. Comm., Kenyon Manuscripts* (1894), p. 88.

[25] W. L. Sachse, (ed.) *Diary of Roger Lowe*, 1663–74 (1938.)

and presented with the business, that he made some sort of a precarious living.

While still indentured, he went, even more than most apprentices, in dread of his master's wrath, but even so that gentle and kindly man, on his infrequent visits to the village, often found the shop shut up, and his luckless apprentice-shopkeeper drinking in the ale-house or bowling in the next hamlet. 'Came to the shop, and thought much I was in Ale. Warned me to take heed. I told him I could not trade if att some times I did not spende 2d.' No doubt the master reminded him of the popular saying of the time, 'Keep your shop and your shop will keep you!' But all too soon after, 'Was invited to go to Gawther Taylor's to drinke Braggod, for wife bought her commodities of me and she said, if I would not come then Farewell, soe I was constrayned to goe. But I stayed but for a short time.' Fortunately Lowe had some education, and besides keeping strict accounts for his master, he often obliged neighbours by writing letters for them, drawing up agreements or making out wills for sick people who usually sent for him for this purpose in the middle of the night. 'To my great greefe my master took of me £3 that I had gotten by writinge and had given me where I lived.'

When he was freed, his master presented him with the business—which again suggests that the 'shop' was a very humble affair, for his master was far from rich. Now he had to pay for his own board, lodging and clothes, and start the grim struggle to make a living. He began with some stock from his master, on long credit, but soon ran into difficulties in replacing it. 'I was at this time sadly troubled for fear of mis-caryinge, and knew not how to get cloth and things. Yet God raised up friends for me, for a Yorkshire man came through the town, and proffered to let me have cloth for three months' credit.' But he was not always so fortunate. Partly because stock was not plentiful anywhere, partly because he lacked good connections and his own credit was poor, he had to spend a lot of time riding about the adjoining towns seeking, often without success, small quantities of goods. His diary is full of entries like this: 'I went to Warrington (7 miles) to buy candles of Richd. Nichols. I had but four dozen and I brought them home upon horseback.' And while he was doing this, of course, his shop was shut.

Sometimes he took what he could from craftsmen hawking their own produce. 'Henry Fielding, the Hower-glass maker whom I had Hower-glasses from, came, and I was ingaged for 1 dozen and ½ of Hower-glasses and this day I payd him . . . I took 30 glasses more. And a very honest man he was to me. I had them of the rate of 10s. and sold them after 12 and he gave me 4½ hower glasses and 6d. in monys when I payd hime.' This seems to have been a good line; his average profits were nearer to 10 per cent than 20 per cent. He does not tell us what he did with half an hourglass, or whether he got rid of them all before the whole village was set up with time-pieces.

His other major difficulty was the familiar one of unpaid bills. 'I went to Wigan. (6 miles) There was a pedlar lived there, one Humphrey Starbotham who aught me some monys. But I gatt nonne.' He repeated this journey many times before he got his money a year later. 'I went to Haddock (2 miles) to seaverall houses to gett monys but I gatt nonne.' His invariable relief at being paid small debts is an indication of how near the margin he lived. 'I was sent for to Brinn (2 miles) and I went and very Joyfully. To my Joy I was payd the debt oweing to me per Mr Brinkes, and very joyfully I came home.' Day after day he left the shop shut up while he went off debt-collecting or trying to get stock, or drinking with his customers or courting. Days when 'I kept shop all day' he thought worth special mention, and once 'being Warrington Fair I kept shop all day'.

So much for Roger Lowe's village shop. In 'lock-up' premises of negligible value, stocked with a heterogeneous collection of any cheap goods the owner could lay his hands on, open for trade intermittently and unpredictably, granting credit as a matter of course to all and sundry, and run by a man who depended heavily upon a side-line—'writinge'—to make a bare living.

A very different sort of shopkeeper was his contemporary, William Stout.[26] He entered trade by the royal road, apprenticed to one of the best shops in the city of Lancaster to learn the grocery trade for a premium of £20 for seven years and providing all his own clothes. At fifteen his nose was put to the grindstone and, it being a good Quaker nose, he never took it off again. While poor Roger Lowe was passing the anxious and idle days of his late 'teens in the village ale-house, William Stout

[26] J. Harland, (ed.) *The Autobiography of William Stout of Lancaster* (1851).

had the company of an older apprentice under a master who 'was very active in trade and a very early riser in a morning, and we apprentices, lying in the shop, were early called up'. ('Early' is a euphemism for about an hour after sunrise in summer.) And he describes how, when he was seventeen 'there was the longest and sharpest frost with snow that had been in the memory of any man then living . . . I attended the shop in winter with the windows open, without sash or screen, till about nine in the evening, and with the windows shut and the door open till ten o'clock, without coming into the house except to our victuals or to the fire, and had my health well all the time . . . For in my apprenticeship we were frequently called up at all times of the night to serve customers.'

Trade came before everything else, before leisure, before comfort, probably even before health. But this was not slavery; this was the accepted way into a lucrative profession, and he followed the same regimen when he owned his own shop, sleeping in it for many years to be always on call, rising at dawn for a short walk before breakfast as his only recreation, devoting (except on Sunday) every waking thought to business. Quakers were becoming noted for shopkeeping; a Quaker had only to be poor, it was said, for his friends to set him up in a shop and give him their custom. This may have been partly true, but since shops were springing up fast in the provinces in the late seventeenth century, it may have been that the Quaker genius for hard work made their ventures successful where so many failed. Of dissenters generally it was said at the Restoration, 'Of all the old Army now, you cannot see a man begging about the streets. But what? You shall have this captain turned a shoe-maker, the lieutenant a baker, this a brewer, that a haberdasher, this common soldier a porter, and every man in his apron and frock, etc. as if they never had done anything else . . .'[27]

Quakers had ideas about the art of trading which were, by the standards of their time, highly eccentric; as William Stout put it:

> I always detested that which is common, to ask more for goods than the market price, or what they may be afforded for, but usually set the price at one word, which seemed offensive to many who think they never buy cheap unless they get abatement of the

[27] *Diary of Samuel Pepys* (ed. H. Wheatley, 1928), III, 337.

first price asked. And its common for the buyer to ask the lowest price, which if answered, they will still insist of abatement; to whom I answered, they should not tempt any to break their words. I observed that such plain dealing obliged worthy customers and made business go forward with few words.

Stout's master was a Quaker too, and the young man obviously took him for a model in all things. ('His wife, my dame, was one who took her ease, and took no notice of trade or of anything but indulging her children.') Being Quakers and unable to take any oaths, neither he nor Stout after him were freemen of the town, and their shopkeeping was therefore technically illegal; both were apparently 'troubled' from time to time by black-mailing threats on this account, but their anomalous position was no secret, it had no effect on their business, and buying off malicious troublemakers was merely a nuisance. Their case is an object lesson in not always accepting the legal position as the true one.

The master was a man in his thirties when Stout describes his shop about the year 1680.

I was mostly employed in the shop on weekdays in making up goods for the market day [Friday] as sugar, tobacco, nails [a local manufacture] and other goods, and particularly prunes which we made up in the summer time about one hundredweight weekly and sold them in 1 lb. and 2 lbs., and sold them 3 lbs. for 4d. commonly, which we bought then for 8s. or 9s. a cwt. Brandy for £10 a hogshead and about £8 a hogshead, foreign produce being then very low in duty. Tobacco at 2d. a lb. retailed at 6d. which caused a great consumption.

As well it might, for at this price it must have been imported direct from Virginia in Lancaster ships and dodged the customs duty altogether, a thing so common in the west-coast ports as to stir no ripple on even a Quaker conscience.

At this time we sold much cheese to funerals in the country from 30 lbs. to 100 lbs. weight, as the deceased was of ability, which was shived into two or three slices to the pound and given with a penny manchet or loaf, and given to all attendants. Also, long Naples biscuits, 20 lbs. to 100 lbs. according to the ability of the deceased . . .

And three or four of us fully employed every market day in delivering out goods [serving], so that we had a full trade then, and the best of customers and might have got an estate if well improved, there being then no taxes except a small excise on ale . . . My master then had a full trade of groceries, ironmongery ware and several other goods, and very much respected and trusted, not only by the people of his own religious profession, but by all others of all professions and circumstances, as well gentry as the most substantial yeomanry. His credit was such that any who had mony, lodged it with him to put out to interest, or make use of, and having great acquaintence he acted much that way and had mony ready to answer his occasions in trade always.

Was this yet another instance of a shopkeeper running a sideline? More likely in this case, as Stout suggests, he handled his neighbours' savings less for profit than to enjoy the great boon of ready money, for it is quite possible that even the owner of a busy shop might otherwise lack 'money ready to answer his occasions in trade always'. His own wholesale purchasing, of course, as a trader of substance, would be all on long credit. When Stout himself set up, he went to London with excellent sponsors, and 'Bought goods of sundry persons to value of £200 paying each half ready mony as was then the custom by any young man beginning trade'. An established trader took credit for a twelvemonth, as a matter of course, in many kinds of manufactured goods. Each trade had its customary time for payment, and this was allowed for in the wholesale price, although many foods wholesaled at fairs, such as cheese or salt-butter, for example, were usually bought for cash.

Judging by Stout's practice, who followed his master's footsteps, the Lancaster grocer bought at the local fairs in their seasons, visited Liverpool twice a year for the New World imports —sugar, tobacco, ginger, indigo—made an annual five-day journey on horseback to London in the company of his fellow-traders to order the bulk of his goods and send them home by sea, and had an understanding with an agent in Sheffield to send 'Sheffield goods' and 'Birmingham wares' from the big Midland fairs, with whom he only settled at long intervals. If the profit rates he mentions above seem large for non-perishables, it must be remembered that the profit had to cover the cost of all these activities, as well as retailing.

Stout's master, like Roger Lowe's, tried opening branch shops in villages, partly, at least, with an eye to his apprentices' future. One twenty miles away was run successfully by a senior apprentice, who bought the business when he was loose, but then 'broke and went mad'. In Stout's native village, six miles away, he opened another shop for Stout to attend two days a week, but, 'finding it did not answer to his expectations, he let it drop, and sold the goods to Roger Hind, the shoemaker, who continued it'. (Presumably, another part-time village shopkeeper.)

From all this diverse evidence about the provinces, two things stand out. The first is that although the number of shops was increasing in both town and country, there were not nearly enough to supply the demand and people still had to rely heavily on fairs and markets for the things they bought and had to travel long distances to get what they wanted.

The other general conclusion is that to run any sort of shop successfully in the provinces, two things were necessary: first the credit, connections and know-how to collect stock; and second, the experience and firmness to get in debts. In spite of his sound training Stout wrote, in 1689: 'It being now a year since I began trade, I find I have been too forward in trusting, too backward in calling, as is too frequent with young tradesmen', and years later, he still lost between one-third and one-half of his profits in bad debts, although Lancashire Palatine courts made debt-collection there comparatively simple. To get the goods, and to get the money, these were the arts of shopkeeping. Merely selling the stuff was child's play, and very often children, or at least young apprentices, were left to do it.

VII

Some Items for a
Restoration Gentleman

> He is a very accomplished person; not that thin sort of animal
> that flutters from Tavern to Playhouse and back again, all his
> life made up with a wig and cravat without one dram of thought
> in his composition.
>
> John Dunton, 1705

THE Restoration gentleman was seldom seen in the market place or the grocer's shop; his wife and his servants bent themselves to the task of supplying his everyday needs, large and small, and extracting the cost from him. Yet, if he was a man-about-town, there were many places where he might be encountered spending his own money on his special pleasures and pursuits. The range of these was being widened in the seventeenth century and new dealers were appearing in the streets of the City and in Westminster to cater for new habits. But foremost, we must put a habit that was far from new: the haunting of the tavern, for this ever-popular resort continued to flourish despite the spread of coffee houses.

London had always been famous for taverns, but their popularity was probably at its peak in this period. Literary mention has kept a handful of famous names alive, the Mermaid and the Mitre, the Nag's Head and the King's Head, Heaven and Hell, the Gaping Mouth and so on. But there were others equally famous in their day and now almost forgotten, and scores of lesser ones. Anyone with a little capital could turn his house into a tavern by putting an ivy bush over his door and getting a few barrels of wine from a merchant and buying a licence from the wine commissioners who were only too anxious to sell. So long as his house avoided riot and disorder, no-one could interfere, and taverns were multiplying fast in mid-century. 'As for Victualling, there is scarce a tavern that does not most frequently use it,' the Lord Mayor reported to the Privy Council in 1633.[1] By 'victualling', of course, he meant serving meals not just retailing food, but the two things came dangerously near together in the eyes of the City authorities. And not without reason. Tavern keepers were notorious for their large purchases on the open market and their secret handing out of scarce items at inflated prices at the back doors of their kitchens. This led, in Charles I's reign, to an attempt to stop them selling meals altogether, which caused such a clamour of indignation from the general public that the idea was dropped.

For as well as being 'the busy man's recreation and the idle man's business' they were now something more. They were becoming pub and club, shop and office, board and all but lodging to all sorts of men; not merely the places where a gentleman could buy a gentleman's drink, they were for long the only places, in a town full of apartment dwellers, to order a decent meal, to entertain one's friends, to learn the news or to arrange a piece of business. Even Pepys, always a busy man, and comparatively a sober one, who could afford a good cellar and a good table at home, nevertheless mentions by name no less than 105 London taverns that he visited at one time or another in the course of eight years, mostly on matters of business. With the first colleagues he met in the morning, he would turn into the nearest tavern to treat or be treated to a 'morning draught' in lieu of breakfast. At Westminster he often dined at one with a court official to pick up the news, or at the Temple with lawyers engaged on navy business. Around the Exchange, he looked into the favourite haunts of merchants he wanted to do business with, and if he took his wife out for a meal, the choice was, to which tavern?

There were fashionable taverns and bohemian taverns, political taverns and business taverns. But in all their variety,

[1] W. H. Overall, ed., *Analytical Index to the Remembrancia of the City of London, 1579–1664* (1878), pp. 540–1.

they were none of them common drinking halls like the modern bar. Their premises retained the layout of the private houses they had once been with numbers of small rooms private to the customer and his friends for the time being, for the price of their pint of wine or their meal. Some idea of what a run-of-the-mill tavern was like in the seventeenth century can be gained from the inventory of the contents of the Mouth tavern in Bishopsgate in 1612.[2] There were eight drinking rooms, called respectively the Portcullis, Pomegranate, Three Tuns, Cross Keys, Vyne, King's Head, Crown and Dolphin; each had movable partitions to further subdivide it and each was furnished with either one or two wainscot tables and an assortment of stools and forms. There was a lodging chamber with two beds and two dice-tables; there was a bar with serving pots and candles and a pair of shove-halfpenny boards; there was a well-stocked cellar with seven or eight kinds of wine and a well-equipped kitchen with a lot of pewter and a little table silver. The contents of the house were worth £135, nearly all of it the value of the wine itself.

In every tavern, the landlord presided from his bar in a strategic position near the entrance; he assessed his customers, allotted the rooms and kept the reckoning. When desirable, only the discreet knock of the pot-boy need interrupt the business deal, the flirtation, the intrigue or the merrymaking. In 1694, one John Lunt made a very full confession about a plot for the return of James II; it is noticeable that in the provinces the places he named for his secret meetings had almost always been in private houses, while in London they were taverns, the Blew Postes, the Figure of Three, the Hole in the Wall and the Great Tavern.[3] At such places, at the end of the century, Tory sympathizers foregathered to toast the absent Stuarts in forbidden French claret at exorbitant prices.

Among other uses, taverns were admirable places for interviewing tradesmen. At various times, and often very late in the evening, Pepys sent for a stationer, a haberdasher, a gunsmith to come and serve him in a tavern. On another occasion he records:

[2] J. Nichols, *Illustrations of the Manners and Expenses of Antient Times in England* (1797), pp. 229–32.
[3] *Hist. MSS, Comm., Kenyon Manuscripts* (1894), p. 292.

> Did go to the Swan, and there sent for my old periwig-maker,
> Jervas, and he did bring me a periwig, but it was full of nits, so as
> I was troubled to see it (it being his old fault) and did send him
> to make it clean, and in the meantime, having staid for him a good
> while did go away by water.

Jervas, undeterred by two abortive trips to the Swan tavern,
brought the wig to Pepys's house a few days later and waited for
his customer before he was up. But all in vain. 'I did now refuse,
having bought elsewhere.'

A discreet landlord could make himself very accommodating
to regular clients. He took messages and letters, effected useful
introductions and prevented undesirable encounters, sometimes
allowed food and drink 'on the score' when a client's cash was
low. Many landlords ran, in effect, a club without subscription,
and one wonders what they got out of it. A few famous establishments like the Mitre or Nag's Head were obviously very busy
caterers with a constant stream of custom and a large sale. (680
quarts a day was a fair average for the Nag's Head even before
the Civil War.) Some, like Locket's or Pontack's, charged
exorbitantly for fine wines and fine food. The *table d'hôte* at
Pontack's ranged from five shillings to two guineas per head in
James II's time.[4] But many seem to have served only occasional
meals, sometimes sent in from a neighbouring 'ordinary' or
cookhouse, and most of the time boasted a dozen or so
customers in half a dozen rooms sitting indefinitely over a
pipe and a quart bottle of wine.

The average consumption of all London taverns in 1639, big
and little, was 212 quarts a day each, including what was
delivered out to customers' houses. Allowing for a handful of
giants this means that many of them must have had a very small
sale. Although they now stood open all round the clock seven
days a week their expenses for a cook and a tribe of apprenticed
pot-boys would be minimal. Nevertheless, they had to pay them
something and to keep up furnished premises, even if only one
cellar or a couple of rooms over a shop, and they warmed and
cleaned them. Ned Ward, for example, going home with the
dawn after a night's merrymaking:

---

[4] C. Wright & C. E. Fayle, *History of Lloyds* (1928), p. 16.

There was no parting without a glass, so we went into the Rose tavern in the Poultry, where the wine, according to its merit had justly gained a reputation, and there in a snug room, warmed with brash and faggot over a quart of claret, we laughed over our night's adventures.[5]

Here was the landlord and a pot-boy roused up to revive the fire, to draw the wine, to await their pleasure, all for the profit on a bottle of claret. How did taverns pay, let alone make fortunes for their owners as so many did?

The answer lies in the high price customers were prepared to pay for their pleasure—the pleasure of sitting as well as the pleasure of drinking. Claret, or just 'French', was for long the cheapest; it was 8d. a quart in 1639, 12d. for most of the Restoration years, and anything up to two shillings during the French wars of William and Anne when it was officially banned. Spanish and Canary were approximately twice as dear as claret until the latter overtook them in the 1690s. This threefold increase in the price of the commonest wine was quite out of line with general prices in the course of the seventeenth century, and was caused initially by increasing taxation, for during all these years the cost of the wine itself—say 2½d. a quart for claret landed on London quaysides—hardly changed at all.[6] But as customs duties went up, so did retailers' margins. In the interests of the consumer, both wholesale and retail prices were 'proclaimed' intermittently by the crown and they allowed both importing merchants and retailing taverner a good margin.[7] For example, if the consumer bought a quart of claret for 8d. in 1639, the wine had cost about 2½d. as far as London, plus 1d. for tax and 1d. importer's profit, leaving the retailer a profit of 3½d. (The taverner who was big enough did his own importing, and from the well-organized port of Bordeaux it was easy enough.) By the 1690s although duty on claret had climbed to the unbelievable height of 13d. on every quart, the current retail price was 2s.; although it was all blamed on the high duty, in fact this now left no less than 8½d. profit to be divided between the im-

[5] E. Ward, *The London Spy* (1698).

[6] R. Davis, 'English Foreign Trade, 1660–1700', *Econ. Hist. Rev.*, VII (1954), p. 157.

[7] R. Steele, ed., *Tudor and Stuart Proclamations, 1485–1714* (1910), *passim*.

porter and the taverner and the taverner still got nearly all of it.

So the taverner gradually increased his margin on every quart, while scarcities were driving his customers more and more to the dearer Spanish, Canary and Rhenish wines. Even then, of course, the retailer's real margin was understated by official prices. He claimed heavy discount from the wholesalers, as well as eighteen months' credit, as a matter of course because, as in so many trades in the seventeenth century, he was in a strong position, being an established London retailer, *vis-à-vis* his supplier. In this case, he had to be licensed to retail; the importer could not retail, but anyone was free to import wine. The typical importing merchant may have been an individual of far greater wealth and consequence than his customer the retail taverner, but his cargoes of wine would often be a sideline to his main business and a seasonal sideline at that. Recurrent wars led to the seizure of wine ships and the public sale of wine cargoes that could knock the bottom out of the wholesale market for an entire season. Then again, the taverner was in a position to charge extra for fine wines, to mix, doctor and manage in selection of wines to his own advantage along lines well understood in the trade. Milk, rice and salt would 'cure' white wines, eggs and salt would sweeten sour sherry, while as for clarets 'there be remedies enough to amend and repair them. Take a Pennyworth of Damsons or else Black Bullaces . . .' and so on. It was inevitable that all vintners were suspected of more sinister adulteration and of using false measures.[8]

So the big London taverns must have made very heavy profits out of their wine sales alone, while even the small ones were making high margins on their slow turnover. Small wonder that they were happy to oblige every customer individually; the snug dens with their club atmosphere were their form of competition with each other in selling a fixed-price commodity. Indeed, compared with, say, the haberdashers, still relying on a 'barker' outside their shop and on haggling within, the wine-sellers were sophisticated right out of their own century. Of course, high profit on what seems by modern standards a small trade was typical of all retailers of the time as we already know, but it stands out in the trade in wine, and has been dealt with here at

---

[8] A. L. Simon, *History of the Wine Trade in England* (1906), II, 54.

some length because here is a trade of which we know something of costs and prices of a fairly standard commodity, and contemporary literature has so much to say about tavern life that it is possible to see clearly just how leisurely their business was.

The taverner made most of his money out of draught wine. He used bottles for the purpose of bringing measured quarts from the cask to the table, where it was drunk from glasses—a seventeenth-century refinement on the old tankard. The habit was growing of householders buying wine for the house in bottles, some stone, some glass. Even before the Civil War, Donald Lupton, describing the old-style country gentleman, had said, 'He had his wine cellar come to him in full butts, but this age keeps her wine cellar in little bottles.'[9] Clearly, buying in bottles was regarded as a mean habit, but over the years the practice grew in London, none the less. People wanted their wine fresher, or they wanted more variety. One's servant could go to the tavern and bring away a dozen quart bottles by himself, but two tavern employees and a cart had to be paid for to get a cask into the cellar and rack it. However, Pepys, as he went up in the world, took a modest pride in the number of casks in his cellar—they put him among the gentry.

Smuggling had not as yet a regular organization. It tended to be active in periods when particular wines were banned, but the wealthy consumer's attitude towards it was still very casual. On 21 January 1694, Sir W. Turnbull wrote to Matthew Prior at the Hague:

> I will venture further to desire you to send me word if there be any French wine of any kind to be had at the Hague. If so I will send you word (when I know the sort and price) what quantity I desire, and hope the captain of some yacht will not deny me the bringing of it safe hither.[10]

In the succeeding century things became more organized. When Sir Robert Walpole was Chancellor of the Exchequer he was responsible for administering the duties on French wine. But that did not deter him from regularly receiving 'his smuggler'

[9] Donald Lupton, 'London and the Country Carbonadoed', *Harleian Miscellany* (1812), IX, 326.
[10] Simon, *op. cit.*, III, 128.

at his country house and giving him regular orders like any other tradesman. How many other country gentlemen did the same we can only guess, but without doubt vast quantities of wine came in illegally in the eighteenth century, and its highly organized distribution throughout the country was condoned, if not actively encouraged, by the classes responsible for keeping the peace.

What happened to wine-buying when the new drinks, coffee, chocolate and tea, suddenly appeared on the scene? For they did come suddenly. Before the Civil War they were unheard of and ale and wine were still the only national drinks. Twenty years later, the new beverages were known and popular with the gentry all over the country. Yet so far as is known, wine consumption did not drop much per head of the population; if the gentry were drinking slightly less, some people were growing prosperous enough to drink slightly more. But the public was ready—had been ready for some time—for a non-alcoholic drink; otherwise it is hard to account for the extraordinary success of the shops that first sold these brews and made them popular.

The first record of coffee for sale is in 1648 in Oxford. Four years later a Turk opened a shop in the City to sell just coffee, either to drink on the premises or as berries to carry home. Almost at once several other shops appeared, and there was noticed a new, pungent smell in the streets outside them that advertised their commodity louder than words. Not everyone was pleased; there were prosecutions for causing nuisance and 'evil smells'.[11] But most people liked it, and coffee acquired a reputation as an *aperitif*. ('The air on Banstead Downs is nothing to it for a whetter!') Soon, the success with selling bowls of hot coffee led to experiments in infusing other exotic herbs. Cinnamon, which came to nothing, cocoa-berries from the West Indies which nearly rivalled coffee, and the very expensive dried leaves of the tea plant brought from China. Coffee shops sold all these, serving them piping hot in bowls, with sugar but not, of course, milk.

In the same shops the enthusiastic customers could buy the materials for making these new brews at home. In 1662 Morat's coffee-house advertised in the news sheets that at his house in

[11] Edward Hatton, *A New View of London* (1708), p. 30.

Exchange Alley could be had Coffee already ground to powder with a pestle and mortar for 3s. to 6s. a pound, as well as tobacco and sherbets. Tea had come down to about 20s. a pound by the close of the century, a luxury still, but fast gaining ground with those who could afford it as an article of elegant entertainment.

The fashion of drinking in coffee-shops caught on rapidly in London with all classes above the actual labouring poor.[12] By 1688 there were at least a hundred coffee-shops there whose names are known: by Queen Anne's reign, at least five hundred and probably many more.[13] Contemporary observers give various reasons for their popularity. 'For persons much concerned in the world,' said one writer, they were superior 'to taverns and ale-houses, where continual sippings, tho' never so warily, would be apt to fly up into their brains and render them drowsy and indisposed for business'.[14] Or again, 'These houses, which are extremely numerous in London are extremely convenient. You have all manner of News there. You have a good fire that you may sit by as long as you please. You have a dish of coffee. You meet your friends for the transaction of business. And all for a penny, if you don't care to spend more.'[15]

In other words, coffee-men had taken a leaf out of the taverners' book and made their shops into social meeting-places. But they had to do more, if they were to draw enough company away from the taverns. It is noticeable that most coffee-shops were known, not by their colourful signs, although they had them, but by the names of their proprietors. Morat's and Nando's, two of the oldest, Tom's and Will's, both familiar in Restoration comedies, White's and Boodle's, the most famous of those that eventually turned into private clubs. These men were not following their masters in an old trade but enterprising in a new one, and their shops were their very personal successes. They mingled their customers democratically in one big, bare room, probably with a sanded floor and the plainest of benches and tables, and they presided over the company from a place behind the bar. And they actively encouraged the dissemination of

12 The history of coffee-houses is extensively discussed in E. F. Robinson, *The Early History of Coffee Houses in England* (1893).
13 John Ashton, *Social Life in the Reign of Queen Anne* (1882), appendix.
14 'Coffee Houses Vindicated' (1675), *Harleian Miscellany* (1812), VI, 472.
15 R. J. Mitchell & M. D. R. Leys, *A History of London Life* (1958), p. 206, quoting from Misson de Valberg's *Memoirs of Travels over England* (1698).

7. View of Cornhill, 1741. The Barrels being unloaded at Swan Passage on the left are presumably for the Swan Tavern, as shown on the map.

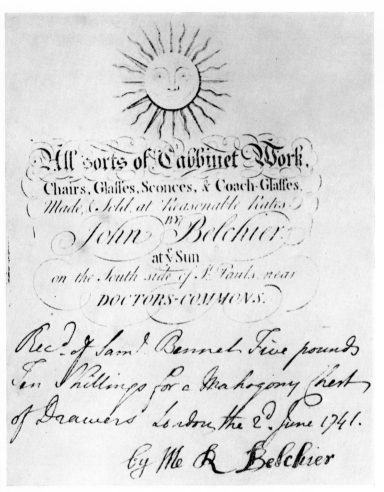

All sorts of Cabbinet Work,
Chairs, Glasses, Sconces, & Coach-Glasses,
Made & Sold at Reasonable Rates
BY
John Belchier
at ye Sun
on the South side of St Pauls, near
DOCTORS-COMMONS.

Recd of Saml Bennel Five pounds
Ten Shillings for a Mahogony Chest
of Drawers London the 2d June 1741.

by Me R Belchier

8(a). Trade card of a London cabinet maker.

8(b). The 'Glasse in a gold frame' he made in 1735 in answer to
the letter on page 233.

news, by circulating the news sheets, such as they were, which were just beginning to appear, and posting up on the walls any interesting items of information, letters from distant places that any customer would lend, 'lost and found' notices and the first rudimentary advertisements. Before the Civil War, the latest news used to be what was 'said on the Exchange' or heard in Paul's Walk; now it was 'the coffee-house talk'.

Coffee-houses did not replace taverns; indeed there is little evidence that they seriously damaged their business, although some started to serve meals and some even took out wine licences. There had been 211 tavern licences (that is, taverns and inns) in London and its suburbs on the eve of the Civil War.[16] A century later, in 1732, Maitland, in his *History and Survey of London*, reckoned up 652 inns and taverns and 551 coffee-houses.[17] Even more convincing is the absence of complaints from ruined taverners. London was still booming and growing and there was room for both.

The start of coffee-houses was also helped by the upheaval of the Great Fire, which destroyed old haunts and old habits and assisted in the formation of new ones. It was during the interval while the Royal Exchange was being rebuilt that the shipping and insurance business of London found a home in the new coffee-houses of Edward Lloyd and his fellows. Many of the City's other retail businesses were shaken up by the Fire and found new quarters in the growing suburbs along the Strand and Holborn where they stayed. While the City was still in ruins, Pepys was

> calling at Bennet's, our late mercer, who is come into Covent Garden to a fine house looking down upon the [new] Exchange, and I perceive many Londoners every day come.
>
> And Mr Pierce hath let his wife's closett and the little blind bed-chamber and a garret to a silk-man for £50 fine and £30 per annum and £40 more for dieting the master and two apprentices.

And on another occasion:

> Thence with my wife to buy linen, £13 worth, for sheets etc. at the new shop over against the New Exchange. [And the

---

[16] Overall, *op. cit.*, p. 548.
[17] W. Maitland, *History and Survey of London* (1756), II, 719, 735.

master who is] come out of London since the Fire, says his and other retail tradesmen's trade is so great here, and better than it was in London, that they believe that they shall not return nor the City be ever so great for retail as it was heretofore.[18]

But there were other new ways for the gentleman of the period to spend his money in London besides drinking. When Raleigh and others brought home the practice of tobacco-smoking from Spanish America, they created a fashion that spread with astonishing speed. Tobacco was very expensive and men smoked it in the seventeenth century with the maximum of ceremony and in the minimum quantity at a time. There were two kinds: Spanish, illegal and dear, but good; and colonial, which began cheaper and much nastier but gradually improved during the century and eventually stole the whole market. Early in the Stuart period, according to Aubrey, Spanish tobacco 'was sold then for its wayte in silver. I have heared some of our old yeomen say that when they went to Malmesbury or Chipenham market they culled out their biggest shillings to pay in the scales against the tobacco.'[19] This would mean paying £4 a pound, more or less. Alongside this there was the Virginian and West Indian product for varying prices around 10s. a pound, and illegal, English-grown tobacco at intermediate rates. All three kinds were scarce in the first years of the century and they were mixed and adulterated and sold at wildly varying prices.

Almost from the beginning, tobacco bore a heavy customs duty. Charles I tried, without great success, to licence retailers so as to control illegal and smuggled tobacco, but at least until the Restoration, demand constantly outstripped supply and a good deal of the tobacco bought was what would nowadays be called 'black market'. Tobacco stalks mixed with 'dyer's liquor', oil and small-coal—all kinds of rubbish sold as tobacco.[20] 'Look to't sirrah, you were best. Threepence a pipeful I will ha' made of all my whole halfe-pound, and a quarter of coltsfoot mixed with it too to eke it out.'[21] This is the master's instructions to his tapster in *Bartholemew Fair*. Thirty years later, the price had improved and the reputation had worsened; in theatres there

[18] *The Diary of Samuel Pepys* (ed. H. Wheatley, 1928), VIII, 57; V, 446.
[19] F. W. Fairholt, *On Tobacco* (1859), p. 70.
[20] *ibid.*, p. 72.
[21] Ben Jonson, *Bartholomew Fair*, Act II, scene i.

were 'the tobacco men that use to walk up and down selling for a penny pipe that which is not worth a penny an horseload'.[22]

However, more and better colonial tobacco arrived in the second half of the century and prices for the best fell to under two shillings a pound. The English-grown and the rare Spanish vanished from the market, and the buying of tobacco became more straightforward and reliable. Apothecaries and grocers and chandlers often had licences and so did all 'ordinaries' and ale-, wine- and coffee-houses. In London, at least, many 'doe keep houses, set open shoppes, that have no other trade to live by but the selling of tobacco . . . and that almost in every lane and in every by-corner around London'.[23] In fact, many that started as tobacco shops took up some other side-line as well—cosmetics, distilled spirits or even an ale-licence—but enough tobacco was sold to keep them in business principally as tobacconists.

There were two signs of a tobacconist that were pretty well universal. One was a painting or carving of a great black ball of 'twist', which was the commonest form in which it was sold. The other was the black boy which lingers still in some present-day tobacconists. On the shop counter there was a maple chopping block and scales, a juniper fire, or perhaps just a candle, tongues to hold the hot coal to the pipe and tables and chairs for customers to enjoy their smoke at leisure. The loan of a pipe was free, for pipes cost only a penny or twopence a dozen, and no-one minded using a pipe that other customers had smoked any more than he objected to a glass that others had drunk from. Pipes, as a rule, were too fragile to last until they got foul, but if they did, the bowls were thrust into a red-hot fire to cleanse them.

In the early days of smoking, little iron or silver pipes had been tried, but then the cheap clay pipes started to be made, a new industry in the districts around Shrewsbury and Bristol, and they held the field for a couple of hundred years. The clay pipe was cooler than metal, and cheaper and lighter, and except that the bowl got bigger over the years, it was the same until the nineteenth century nicknamed it a 'churchwarden'. To begin with, bowls were minute. Twenty-five pipefuls to the ounce was a fair average in James I's time, compared with a modern briar's

[22] Anon. *The Actor's Remonstrance* (1643), quoted in J. Dover Wilson, *Life in Shakespeare's England* (1926), p. 188.
[23] Fairholt, *op. cit.*, p. 76.

eight or ten when new. There were pipe-hawkers who made a continuous round of their regular customers, mostly taverns, coffee-shops and tobacconists, but no doubt a few private consumers as well who were prepared to buy them by the bundle— that is a gross at a time. Thus, the Duke of Rutland in 1664, 'For a grose of tobacco pipes, 1s. 6d.' And again in 1680, 'For burning my Lord's pipes, 6d.' This would be a matter of having them cleaned by some tradesman with a furnace; it hardly seems worth while.

In 1698, Ned Ward in *The London Spy* gives his account of buying tobacco:

'We have a rare opportunity of replenishing our boxes with a pipe of fine tobacco, for the greatest retailer of that commodity in England lives just over the way and if you dare run the hazard of crossing the kennel we'll take a pipe in his shop.' We ventured to shoot ourselves through a vacancy between two coaches and so entered the smoky premises of the famous fumigator. There a parcel of ancient worshippers of the wicked weed were seated. There was no talking amongst them but that Puff was the period of every sentence and what they said was as short as possible for fear of losing the pleasure of a whiff. Behind the counter stood a complaisant spark who, I observed, showed as much breeding in the sale of a pennyworth of tobacco or the change of a shilling as a courtier's footman. He is very generous of his small beer to a good customer, and will show a man more courtesy for the taking of a penny than many will do for the taking of a pound. By this time the motion of our lungs had consumed our pipes and our boxes being filled, we left.[24]

Thus the townsman buying tobacco. Here is a description from about the same date of how it was often sold in the country:

Thomas Woods is a dealer in tobacco after this manner, viz. He is a settled housekeeper in the country and hath tobacco brought down to him in hogsheads, and at his own house, by himself and servants, he stripps it and cuts it and in all other respects prepares it for use and sale. When it is so manufactured and prepared, he carries it out to his customers in several neighbouring parts of the country in parcels whither he goes with it on horseback and

[24] Ward, *op. cit.*, p. 156.

always returns home at night. And this hath been his trade and way for twenty years or more.[25]

With his fill of good wine and tobacco, a man of those days might feel like a gentleman, but he would not look like one until he was clean-shaven and wearing a wig. One of his most important tradesmen, therefore, was the barber:

> His pole with pewter basins hung
> Black rotten teeth in order strung
> Ranged cups that in the window stood
> Lin'd with red rags to look like blood
> Did well his threefold trade explain
> Who shaved, drew teeth, and breathed a vein.[26]

Barbers had ceased to be general surgeons in the sixteenth century although for many years afterwards they were prepared to undertake any number of small personal services of a similar nature along with shaving and hair-cutting and, as the verse above indicates, blood-letting and dentistry. Philip Stubbes in 1583 allows barbers to be expensive but necessary tradesmen, 'or we should be ugglesome to behold'. But in Restoration times, the fashion of wearing wigs came over from France, and the barber's trade took a sudden upward flight into dizzy prosperity. At first they charged £2 or £3 for a good wig, but the elaboration and the price increased over the years, so that £10 or £15 was a common price in the early eighteenth century. A dandy might go to £40 or £50 for an exquisite creation—the sort that 'the touch of a hat never profaned'—but even this did not save him from buying a hat, for he still needed one to tuck under his arm.

One thing that drove up the price of ordinary wigs was the increasing scarcity of hair. 'Money for live hair' was a common notice in a barber's window. And although it was the thing to do when first embarking on a wig, to trade in one's own hair for part of the price, this was obviously a once-and-for-all economy. *The Protestant Mercury* of 1700 mentions £3 an ounce as the price offered by wigmakers that year for fine hair,

---

[25] 'A Case Stated re the Act for Licensing Hawkers, 1684' (1705), in *A Collection of Acts Relating to Hawkers and Pedlars* (1726), Goldsmiths' Library, London.
[26] G. Lambert, *History of the Barbers' Company* (1881), p. 30.

and 'when human hair was scarce, a little horse-hair supplied the place in the parts least in sight'. When wigs were still in their infancy the Great Plague occurred and there was some fear that the hair of plague victims might be used or even that the fear of such a thing might drive wigs out of fashion. Vanity triumphed, however, over the darkest suspicions. And was there an element of laziness? The night before he had audience of the Queen, and before he owned a wig, Pepys sent for his barber after supper to come and trim and curl him. The barber's task took so long that he was locked in the Admiralty building where Pepys lived and a porter had to be fetched out of bed to let him out.

Pepys explains, with characteristic frankness, his feelings about wigs:

3 May 1663
I did try two or three borders and periwigs, meaning to wear one, and yet I have no stomach for it but that the pains of keeping my hair clean is so great. He trimmed me and at last I parted, but my mind was almost altered from my first purpose, from the trouble that I forsee in wearing them also.
26 October, 1663 [The day he deserted poor Mr Jervas at the Swan]
Being resolved to go a little handsomer than I have hitherto . . . to one or two periwig shops about the Temple, having been much displeased with one that we saw, a head of greasy old woman's hair, at Jervas's this morning. And I think I shall fit myself with one very handsomely made.
30 October, 1663
. . . . . calling at my periwig-makers and there showed my wife the periwig made for me, and she likes it very well.
2 November, 1663
To the periwig-makers, but it being dark, concluded of nothing.
3 November, 1663
By and by comes Chapman the periwig-maker, and upon my liking it, without more ado I went up, and he cut off my haire, wich went a little to my heart, at present, to part with it. But it being over and my periwig on, I paid him three pounds for it, and away he went with my haire to make up another of.

It was very usual to avoid, as Pepys did, buying anything by candlelight that needed inspection. But it was most unusual to pay cash for so large an item; to 'even' with one's tradesmen once every six months was the mark of a scrupulously honest man. Barbers, however, were long accustomed to holding out the hand for their money immediately after performing their services, and no doubt the habit persisted now they had commodities to sell as well.

One wig led to another. Indeed, when a man had given up his own hair he had no choice in the matter. Pepys bought his second pair in 1664 but delayed wearing them because of the Plague. This year, the King and the Duke of York first took to periwigs. In 1667, his third pair came from a French periwigmaker. ('Mighty fine. Indeed too fine I thought, for me, but he persuaded me.') And a year later, 'being now come to an agreement with my barber to keep my periwig in good order for 20s. a year, I am like to go very spruce, more than I used to do'.

Men's wigs did not gain the day without a good deal of criticism. 'How many bad women have laid their heads together to complete that mane of yours?' asks a character in a play of 1690. 'It is a most monstrous piece of prodigality! Pray, what might it cost you the pound?' Or again, 'Forty or fourscore pounds a year for periwigs, and ten to a poor chaplain that says grace to him that adores hair, is sufficient demonstration of the brains they keep warm.'[27]

But there were, nevertheless, plenty of brains warming under periwigs in the reigns of the later Stuarts, the age of Wren and Newton, the age that first read and appreciated Bunyan and Milton and Dryden. Book publishing was at last getting into its stride. The arbitrary censorship which had cramped literary enterprise for so long was increasingly evaded, and fell into disuse in the 1680s. For twenty years the booksellers made hay with a free market, an eager public, and no authors' rights whatsoever, until the first copyright act in Queen Anne's reign at last put the trade on a steady footing.

When Charles II came to the throne, London booksellers were already numbered in dozens, with a few odd ones scattered in the chief provincial cities. By Queen Anne's reign, the estimate of John Dunton, himself a bookseller who knew most of them personally, was some 150 in London and '300 now trading in the country towns'.[28] Most of these provincial booksellers, of course, were only doing it as a sideline; in many cases their chief

[27] J. P. Malcolm, *Anecdotes of the Manners and Customs of London* (1808), p. 404.
[28] J. Dunton, *The Life and Errors of John Dunton* (1705), p. 239.

trade was in stationery, paper, quill pens by the dozen, almanacks, penny-books, and perhaps a little bookbinding as required. In London, on the other hand, they had risen above the stationery-trade long before this, and very few of the 150 named and described by Dunton in his autobiography dealt in anything but books.

They were thickest on the ground, as they had always been, around St Paul's and the streets to the north of it. At the time of the Great Fire there were about twenty-three booksellers in St Paul's Churchyard alone, but even then they were to be found scattered all over the town as well and some of the best known were nowhere near St Paul's. After the Fire, when newcomers were entering the business in numbers, certain localities began to be favoured: the Temple and the vicinity of Westminster Hall for Law books, the Tower district for technical books, almanacks, practical manuals, the Strand for the latest plays and poetry and music. St Paul's Churchyard, losing its pre-eminence in general bookselling, remained the place to buy divinity books and ancient classics although these no longer formed the bulk of the book-trade as they used to do before the Civil War. 'Parsons,' says Ned Ward, 'were busily searching after the venerable conceits of our wormeaten ancestors as if they came hither for want of brains or a library, to patch up a seasonable discourse for the following Sunday.'[29] And Paternoster Row, which had once been an exclusive shopping street where 'the quality used to choke the street with their carriages' outside the mercers' and lacemen's and haberdashers' was also invaded by the booksellers. After the Fire it was rebuilt with 'spacious shops, back warehouses, skylights and other conveniences made on purpose for their trade' but the fashion-shops were slow to return and the bookshops were eager and within twenty years of the Fire they had taken over the whole of Paternoster Row and Little Britain and Duck Lane behind, and formed an enclave of the book-trade that retained its character until the next great fire in 1940. (But they never needed a private beadle to regulate the traffic of carriages in their street as their predecessors, the mercers, had done.)

What sort of shops were all these bookshops? It might be supposed that they bore some resemblance to their modern

29 Ward, *op. cit.*, p. 98.

counterparts since, saving their dust-jackets, books are very much the same now as then. In fact, the shops must have looked very different because, until well into the eighteenth century, all their new stock was unbound, and lay about in loose sheets, looking, one must assume, like a proof-reader's Monday morning. For the booksellers were the publishers of those days; it was they who employed the printers and commissioned the authors. Even Dryden, Defoe, Marvel and Pope wrote for the proprietors of bookshops and were paid by the hundred lines.

The retail booksellers were the aristocracy of the new literary trade that was fast coming into being by way of their capital and their enterprise. Shakespeare had never made a penny from the printed word. Half a century after him things were improving; Milton, for example, received £5 initially for *Paradise Lost*. Soon after this, Bunyan might have made a comfortable sum from writing had not a rival bookshop commissioned a hack writer to produce *The Second Part of the Pilgrim's Progress* before he could write it himself, and so stolen some of his market. But a little later still, by the end of the century, Dryden made a reasonable living from writing alone, and Pope in the eighteenth century made a handsome one. In a similar way, bookselling changed during the second half of the seventeenth century from an obscure trade to one where leading practitioners could make a fortune. The wealthy founder of Guy's Hospital started life selling books in Cornhill in 1667 with a capital of £200. Tonson, a 'poor apprentice', rose to keep his carriage and mix with the quality. Keeping a bookshop grew 'to be esteemed a very polite and profitable trade in the shopkeeping way'.

But along with the high profits went big risks, and so some of the more ambitious publications were launched by subscription. Here is how Curwen in his *History of Booksellers* describes the arrangements in 1696 for a translation of Virgil:

> As usual, the preliminary terms were to be settled in a tavern, a custom between authors and booksellers that seems to have been universal. 'Be ready' writes Dryden 'with the price of paper and of the books. No matter for any dinner, for that is a charge to you and I care not for it. Mr. Congreve may be with us as a common friend.' There were two classes of subscribers, the first of whom paid five guineas each, and were individually honoured with the dedication of a plate and their arms engraved underneath. The

second class paid two guineas only. The first class numbered 101 and the second class 250.[30]

In the eighteenth century the practice of asking customers to subscribe to proposed publications was extended and became very common, but the onus of enlisting subscribers was transferred from the booksellers to the authors.

John Dunton, who failed in the bookselling business, wrote somewhat enviously: 'The Booksellers in the country cannot in a settled way either ruin or enrich themselves so soon as those in London in regard they have not the temptation, nor indeed the opportunity, to print much.'[31] He himself printed too much, most of it unsaleable, but he gives an interesting hint as to how booksellers provided themselves with stock in the days before wholesaling was organized. He opened his first shop in the Poultry as soon as he was out of his time, and published his first book right away in 1685. 'This book fully answered my purpose for exchanging it through the whole trade it furnished my shop with all sorts of books saleable at that time.' But he goes on:

> Were I to begin the trade of bookselling once again, I would never give myself the trouble to keep open shop. Unless a man can haggle half an hour for a farthing, be dishonest and tell lies, he may starve behind his shop-board for want of subsistence. There is no certainty in a *dropping* trade . . . yet this I can say for myself, that I never printed another's Copy, went upon his Project, nor stole so much as his Title Paper or his Thought.[32]

If the customer liked the look of a book, he could sit down in the shop and read it on the spot. Stools were provided for the purpose. Or he could buy the loose sheets and take them home to read and get them bound privately later if he decided they were worth keeping. Or he could take a bookseller's word for it and order a book to be bound for him right away, plain or fancy 'according to the price the purchaser has a mind to bestow on it'. Pepys mentions waiting a fortnight for this job to be done. John

[30] Henry Curwen, *A History of Booksellers* (1873), p. 28.
[31] Dunton, *op. cit.*, pp. 316–7.
[32] *ibid.*, p. 87.

Dunton patronized several binders who did different classes of work for him. 'Mr Steel, I may call him my Occasional binder, for when I met with a *nice* customer, no binding would serve him but Mr Steel's which, for the fineness and goodness of it, might vie with the Cambridge binding . . .' And so on.

This custom of offering unbound sheets as the normal sale had several minor advantages. The fastidious book-collector could have all his volumes in a uniform binding if he wished, just as with the buyer of continental paper-bound books today; while from the bookseller's point of view, title-pages were easily lifted and stuck up on the walls as advertisements, or the Contents pages were sometimes given away as handouts.[33] When shops were open to the street, these useful notices were nailed to the corner posts, and later they decorated the insides of bookshops. For some reason, authors seem to have resented the implied need to advertise their work. Pope in the *Dunciad* as late as 1728, ridiculed his own bookseller for, among other things, 'filling his shop with rubric posts'.

> What though my name stood rubric on the walls
> And plaistered posts, with clasps in capitals?

Compare this with Ben Jonson almost a century earlier:

> *To My Bookseller*
> Thou that mak'st gain thy end, and wisely well
> Call'st a book good or bad as it doth sell,
> Use mine so too. I give thee leave. But crave
> For the luck's sake it this much favour have,
> To lie upon thy stall till it be sought
> Nor offer'd as it made suit to be bought.
> Nor have my title leaf on posts or walls
> Or in cleft sticks advanced to make calls.
> If without these vile arts it will not sell
> Send it to Bucklersbury. There t'will, well.[34]

This last reference is to the common fate of all unsuccessful books throughout the seventeenth century which was to be sold off to the grocers and apothecaries (who in Jonson's time clustered

[33] *ibid.*, pp. 496–509.
[34] Ben Jonson, *Epigrams* (*Works*, ed. F. Cunningham, 1873), III, 226.

in Bucklersbury) for use as wrapping-paper, or alternatively, to the cookshops to make pie-cases.

> One common fate all imitators share
> To save mince-pies, or cap the grocer's ware.

Unscrupulous booksellers tried to put off this evil day by putting slow sellers under new title-pages with new author's names, so that the unwary buyer sometimes bought the same thing twice over, and the too successful author sometimes found himself credited with someone else's sorry rubbish.

This great spurt forward in the trade of literature during the later Stuart period coincided with a passion for private library-making among the more studious of the gentry. There were, of course, no institutional libraries yet (if we exclude the nucleus of one already started at Oxford by Bodley), and as books continued to pour forth the ambition to own a collection, a balanced, representative, yet discriminating collection, fired a number of wealthy men. Bishop Cosin took endless pains over the assembling, cataloguing, furnishing and arranging of his private library, now in the University Library at Durham. Pepys took the same pride and pleasure in his, still preserved in Magdalen College, Cambridge, having the volumes all bound to match, discarding copies ruthlessly when any work came out in a second edition that he thought might be better produced than the first. And these two were but typical of many others.

Apart from the cost of such a hobby, it was not an easy task to acquire books that were wanted. Editions were small—thirteen hundred was a common size in the seventeenth century—and stock-carrying in the trade was very limited. Books appeared, were praised by their readers, sold out and disappeared. The correspondence of country gentlemen is full of requests to friends to seek out particular books in likely places. So a second-hand book-trade started. These were the dealers 'who often purchase whole libraries and keep large warehouses besides their shops for exposing them to sale'. It was this kind of bookseller, too, who started public auctions of books, very often 'by inch of candle' where the last bid before the flame died was the decisive one. Another way of dealing with second-hand books was to hold lotteries. In one of these Pepys won two books that he owned already, but he soon traded them in for something else. And many London booksellers of both old and new books 'kept the fairs'. Book-publishing was so much concentrated in London that there was a lively market at fairs. The book section at Stourbridge Fair was nationally famous at this time, and all the big fairs would attract some London dealers to take stalls.

The dealers in old books might have in their warehouses several rooms full of books, and they encouraged their customers to come and browse amongst them, meeting with congenial company and 'agreeable conversations', and they put half-read books aside for them until their next visit. This sounds an unprofitable side to any bookselling business—no wonder they resorted to auctions and lotteries. While it may have been agreeable to the idle customer, for the searcher after a particular book it was probably unsatisfactory. 'Mr Shrowsbury keeps his stock in excellent order and will find any book as ready as I can find a word in the dictionary.' It is clear that Dunton regarded this much order as bordering on the eccentric, as was the honesty of another of his colleagues who 'if a child came to his shop would not charge him a penny over the price'.[35]

London booksellers were of all kinds and sizes. There were some who ran 'literary lounging places' like Herringman at the Blue Anchor in the New Exchange, where poets, playwrights and wits met to hear literary gossip. There were grave emporia of learning in Little Britain where elderly bibliophiles browsed over the classics. There were open stalls dotted about at the corners of busy streets, where booksellers who could not afford to 'print' themselves sold the more popular of other people's books. And there were the hawkers with their 'Long Boxes' haunting every place where crowds gathered, the cockpits, the hangings, the playhouses, the Exchanges, with their pamphlets, their penny sermons, the latest ballad or political tract.

But all of them, even the grandest High Priest of the Muses, were mere tradesmen in the eyes of their customers. However much they might hector their authors, swindle their printers and cut each other's throats, when a gentleman crooked his finger to be served, they came running:

[35] Dunton, *op. cit.*, p. 299.

24 July, 1694. For My Worthy Friend, Mr. John Dunton, Bookseller, at the Raven in the Poultry, London.

Sir,

I have taken notice of the second volume of the French book of Martyrs, and when your man comes my way I shall be glad if he will bring me one to read for a week. If I keep it a day longer (provided he then calls upon me for it) or if there be the least damage done to it, I shall be content to pay for the book.

I wish you health and happiness, and am,

Your very humble servant,

[Sir Peter Pett][36]

[36] *ibid.*, p. xvii.

THE EIGHTEENTH CENTURY

VIII

◇◇

Bright Lights and Bow-Windows

◇◇

The Retail Tradesman must furnish himself with a competent stock of patience; I mean that patience which is needful to bear with all sorts of impertinence. A tradesman behind his counter must have no flesh and blood about him; no passions; no resentment. He must never be angry, no not so much as seem to be so, if a customer tumbles him 500 l. worth of goods and scarce bids money for anything.

Daniel Defoe, The Complete English Tradesman, 1727

W E have lingered so long in the seventeenth century because this was the decisive period when shops emerged as the normal places for the consumer to spend a large part of his money. By the eighteenth century shops were well established as an important part of the country's economy and as a familiar part of the urban scene. In many respects shopping was very much what it is today. (Or rather, what it was until yesterday.) But although the retail shop in country towns as well as in large cities was now a commonplace, it was still a very crude establishment by our standards, and was to see a lot of development in the next two centuries.

If the present-day consumer were to be suddenly transported into the middle of the eighteenth century, he would not find it by any means easy to turn his income—big or little, whatever it happened to be—into the appropriate standard of living. There were plenty of goods, and plenty of shops, but using them was no simple, impersonal routine, like putting down sixpence for a

181

tin of beans, or consulting a copy of *Which?* and then signing a cheque for a well-known brand of washing-machine. The shopper of those days, whatever he needed, had to buy a lot of personal service along with the goods, for he depended very heavily on the shopkeeper's knowledge and skill and honesty. To shop successfully it was important to choose a reliable shopkeeper and come to terms with him. Not necessarily friendly terms; acrimonious terms would do just as well; but at least to personal terms. Even the simplest purchase was a cautious bargain struck between two mutually suspicious individuals. It was the customer's job to keep his end up and impress the salesman, even (or perhaps especially) an apprentice; to make it clear that he was a good judge of whatever he was about to buy and had ample means to pay for it; and this applied whether he was a poor man buying a pig's foot in the market or a wealthy one ordering a suite of Chippendale furniture from the great master himself.

Nothing, of course, was branded, or standardized, or guaranteed. No two manufactured articles could be relied on to be exactly alike. About their materials, their design, their workmanship, the buyer could only guess; he had to rely on the shopkeeper's word as an expert. And this was not always easy. Shopkeeping at this time attracted more than its share of the ignorant, the careless, and the dishonest, especially in London. If many traders were scrupulously honest, probably as many again were downright rogues, for the public regulation of inland trade was at a minimum in this century; the old company and civic controls were discredited and enfeebled, while national laws to safeguard standards were still to come. So the majority of traders were simply more or less honest by the currently accepted standards of trading, and these gave them plenty of latitude for sharp practice. Society, under its veneer of cultured elegance, was violent, crude and very tough and trade reflected these rough social conditions. Although easy and tempting to enter, it was an unregulated jungle in which, in spite of some fat pickings, the penalty for failure was often disaster and the debtors' prison. Shopkeepers started and broke, came and went, with bewildering rapidity. There was no limited liability for the shopkeeper to fall back on and on the other side there were virtually no laws to protect the consumer; so caution and trouble were needed on both sides all the time, and, since the shopkeeper tended to have more at stake than the consumer, no customer could afford to relax. The lazy, trustful shopper typical of our own time, even if miraculously preserved from outright swindling, would have received more and more contempt and less and less value from even the most honest and God-fearing shopkeeper of the eighteenth century.

Two disagreeable hazards in particular attended the shopper on every occasion. The price of nearly everything had still to be settled by argument, and then it had to be paid in coins whose validity was often the subject of still further debate. As regards the first of these difficulties:

> It is necessary if the Tradesmen would carry on his affairs with Ease and Satisfaction that his customers should entertain the Opinion that he sells them as cheap as he can afford, and live with becoming Decency. And nothing will contribute more to it than asking within a small matter of what he will take and not going below it, except the Quantity, and Ready Money are a Balance to the Profit he would have made according to his first Demand.[1]

But this was not easy, according to another writer:

> If the customer would expect the tradesman should keep strictly to his demands, they should not stand and haggle and screw the shopkeeper down, bidding from one penny to another.[2]

One reason, it was said, why a shopkeeper should not leave his apprentices to serve the shop any more than necessary, was that whereas the customer was usually convinced that he got things cheaper from the master himself, in fact the master generally obtained a higher price than the apprentices did. Even the Quakers, who had been used on principle to ask a firm price and stick to it, had been obliged, by degrees, 'to ask and abate, just as other honest tradesmen do'.[3]

The plague of a poor coinage, however, was a much more serious trouble. Bad money was still a trap for the unwary. Writing in 1727 Defoe had a lot of warnings about the reappear-

---

[1] Anon., *The Tradesman's Director* (1757), p. 9.
[2] Daniel Defoe, 'The Complete English Tradesman' (1727) in *Works*, ed. J. Skeltie (1870), p. 566.
[3] *ibid.*, p. 566.

ance of counterfeit money which, after a slight reform, was
becoming an even graver nuisance than it had been in the
seventeenth century. If you took it, Defoe said, by mistake, you
were put to the trouble of palming it off again 'on some poor
raw servant or ignorant woman', but he had the grace to add:
'As to the dishonesty of the practice, I think it is out of the
question: it can have nothing but custom to plead for it.' He
went on to recall how, 'If you went but to buy a pair of gloves
or stockings or any trifle at a shop, you went with bad money
in one hand and good money in the other, proffering first the
bad coins to get them off if possible, and then the good if the
other was rejected'.[4]

The silver shillings and sixpences had been in good condition for a while after they were re-minted in William III's
reign, but for most of the century no new silver was struck, and
while trade and population were increasing, the existing silver
coins, so far from keeping pace with the need, were wearing out
and getting lost. By George III's reign, for example, even
genuine silver shillings (and these were said to be actually in a
minority) were worn down to about three-quarters of their
proper size, and sixpences were even worse. Yet because it was
their silver, not their nominal value, that was thought important,
anyone paying a large sum in silver to a shopkeeper had to be
prepared for it to be put on the scales and to be asked to make up
the true weight. It is true that gold guineas, once so rare, were
now minted more often than new silver coins, but these did not
help with the payment of small amounts. Think of it in terms
of present-day prices; imagine pennies non-existent, three-
penny and sixpenny pieces very scarce and mostly illegal,
silver five- and ten-shilling pieces largely devalued by clipping
and often false, ten-pound notes alone plentiful and reliable—
and no cheque-books.

Foreign coins in bewildering variety and bills and pro-
missory notes for larger transactions were accepted among
business men as real money, but although they circulated they
usually represented odd and awkward sums. Private banks issued
their own notes, sometimes for denominations down to a
shilling, but they were only accepted locally. Small wonder then
that large numbers of privately made coins of all kinds were in

[4] *ibid.*, p. 569.

circulation, numbers of them issued for giving change by substantial shopkeepers. Some copper farthings and small silver
coins, although illegal, were made of metal worth their face
value and so were accepted by most people except the government. Many more were thoroughly counterfeit brass or lead
thinly washed over. If the guinea you accepted in good faith was
the next day bitten or broken in your face by an indignant
shopkeeper, the loss was irrecoverable. Or virtually so, for bad
money could be saved up to await the cry of one of the most disreputable of all street hawkers: the men who bought 'Brass
Money! Broken or Whole!' These merchants bought it to sell
back to the coiners whose numbers and output were increasing
all through this century and whose activities amounted to a
minor industry. There were constant complaints, of course,
about the general coinage situation; here is a typical press
article from the *Gazette and London Daily Advertiser* for
30 March 1762.

> The scarcity of silver coin is now become so exceedingly great
> among all degrees and classes of people that they cannot without
> continual vexations carry on their respective branches of manu-
> factory, trade or other dealings. For partly by trusting some
> people who would pay ready money and partly by turning away
> others for want of necessary change, all traders are daily sub-
> jected to losses and obstructions which want nothing but the name
> to make them a vexatious tax.

One result of the perpetual shortage of coin was that credit
was still very free in all branches of trade. Shopkeepers themselves received credit from their suppliers, not for a month or
six weeks as nowadays, but for three to four months as a matter
of course and six to nine months quite commonly, while 'it may
be said that almost every country shopkeeper has credit for a
year if not more'.[5] In their turn they trusted their customers, all
except the casual stranger making an odd purchase or the very
poorest. Established householders were offered credit with
astonishing freedom and for very long periods. Shopkeepers
were perpetually harassed by the risk, and indeed it often ruined
them, but it continued to be the universal practice. An Act of
James I, alleging that shopkeepers' books were often faked, had

[5] Anon, *The Tradesman's Director* (1757), p. 54

made them inadmissible in courts of law as proofs of debt over a year old,[6] and in the seventeenth century the 'trusting' shop-keeper had run grave risks of being let down by the death of even his rich and honest debtors, for when most substantial incomes still came from land entailed upon the heir, and widow's jointures had taken precedence out of the remaining assets, there was often little left to pay huge debts to tradesmen.[7] These risks still remained in the eighteenth century, although now they were lessened because there were far more varied sources of income and wealth, as well as far more personal possessions to claim from when customers died.

> How many families have we in England that live upon credit, even to the tune of two or three years' rent of their revenue before it comes in, so that they may be said to eat the calf in the cow's belly? Thus, I have known a family whose revenue has been some thousands a year pay their butcher and baker and grocer and cheese monger by a hundred pounds at a time and be generally a hundred more in each of their debts. And yet the tradesmen have thought it well worth while to trust them, and their pay has, in the end, been very good . . . Yet they do not lose by it neither, for the tradesmen find it in the price, and they take care to make such families pay warmly for their credit in the rate of their goods. Nor could it be expected that it should be otherwise, for unless the profit answered it, the tradesmen could not afford to be so long without their money.[8]

Not all families were as dilatory as this, of course, but all respectable households expected the tradesmen to call to receive orders and to be paid. For example, the household accounts of the Earl of Halifax's London house contain a very typical receipt-book for the mid-eighteenth century signed by all sorts of tradesmen who called at the house for their money. They came, presumably when they were summoned for the purpose, at long intervals. It consists of hundreds of entries of this sort:

Janry. ye 16th 1715–6.   Rec'd. then from ye Rt. Honble ye Earl
                            of Halifax by ye hand of Wm. Beevor, a
                            Bill of Medicons for ye family use. Nine

[6] 7 James I, c. 12.
[7] N.H., *The Compleat Tradesman* (1684).
[8] Defoe, *op. cit.*, p. 575.

> pounds seven shillings. In full of all
> Accts. by me. Chas. Wolf[9]

Few salesmen in this century realized the possible commercial advantages of cash sales at fixed prices (except, perhaps, the publicans whose trade was somewhat specialized), but in the second half of the century the idea must have been in the air, for two shopkeepers at least became famous for this eccentric method of doing business, and there may of course have been others who tried it with less success. One of them, James Lackington, the first large-scale bookseller, whose shop, the 'Temple of the Muses', became something of a legend.

It was some time in the year seventeen hundred and eighty that I resolved from that period to give no person whatever any credit. I was determined to make this resolution from various motives. I had observed that when credit was given, most bills were not paid within six months, some not within a twelvemonth and some not within two years . . . The losses sustained in interest of money in long credits and by those bills that were not paid at all; the inconveniences attending not having the ready money to lay out in trade to the best advantage, together with the great loss of time in keeping accounts and collecting debts, convinced me that if I could but establish a ready-money business without exceptions, I should be enabled to sell every article very cheaply . . . When I communicated my ideas on this subject to some of my acquaintances I was much laughed at and ridiculed. It was thought I might as well attempt to re-build the Tower of Babel as to establish a large business without giving credit.[10]

Cash sales involved fixed prices; the two were generally regarded as inseparable, but though all books were now sold ready-bound, prices of new books were not fixed since little distinction was yet made between new and second-hand books. There were simply 'neat' copies and 'damaged' copies, in good or bad bindings.

I determined to make the experiment, and began by plainly marking in every book, facing the title, the lowest price that I

[9] State Papers, Domestic, 9–48.
[10] James Lackington, *Memoirs of the First Forty-five Years* (1830), p. 214.

would take for it . . . But you can scarce imagine what difficulties I encountered for several years together. I even thought of relinquishing this, my favourite scheme, altogether, as by it I was obliged to deny credit to my very acquaintance. I was also under a necessity of refusing it to the most respectable characters, as no exception was (or now is) made, not even to the nobility.

Lackington made a vast fortune, and he really believed that his system was unique. But it wasn't, for a draper and haberdasher had beaten him to it by a few years. Haberdashers have always been in the forefront of innovations in retailing; in Elizabethan times, in nineteenth-century department stores, in bazaar-trading and postal shopping in recent times. It is true that their goods are numerous, cheap, and universally in demand, and perhaps this means that competition had tended to sharpen their salesmanship. Or it may simply be that there have always been so many of them that one or two were almost bound to have original ideas occasionally. But butchers, for example, have always been just as numerous, and when did butchers do anything to improve retailing? However that may be, the first undoubted fixed-price cash shop that history can record was a haberdashery and drapery, Flint and Palmer's on London Bridge. Robert Owen the philanthropist worked there as a boy, and he describes the shop in his autobiography:

> It was a house established, and I believe the first, to sell at small profit and for ready money only . . . Not much time was allowed for bargaining, a price being fixed for everything and, compared with other houses, cheap. If any demur was made or much hesitation, the article asked for was withdrawn, and as the shop was generally full from morning till late in the evening, another customer was attended to.[11]

The type of custom Owen describes as 'inferior'. But for all that, the many shop assistants, who all of course lived in, had to be very sprucely turned out and have their hair curled and powdered by the barber every morning before entering the shop at eight o'clock. This shop, like Lackington's cheap bookshop,

11 Robert Owen, *The Life of Robert Owen, by Himself* (ed. M. Beer, 1920), pp. 25-7.

was a goldmine for its owners. Owen and his fellows served like beavers until the last customers were turned away at ten-thirty at night, and he eventually left because 'the slavery every day of the week seemed more than my constitution could support'. But in spite of their success both shops were regarded rather as curiosities than as examples to be followed. Even the clear-headed Robert Owen looked back with contempt on Flint and Palmer's because the custom was not very 'genteel'.

London was now a vast and busy commercial city. In 1732, Maitland estimated that nearly a quarter of all the houses in the metropolis were shops or taverns selling some kind of food or drink, not counting all the shops of other kinds.[12] While estimates of the total vary very greatly, it is clear that there were now many thousands, probably scores of thousands, of shops of one sort or another. Most of them would hardly deserve the name of shop by present standards, for there were no special taxes or rates to discourage anyone who occupied the ground floor of a house and could get a few goods together, from keeping a shop and leaving his wife to run it. But more genuine businesses were thick on the ground for another reason; the shops of London still served, besides the inhabitants of a big city and a constant stream of visitors, a great many small, country shopkeepers who came to the capital to buy their stock. Specialized wholesale houses were coming into being in the eighteenth century but the majority of provincial shopkeepers still came to ordinary London shops for their supplies.

The identification of addresses among such large numbers of tradesmen was now becoming a matter of some confusion, for houses were still known by signs instead of numbers. Originally a simple device carved over the door, the tradesman's sign had grown in size and elaboration over the years as each shopkeeper strove to make his premises more conspicuous than his neighbours'. In the seventeenth century, the favourite sign had been a painted board hung out on brackets, and Cheapside then had been described as 'like the Medici gallery'. By the eighteenth century, these had developed into models, enormous, carved, gilded and painted symbols that hung out over the streets, and in narrow thoroughfares actually met overhead. Some of these cost over a hundred guineas, some were so monstrously heavy

12 W. Maitland, *History and Survey of London* (1756), II, 719, 735.

that they pulled out the house-fronts, and several fell down and injured passers-by. By mid-century, public opinion was demanding some sort of control.[13]

For however grand the signs themselves became, they were now hopelessly inadequate as a means of finding a particular shopkeeper or even a particular kind of shop. A few still indicated the shopkeeper's trade: the three sugar-loaves for the grocer, the three tents for the upholsterer, the three hats for the hatter and so on. But houses changed hands, men changed trades, and the majority of signs had lost all connection with the shop underneath. Addison in the *Spectator* was only slightly exaggerating when he said:

A cook should not live at the *Boot* nor a shoe-maker at the *Roasted Pig* . . . I have seen a *Goat* set up before a perfumer and the *King's Head* before a sword-cutler's.

Another writer described signs as 'very large, very fine, and very absurd, golden periwigs, saws, axes, lancets, razors, trees, knives, salmon, cheeses, blacks' heads, half-moons, sugar-loaves and Westphalian hams . . . repeated without mercy from the Borough to Clerkenwell'.[14] Repetition, of course, was inevitable. (And sometimes downright malicious; it was necessary, for instance, to put an advertisement in the paper to point out that the old *Three Bibles* on London Bridge was the original shop and not to be confused with the new *Old Three Bibles* just opened opposite.)

Hanging signs had outlived their useful functions, but their splendid profusion of colours and shapes had become the most conspicuous feature of the city streets; they had dripped on rainy days and creaked on windy nights for as long as anyone could remember and in 1762 they clustered sparkling overhead in their thousands, more elaborate, more beautiful than ever before. When they were suddenly removed that year in one clean sweep, by order of the authorities, London must have looked bleak and ugly. Most signs passed out of use at once, except where inns and taverns clung to familiar names, and they would have been lost without trace had it not been for their pictures on shop-bills

[13] F. G. Hilton Price, 'Signs of Old London', *London Topographical Record*, IV (1907).

[14] J. P. Malcolm, *Anecdotes of the Manners and Customs of London* (1808), p. 469.

and trade-cards, many of which still survive. These trade-cards, as they were called, were not cards at all but a kind of hand-bill passed out to the public as an advertisement, often beautifully designed and engraved, and simply stating the shopkeeper's whereabouts and line of business, and they give the best impression now surviving of this picturesque feature of old shops.[15]

Shop premises were changing and improving slowly, but many of the old ones, especially those in the eastern parishes and those that had escaped the Great Fire, were still dark and cramped. Sales across open windows were still very common, and the phrase for starting and finishing the day's business was still to open and close 'the window'. Defoe's *Colonel Jack*, a ten-year-old beggar boy in Ratcliffe Highway, was often given a penny to guard a window and save the trouble of putting up shutters while the shopkeeper went into the ale-house. But open windows were not confined to the East End:

> The cheesemongers should not set out their butter and cheese so near the edge of the shop window, nor put their firkins in ye pathways, by which many a good coat and silk gown may be spoiled. As by advertising in the papers his shop may be sufficiently known without carrying home the shop-bill upon their clothes.[16]

Stalls in sheds or 'bulks' set up against house or shop walls were still very common. All sorts of poor tradesmen were to be found sitting in these, especially cheap tailors, shoe-menders, seamstresses who took in mending, and the like. Some were only big enough to provide seat and roof; some were slept in at night by vagrants; some had a door and a bed on the floor and their tenants had no other home. One cold night in 1768, for instance, a cobbler was found frozen to death in his pavement stall.

The politer trades were now beginning to take advantage of the new plate-glass for windows in place of the old ring or bottle glass. Panes of twelve inches by sixteen enabled the passer-by to see into the shop, and about mid-century we begin to hear of 'the ambition of the shopkeepers who encroached upon the

---

[15] Ambrose Heal, *London Tradesmen's Cards of the Eighteenth Century* (1925); *The Signboards of Old London Shops* (1947), *passim.*
[16] Malcolm, *op. cit.,* p. 191.

footways with bow-windows; when an example was set, the whole fraternity, fired with emulation, thrust each one beyond his neighbour'.[17] And what were the bow-windows used for?

> Behind the great glass windows absolutely everything one can think of is neatly, attractively displayed, in such abundance of choice as almost to make one greedy. Now large slipper and shoe-shops for anything from adults down to dolls, can be seen; now fashion-articles or silver or brass shops, boots, guns, glasses, the confectioner's goodies, the pewterer's wares, fans, etc. . . . There is a cunning devise for showing women's materials. They hang down in folds behind the fine, high windows so that the effect of this or that material, as it would be in a woman's dress, can be studied.[18]

That was said in 1786, but lest it sound too modern to be credible, consider that such windows might have been fitted into premises such as the following, a 'modern' shop in a good position advertised in 1712:

> To be Lett, near Cheapside, a large new-built House that fronts two streets of great Trade. The Shop is lined with deal all round, and is about 60 foot deep one way. There is under the shop a very good dry Warehouse that is brickt at bottom. Joyce and boarded over it, the sides and top lined with Deal. It is 9 foot between Floor and Top. There is above Stairs, 4 rooms on a Floor almost all Wanescotted, and a large Staircase all Wanescotted. All the Flat [i.e. roof] is covered with very thick Lead, with Rails and Bannisters round the leads and a large Cupolo on Top. Enquire of Mr. Richd. Wright at the Periwig in Bread Street.[19]

Such a shop would be expensive and fit for the highest class of trade—the lead roof and cupola where the family could take the air were marks of real distinction. All the same, it is notice-able that there was no kitchen on the ground floor, and no water-supply except the public pump in the street. And no yard for a privy; the 'night man' would be paid to call daily for what must be carried down the 'large staircase' (i.e. not enclosed between walls) and out through the shop past the customers. There must have been hundreds of City shops like this, built in

---

[17] *ibid.*, p. 468.
[18] S. Von La Roche, *Sophie in London* (1786) (ed. Clare Williams, 1933), p. 87.
[19] John Ashton, *Social Life in the Reign of Queen Anne* (1882), p. 48.

the latest fashion after the Great Fire in conformity with the new building standards and in use throughout the eighteenth century.

It had always been the rule with shopkeepers hitherto that their capital was in their stock, and in the credit allowed to customers, and not wasted in fitting up shop-furniture to house and display goods. There was plenty of time to spare for rummaging through boxes and parcels and bringing out what the customer inquired for. And a splendid muddle some of their shops must have been in. Even as late as the 'seventies, in a progressive shop like Flint and Palmer's it took numerous assistants hours every night to tidy away the goods 'tumbled' during the day, and this tedious sorting does not sound as though shelves and cupboards and drawers were plentiful; it is more suggestive of brown-paper parcels heaped in back rooms and attics. Moreover, shoplifting was the commonest of crimes even in small, one-room shops where little was put on display, which indicates that the shopkeeper's back was turned a good deal while he hunted for goods.[20] But in the first half of the eighteenth century, new luxury goods were giving rise to new kinds of shop and changing tradesmen's ideas about how to fit up a shop and attract custom.

> It is a modern custom and wholly unknown to our ancestors to have tradesmen lay out two-thirds of their fortune in fitting up their shops. By fitting up, I do not mean furnishing their shops with wares and goods to sell; but in painting and gilding, fine shelves, shutters, boxes, glass doors, sashes and the like, in which, they tell us now, 'tis a small matter to lay out two or three hundred pounds . . .[21]

Defoe, who distrusted the new fashions because he thought they gave rise to unsound, ephemeral business which would damage traditional trades for no lasting benefit, described the new frivolities better than anyone. Here he is at the now-familiar grumble about the 'good' shopping streets that are going down in the social scale.

[20] R. J. Mitchell & M. D. R. Leys, *History of London Life* (1963), p. 214; Defoe, *op. cit.*, p. 550.
[21] D. Defoe, *op. cit.* (1732), I, 257.

Let any man who remembers the glorious state of our Trade about 30 or 40 years past, view but the streets of this opulant city . . . Here in the room of a trifling Banker or Goldsmith, we are supplied with a most eminent Brandy Shop (*Cheapside!*). There, in the room of ditto, you have a flaming shop for White Teapots (*Cornhill!*). It is impossible that Tea, Coffee and Chocolate can be so enhanced in their consumption without an eminent increase in those trades that attend them, whence we see the most noble shops in the City taken up with the valuable Utensils of the Tea-table . . . The eminent Corner Houses of the chief streets in London are chosen out by the town tinkers to furnish us with Tea-kettles and Chocolate Pots (*vide Catherine Street and Bedford Buildings!*). Two thousand pounds is reckoned a small stock in copper pots and laquered kettles, and the new fitting-up one of the brazen people's shops with fine Sashes etc. to set forth his Ware costs above 500 l. Sterling, which is more by half than the best Draper's or Mercer's shop in London requires . . . It will hardly be believed in ages to come that a pastry cook's shop, which twenty pounds would effectively furnish at one time with all needful things for sale, yet that fitting up one of these shops should cost upwards of 300 l. Anno Domini 1710, let the year be recorded![22]

We do in fact believe it, and we note the year, for pastry-cooks' shops went from strength to strength after that and were commented on by many writers. Sugar and dried fruits, once the luxuries of the rich, lent to ready-made cakes and confectionery a wide appeal. In the fashionable districts these shops were elegantly appointed, furnished like drawing-rooms with candelabra and mirrors and snowy tablecloths on which the food was set out for the customers to stand about and eat it on the spot. Another writer said of them, 'Notwithstanding that this seems to be almost an unnecessary Business yet as they now stand they are considerable shopkeepers and traders, and there are more of them than any body can presently conceive'.[23] And the same might have been said of all the new shops that Defoe so disliked—they seemed unnecessary, but they flourished. All the sedan-chair makers, and looking-glass shops and wig-makers and china-, brass-, tea- and coffee-shops, 'whose trades used to be found only in lanes and alleys and back streets and by-places and are fittest for such places'.[24]

[22] D. Defoe, *The Review*, 8 Jan. 1713.
[23] Anon., *A Description of Trades* (1747).
[24] D. Defoe, *The Review*, 8 Jan. 1713.

While the old City still held thousands of shops, the biggest and finest shops, especially for apparel and luxury goods, were increasingly to be found in what is nowadays called the West End. A division, apparent in the seventeenth century, grew very marked in the eighteenth between the two Londons. There was the London of the poor, of the City's back streets and industrial parishes and fringe of eastern suburbs, all crowded with artisans and labourers; and there was the London of the upper classes who knew the City only for its principal streets and public buildings, but lived west of Temple Bar in the new suburbs of Bloomsbury and St James'. In the newer suburbs of the West End the shops were becoming very specialized to particular commodities, and they stocked the finest of English manufactures which in many lines were unmatched in Europe. Sophie von la Roche in 1786 wrote home to Germany about 'lovely Oxford Street', brilliantly lit by oil-lamps and lined with shops open until ten in the evening.

> First one passes a watch-making, then a silk or fan store, now a silversmith's, a china or glass shop. The spirit booths are particularly tempting for the English are in any case fond of strong drink. Here crystal flasks of every shape and form are exhibited; each one has a light behind which makes all the different coloured spirits sparkle. Just as alluring are the confectioners and fruiterers, where, behind the handsome glass windows pyramids of pineapples, figs, grapes, oranges and all manner of fruits are on show. We enquired the price of a fine pineapple and did not think it too dear at 6s. Most of all we admired a stall with Argand lamps, situated in a corner house and forming a really dazzling spectacle. Every variety of lamp, crystal, laquer and metal ones, silver and brass in every possible shade.[25]

Adequate street lighting, even in main thoroughfares, was of course a rarity until the nineteenth century. Oxford Street was a wonder, but elsewhere trade fell away sharply after dark because the streets were unsafe. The same writer mentions that the living-rooms of the Oxford Street shopkeepers were perfectly visible through the backs of their shops, a reminder that these were new buildings, spacious and elegant. Hitherto, it had been almost unknown for a shopkeeper to live anywhere else but

[25] Von la Roche, *op. cit.*, p. 141.

upstairs, for few shops had occupied enough ground space to waste any of it on living quarters; in the City the most prosperous tradesmen were now beginning to take houses for their families in the country, and travel in each day. But it was the shopkeepers in the fashionable West End who were the targets for all the popular jibes about tradesmen trying to live like gentlemen, with their long wigs and silk waistcoats; with their genteelly furnished apartments and servants in livery; with their well-born wives who had set them up in trade by their large dowries but were too ladylike to be seen in the shop themselves; and with their high-premium apprentices whose condescending airs were alleged to be so insufferable to any customer without a title. All these allegations about shopkeepers and many more in the same vein abound in eighteenth-century writing, and they suggest that some, at any rate, of the West End shops were extremely profitable businesses.

It is interesting to trace, in Miss Scott-Thompson's books about the Russell family, how the shopping for that household changed its locale over the years. In the seventeenth century, when the family had Bedford House in the Strand, the buying was done almost entirely in the City, but gradually in Restoration times they came to accept tradesmen who had set up in the Covent Garden district after the Fire. By the mid-eighteenth century, the family residence had been moved back from the increasingly commercial bustle of the Strand to a new mansion in Bloomsbury, and its patronage was spread wide, not only over shops in the City and Covent Garden but in St James's and Piccadilly too. Family tradesmen's bills in George III's reign came from all over the town and included at any one time the names of several grocers, several mercers, several haberdashers and so on and no doubt represented a nice discrimination in prices and qualities.

But important as were the new shopping districts in the West End, the centre of gravity, as it were, of London's retail trade remained in the City itself. There, many a draper, or mercer, or grocer of the old school, in a cramped, dark, muddled shop but with a good reputation in London and a sound connection among country gentry or village shopkeepers, still did a bigger trade than his more showy colleague in Oxford Street who depended much more on what was contemptuously called a 'dropping trade' meaning the casual trade from passers-by. The old style and the new existed side by side, but in different worlds, as each was different from the hundreds of mean shops in the poor quarters.

London's shopping habits and London's shops, then, were still changing even if somewhat less dramatically than in the previous century. In one respect, however, change was sweeping on as vigorously as ever; new articles of trade were continuously appearing, either the products of English craftsmanship or exotic new foodstuffs. Their effects on shopkeeping practice did not offend everyone as they did Daniel Defoe, and some of these new trades deserve a less partial view.

Prominent among the luxury shops of the eighteenth century were the furniture-makers. Besides the cabinet-making and chair-carving for which they are now remembered, they commonly dealt in all the elegant parts of house-furnishing, in carpets, hangings, mirrors, and the equipment for funerals. (Cheap wooden furniture for more humble requirements was the business of the turners' shops.) This was the century when the London furniture-makers' craft was brought to a peak of perfection by an era of general prosperity, and an abundance first of walnut and later of tropical hardwoods. The gentry from all over England were coming to London for the latest styles by the middle of the century and the trade was booming, for in furniture, as in so many more important things, this was an age of self-confidence, when men looked forward, not back, for the best.

Many shopkeeping cabinet-makers worked with their own hands in small businesses, specializing in particular articles, chairs or chests, etc., and trading in the others. Most of their work seems to have been to customers' orders, but they kept stocks for display. It was said in 1753 that £40 to £50 would buy an apprenticeship and £200 to £300 would set up a shop— not one of the most expensive of retail trades to enter, by any means.[26] But 'many of their shops are so richly set out that they look like palaces and their stocks are of exceeding great value. But this business seems to consist, as do so many others, of two branches, the Maker and the Vendor, for the shopkeeper does not always make every sort of goods that he deals in, though he

[26] Anon., *The General Shop Book* (1753).

bears away the Title'.[27] Francis Place's brother-in-law was a journeyman chair-carver, 'a good workman and remarkably swift', and he received chairs and other small pieces from shops to make at home, and could, if he worked hard, earn £4 a week all the year round—remarkably high wages.[28] No doubt this is why so much of the finest surviving work of this period is unmarked by any maker's name and is now unidentifiable, while the now-famous names of eighteenth-century furniture-making were by no means the owners of the biggest workshops or even of outstanding reputation in their own day.

Some prosperous cabinet-makers undertook the whole task of interior decoration for wealthy customers, employing upholsterers, carvers, gilders, glass-makers and so forth. A similarly comprehensive task at a less exalted level was the usual work of upholsterers. Here is an upholsterer's bill for undertaking the main items in a fine new bedroom. Notice that he has been responsible not only for curtains and bedding, but for paperhangers and cabinet-makers under his directions, although there is no doubt that he would make most of his profit on the sixty yards (sixty yards!) of silk damask.

Mr. John Crook.   *Bought of Thos. Townsend, Upholsterer,*
                              Feb. 8th 1761

	£	s.	d.
65 yards red & white Sprig'd paper	2	8	9
Putting up the same & Paste included		11	3
30 yards fine Ticking	3	1	6
60 yards Green Silk Damask	34	15	0
14 Dozen of Green Silk Binding Lace	4	2	0
Buckram to line Vallens, Basses & Paper for Tester		10	6
6 yards Green Stuff to line Vallens		9	6
A set of Carved Cornices		14	0
A Four Post Bedstead, Sacking, Bottom & Casters	3	10	6
Making the Bed and Window Curtains ..	2	14	0
A large Feather Bed & Bolster & Fustian Pillows	8	10	0
3 Large fine Blankets	3	12	6
A Large Linen Quilt & Large Cotton Counterpane	1	10	0
	£66	9	6[29]

[27] Anon., *A Description of Trades* (1747).
[28] Dorothy George, *London Life in the Eighteenth Century* (1925), p. 367.
[29] P. Hudson, *On Trade* (1761).

For those of modest means, the drysalter sold the ingredients for do-it-yourself house decorating. He was a dealer in all sorts of household cleaning materials like starch, soap, sand, brickdust, oil and so forth, and he sold raw linseed oil, white lead, dyes, etc. Books of the style of *The Compleat Housewife* explained how to boil up various kinds of paint and varnish (out of doors, of course, for fear of setting fire to the house) and for paintpots 'there must be bought six chamber pots of earthenware and keep them to what they belong to'.[30]

After the furnishing and decorating, came the ornamental embellishments. The cargoes of the East India Company's ships, auctioned off at East India House, contained not only coffee and tea and spices but many ornamental goods from both India and China, and many traders, but especially tea- and coffee-dealers, bought some of these to sell in their shops. There were even one or two specialist India or China shops (the two far-away countries and their products seem at first to have been somewhat confused in the popular mind). Peter Motteux, now remembered for his translation of *Don Quixote*, ran one such shop in Leadenhall Street quite early in the century.

> Straight then I'll dress and take my wonted range
> To India shops, Motteux's or the 'Change
> Where the tall jar erects its costly pride
> With antique shapes in China's azure dyed.
> There careless lies the rich brocade unrolled
> Here shines a cabinet with burnished gold . . .[31]

The passion for table china grew alongside that for tea. (Indeed there was at first nothing but imported china suitable to drink tea from.) And when the fashionable household had its porcelain tea-service and brass or copper tea-kettle it required a dainty little table on which to set them out, and this too came at first from the Far East before it was copied by English makers. China soon started to be bought for ornament as well as for use; dishes, bowls, vases were set up for show, though not all of them were of the kind referred to in this advertisement from Queen Anne's reign:

[30] Eliza Smith, *The Compleat Housewife* (1727).
[31] John Gay, *Eclogues* (1720) (*Poetical Works*, ed. John Underhill, 1893), I, 235.

> Whereas the New East India Company did lately sell all their China Ware, these are to Advertise that a very large parcel thereof (as Broken and Damaged) is now to be sold by wholesale and retail extreemly cheap at a Warehouse in Dyer's Yard. *Note.* It is very fit to furnish Escrutores, Cabinets, Corner Cupboards or Springs where it usually stands for ornament only.[32]

English-made china improved very quickly to meet this demand, not only the exquisite Chelsea and Worcester and Derby but the commoner and cheaper pottery of Staffordshire where Wedgwood made his fortune in the middle of the century. Like all really great men, Josiah Wedgwood was too far in advance of his times to be called typical, but he is of interest here because as well as being a great potter, he was, as Mr McKendrick's researches have recently shown, a brilliant salesman.[33] Among his many original schemes for promoting the sales of his wares, which he felt were badly served by travelling packhorse salesmen supplying country shops, he opened a London showroom in 1765 in Grosvenor Square. It was aimed deliberately at securing the patronage of the nobility and gentry. 'Fashion,' he told his partner, 'is infinitely superior to Merit in many respects.' In this shop he did such a thriving retail trade that in two years he was looking for bigger premises. 'We must have an Elegant, Extensive and Convenient showroom,' he wrote, but he thought one suggested in Pall Mall was too accessible to the common folk 'for you know that my present sett of Customers will not mix with the rest of the World'.

He chose Portland House in Greek Street for his new shop and made it a fashionable resort. No doubt he was more efficient than most shopkeepers, but his methods throw some light on contemporary attitudes to selling luxury goods. The watchword was lavish display and showmanship. Whole dinner services were set out on tables as if for a meal

> as if to *do the needful* for the Ladys in the neatest, genteelest and best method. The same, or indeed a much greater variety of setts of Vases sh'd decorate the Walls & both these articles

[32] Ashton, *op. cit.*, p. 57.

[33] N. McKendrick, 'Josiah Wedgwood: An Eighteenth Century Entrepreneur in Salesmanship and Marketing Techniques', *Econ. Hist. Rev.*, XII (1960), pp. 408–33.

may every few days be so alter'd, revers'd & transform'd as to render the whole a new scene, even to the same Company every time they shall bring their friends to visit us.

I need not tell you the many good effects this must produce, when business and amusement can be made to go hand in hand. Every new show, Exhibition or rarity soon grows stale in London and is no longer regarded after the first sight, unless utility or some such variety as I have hinted at above continues to recommend it to their notice . . . I have done something of the sort since I came to Town, and find the immediate good effects of it. The first two days after the alterations, we sold three complete Setts of Vases at 2 & 3 Guineas a sett, besides many pairs of them, which Vases had been in my Rooms 6–8 and some 12 months & wanted nothing but arrangement to sell them . . . I need not tell you that it will be our interest to amuse and divert & please & astonish, nay, even to ravish, the Ladies.[34]

In 1769 he was taking about £100 a week in the shop, apart from extensive orders from the pattern-books, and he seems to have established, at least to some extent, cash sales for fixed prices according to a letter he wrote that year to his partner: 'I think that what you charge 34s. should be . . . a Guinea and a half. 34s. is so odd a sum, there is no paying it genteely . . .' (Those elusive silver shillings again, and Wedgwood was not a man to lower his price without good reason.) Gentility was essential to his brand of showmanship; when it was suggested that he issue trade-cards he retorted, 'We have hitherto appeared in a very different light to common Shopkeepers, but this step (in my opinion) would sink us exceedingly . . .' In this snobbish avoidance of the word shop, he was not alone. 'Have we now any Shops?' asks a correspondent in the *London Chronicle* in 1765. 'Are they not all turned into Warehouses?'

The exclusive and expensive pottery shops of Wedgwood, and later of Spode and Minton, were exceptional, but there were plenty of more ordinary china-shops appearing, to sell all kinds of glass and pottery. All through the eighteenth century, however, it was usual for them to sell china and tea together. It is a most mysterious thing that, having embraced coffee with such enthusiasm at the end of the previous century, the English alone among European nations, deserted it permanently for tea. In the

[34] *ibid.*

eighteenth century, the sale of tea was not particularly associated with grocers. Apothecaries and coffee-houses were the chief sellers, it was sold along with china, and all other sorts of shops kept it as a sideline. In 1713, the famous Tom's Coffee-House in the Strand did so much business selling tea by the pound that it interfered with normal coffee-house trade, and its proprietor, Tom Twining, thought it worth his while to take the shop next door especially to deal with this sideline; his descendants, the present Twinings tea firm, are still engaged upon it.[35] Other coffee-house proprietors, however, fared less well; except for a few that became successful private clubs (like White's) most of them disappeared in the course of the century.

All the tea drunk before Victoria's reign was, of course, China tea, although it was never called that because there was no other sort. Instead it was known by a great variety of fancy names that are now unknown except to professional tea-blenders. Then, there were no professionals; every customer bought and blended his own choice, mixing the cheaper Common Bohea or Common Green with the dearer Hysons or Gunpowders or Congos. Prices, and no doubt qualities too, varied critically with every season and every auction. The precious ounces were stored away in the separate compartments of little tea-cabinets fitted with porcelain mixing bowls and good locks to keep the servants out. Not that the servants were denied their tea, for they were usually allowed the second brewing of the leaves, which they could then give away to someone else if they wished.

For although it was so dear, the craving for tea spread like a vice:

> Being the other day at the grocer's, I could not forbear looking earnestly and with some degree of indignation at a ragged and greasy creature who came into the shop with two children following her and in as dismal a plight as their mother, asking for a penny worth of tea and a halfpennyworth of sugar, which, when she was served with, she told the shopkeeper, Mr. N., I do not know how it is with me, but I assure you I would not desire to live if I was to be debarred from drinking every day a little tea.[36]

[35] S. H. Twining, *The House of Twining* (1956), *passim*.
[36] Dorothy Marshall, *English People in the 18th Century* (1956), p. 172, quoting Charles Deering, *Nottingham Vetus et Nova* (1751).

This was in 1751. These cheap pennyworths would be at best a meagre teaspoonful, partly dust; at worst, made from the dried leaves of English bushes coloured with copperas or tanner's fluid. It may have been partly because it lent itself to such reckless adulteration by shopkeepers that tea was so widely denounced (far more than coffee) as a 'destroyer of health' and 'enfeebler of the frame' and so forth by the wine-drinking classes who thought the lower orders should stick to ale. But tea, like coffee, had two great advantages, especially for the poor; it was a warm drink in a cold climate, and to make it at all involved boiling the drinking water and so making it safe. In 1722 the English were buying tea at an average rate of an ounce a head per year and over the next hundred years this increased steadily to an ounce a head per week, while over the same period the drinking of beer was almost exactly halved. [37]

The shops that catered for the well-to-do in the West End now included a good many food shops; grocers were becoming more important, and there were many good-class butchers' and fruiterers' shops. Cheesemongers now sold cheese and butter, eggs, bacon, hams and in fact the whole 'provisions' side of the modern grocery, a notoriously risky stock to hold in quantity in the days before refrigerators. The 'oilman' overlapped some-what with the cheesemonger, besides selling many foreign dainties in vinegar-pickle and 'a vast number of articles for family supply chiefly in the service of the kitchen'. Bread, too, was becoming a shop article in the West End; it was still nominally controlled in size and weight but it was more often sold over the counter now or delivered out to customers' houses than carried into the open market. But perhaps the most signi-ficant pointer to the way in which food-retailing had left behind the old rigid controls of the market-place was the way in which the many new bun-shops and pastry-cooks were allowed to spring up anywhere, charging what they could get and selling what they liked. But it must not be thought that shops had taken the place of the markets; on the contrary, most perishable food was still bought as it had always been from trestle stalls in the open street or market-square and many of the most prosperous butchers and cheesemongers and poulterers and so forth, who

---

[37] Peter Mathias, *The Brewing Industry in England, 1700–1830* (1959), p. 375.

were referred to as 'shopkeepers' and served very good families, never sold under a roof in their lives.

Food of all kinds was more plentiful and relatively cheaper than it had ever been, and while this was a century of unparalleled gourmandizing, there was less preoccupation than formerly with food and how to get it, and more of people's income and interest was going in other directions. (For example, in the household account of a tradesman quoted at the end of this chapter, food and drink represent only 29 per cent of the total outlay.) Only towards the end of the eighteenth century, when bad harvests and the hardships of the Napoleonic wars were causing alarm, did the old cries of scarcity come back. Then there was a panic for a few years to have food prices controlled and to hunt out the three ancient bogey-men, the engrosser, the forestaller and the regrator, and in fact numbers of food-dealers were prosecuted under old laws for speculating in the markets and the bakers were driven to despair by abrupt attempts to enforce the Assize of Bread. It was a brief phase, but a revealing one; although many years of plenty had relaxed food controls and there were now many middlemen handling the commodities for London's growing population, yet on the whole, the organization of London's supply of home-produced foods had not changed fundamentally since Restoration times.

Fresh vegetables and fruit were eaten in greater quantities in the eighteenth century than ever before, and dainties in this line fetched enormous prices. Early garden peas, for instance, came into Covent Garden and sold there at two guineas a quart, retail. Sea-kale was advertised 'daily fresh-cut for the short season it may last. Printed directions for dressing it are tied up with each bundle.' The consumer who wanted the best and freshest fruit and vegetables bought them directly from the market gardeners or their agents in one of the wholesale markets, especially Covent Garden. Inferior produce that had failed to sell in the Stocks or Covent Garden to the better-off customers or the high-class West End shops, went more cheaply to the barrow trade or basket hawkers who between them still formed the biggest outlet for fruit and vegetables.

It was but yesterday that I saw a dirty barrow-bunter in the street, cleansing her dusty fruit with her own spittle; and who knows but some fine lady of St. James's parish might admit into her delicate mouth those very cherries which had been rolled and moistened between the filthy and perhaps ulcerated chops of a St. Giles' huckster?[38]

Butter and cheese were both cheap and plentiful because although milk production had greatly improved there was as yet no means of distributing fresh milk that was not actually produced on the outskirts of a big town; so most of it went into butter and cheese that would keep a while. Best London butter was fresh and local, usually styled 'Epping butter' for courtesy, but the ordinary kind was the cheaper 'Cambridge butter', not made in Cambridge but marketed there from all over the eastern counties and bought there by London dealers, salted in barrels. Smollett's *Humphry Clinker* describes it as 'the tallowy rancid mass called butter, manufactured with candle-grease and kitchen stuff', and even a sober writer on the art of marketing in 1788 advised 'butter should be bought by the taste and smell'.[39] The same writer has a word on the new pork-butchers who were appearing in London to sell bacon, ham and so forth which everywhere else in the country were made at home; a ham at the butcher's, he says, should be tested before being bought by running a knife under the bone to see if it smells when withdrawn. The beef-butcher was not expected to charge for the odd half- and quarter-pounds in the price of a joint, but as to the meat itself, consider the advice on etiquette which deprecates

> Smelling to the meat whilst on the fork, before you put it in your mouth. I have seen many an ill-bred fellow do this . . . If you dislike what you have, leave it. But on no account by smelling to or examining it, charge your friend with putting unwholesome provisions before you . . .[40]

These were by no means the only writers to criticize the state of food on sale in London compared with that available in the country, but Smollett's diatribe against London milk is perhaps the most nauseating as well as the most convincing contemporary description of the town's fare:

[38] T. Smollett, *The Expedition of Humphry Clinker* (1775).
[39] John Trusler, *The Honours of the Table* (1788).
[40] *ibid.*, p. 172.

But the milk itself should not pass unanalysed, the produce of faded cabbage leaves and sour draff, lowered with hot water, frothed with bruised snails, carried through the streets in open pails, exposed to the foul rinsings discharged from doors and windows, spittle, snot and tobacco quids from foot-passengers, overflowings from mud-carts, spatterings from coach wheels, dirt and trash chucked into it by roguish boys for the joke's sake, the spewings of infants who have slabbered in the tin measure which is thrown back in that condition among the milk for the benefit of the next customer; and, finally, the vermin that drops from the rags of the nasty drab that vends this precious mixture, under the respectable title of milk-maid.[41]

Was London's food in general getting more stale and dirty than it had been? Or were observers merely more fastidious than they were? It is impossible to judge from mere verbal description, but it does at least seem probable that, as the size of London grew and its food came from farther afield by slow and unreliable transport, the quality of much of it should have declined. Moreover, official regulation or interference with retail trade was out of fashion.

Far more sinister, however, than all the complaints about frowsy meat and dirty fruit which the customer could at least see and judge for himself, was the opportunity the situation offered to the small trader to make money by deliberate adulteration and fraud. It was in this century of plentiful food that the first mutterings against poisonous contamination were first heard; against beer that was 'pernitiated' with vitriol, and wine with copperas, and that boiled sweets sometimes contained a species of rat's bane to give them 'a fine but excessively dangerous sparkle'. Cupidity, ignorance and irresponsibility combined to tempt shopkeepers and stallholders not only to mingle harmless dust with the tea but brickdust with the cocoa; not only sand with the sugar but lime with the flour; not only to cheat on their own account but also to buy cheap food without question from rogues with more specialized cunning like the manufacturers of imitation vinegar from diluted sulphuric acid coloured with oak chips or the makers of bright green pickles who poisoned them with verdigris.

41 Smollett, *op. cit.*, p. 172.

But the only case of adulteration that really aroused wide-spread public alarm was the state of London's bread, for a great deal of it was eaten by all classes and nearly all of it was bought. Potatoes, although now a common vegetable, were not yet a substitute for bread as a bulky filler except in the north. Consequently, when a pamphlet was published by a doctor in 1757, entitled *Poison Detected or Frightful Truths and Alarming to the British Metropolis*,[42] which catalogued a nauseating list of the ingredients mixed into bread and an even more frightful list of the illnesses and deaths attributed to them, it succeeded in its author's intention of raising a widespread scare. Other doctors rushed into print with even more hair-raising accusations against the millers and bakers, while the spokesmen for the trade repudiated all the charges out of hand.[43] In the long controversy that followed, the only thing that emerges conclusively is that there was certainly a widespread and reckless use of alum in flour to make bread white, and this alone was bad enough to justify a good deal of the public alarm.

But no action was taken by the authorities. The public liked its bread white and would not be reconciled to any other sort, although truly white flour was only to be had in very small quantities at a high price. On several occasions in the eighteenth century, in years of bad harvest, the bakers had been specifically ordered to bake 'standard bread' that is brown bread to save flour, and to sell it a penny cheaper, and every time this economical bread had proved most unpopular. So the authorities took no notice of the 'poisoned bread' uproar. As for the other allegations, for example that the alum used was often dissolved in human urine; that often one part in six of a loaf was either lime or chalk or whiting and ground bones from the graveyard; that purgatives were sometimes added to offset the constipating effect of the alum; that 'the destruction of Infants from this cause is Terrible, for their food is principally Bread [i.e. weaned on pap], and according to the chance mixing of the Ingredients we see them carried off by obstinate Costiveness or Unconquerable Diarrhoaeas',[44] these and many similar charges were never either proved or disproved. But the fact that some of them

[42] Anon., *Poison Detected* (1757).
[43] M. D. Manning, *The Nature of Bread* (1758).
[44] *ibid.*

involved crude frauds easily detected makes it no less probable that the more stupid small bakers indulged in such bread-doctoring without regard for the consequences.

'The practice of using hurtful ingredients with flour,' wrote Dr Manning in *The Nature of Bread*,[45] 'though very common is not universal, and as there is some trouble and difficulty in making the bread at home, the family should not be put to it except where there is cause.' He went on to advocate that every household should analyse the bread it bought by removing the crust and heating the soft part in water for twenty-four hours. Various simple means were then described for testing the sediment and the scum for whiting, chalk, alum, bone-ash and jalap, and if this home chemistry revealed the worst, then the remedy was a change of baker. Not for another hundred years, until 1860, did the first Food and Drugs Act begin the slow process of relieving the consumer of the hazard of impure food.

The regular custom of a substantial household was a valuable favour to any food-seller in the days when families tended to be much larger than today with numbers of children and servants. One way of competing for regular custom was to bribe the servants who did the buying, and another, very common towards the end of the century, was to make a contract for a year's supply at regular prices, particularly in the case of meat. One contractor catered for the whole household of the Marquis of Anspach for 10s. per head per day in the 1790s, and since he reclaimed all the broken meats, the servants had 'nought to give away but bread and cheese and kisses', clearly a hardship for servants in a decent house.[46] This practice of making fixed-price yearly contracts was evidently quite popular even among very modest middle-class householders and was intended to put the risk of fluctuating prices on to the shopkeeper in return for regular custom. Inevitably, it led to accusations of cheating, and several late-eighteenth-century writers denounced the system of yearly contracts with butchers as an open invitation to them to charge for joints that were never delivered. One writer even suggested that butchers usually kept one specially heavy leg of beef to weigh before each customer at their stalls, but delivered smaller

---

[45] *ibid.*
[46] John Ashton, *Old Times* (1885), quoting *The Times* of June 1795.

ones to their houses. [47] How many customers kept scales capable
of checking the weight of 'a leg of beef'?

The servant who connived with cheating tradesmen was an
even commoner cause of complaint. Consider, in this connection,
an illuminating notice in *The Times* for 1795; almost identical
statements were made at the same time by the bakers, the
brewers, the publicans and the butchers of this parish:

CHRISTMAS BOXES

The butchers resident within the Parish of Hackney beg leave
respectfully to inform their customers and the Public, that, on
account of the excessive high price of Provisions, they find it
impossible to continue the practice of giving Christmas Boxes
to the servants of their Customers, without sustaining on the one
hand a deduction of their profits which the trade will not allow, or,
on the other hand, increasing their charges. They have therefore
unanimously resolved to discontinue the practice in time to come,
and hope that their conduct on this occasion will not be deemed
improper or disrespectful. [48]

Which raises once again the question with which this chapter
began; how would the modern householder cope with the
shopping conditions of the eighteenth century? Suppose him
to be a family man, with an income, by modern standards,
upwards of three thousand pounds a year; could he pick his way
through the confusions mentioned in this chapter to make some
such provision as the following?

An Estimate of the Necessary Charge of a Family in the Middling
Station of Life, consisting of a Man, his Wife, four Children and
one Maidservant. (The Station in Life of a Tradesman who sets
up Business on £1,000, a Very Substantial Start in Life.) [49]

	per head per day d.	Daily Expense s.　d.	Weekly Expense s.　d.	Yearly Expense £　s.　d.
Bread for 7 persons per head per day	$\frac{3}{4}$	5$\frac{1}{4}$	3　0$\frac{3}{4}$	
Butter	$\frac{3}{4}$	5$\frac{1}{4}$	3　0$\frac{3}{4}$	
Cheese	$\frac{1}{4}$	1$\frac{3}{4}$	1　0$\frac{1}{4}$	
Fish & Flesh Meat	2$\frac{1}{2}$	1　5$\frac{1}{2}$	10　2$\frac{1}{2}$	

Carried forward

[47] *ibid.*
[48] *ibid.*, 9 December 1795.

	per head per day d.	Daily Expense s. d.	Weekly Expense s. d.	Yearly Expense £ s. d.
Roots & herbs, salt, vinegar, mustard, pickles, spices and grocery (ex. tea & sugar)	½	3½	2 0½	
Tea & Sugar	1	7	4 1	
Soap for the Family Occasions & Washing all manner of things both abroad & at home	1½	10½	6 1½	
Threads, needles, pins, tapes, worsteds, bindings, & all sorts of haberdashery	½	3½	2 0½	
Milk, one day with another	¾		5¼	
Candles, about 2 lbs per week the year round			1 3	
Sand, Fuller's Earth, whiting, Smallcoal & brickdust			2	
'Ten shilling small beer' a firkin & quarter per week [= 11¼ gall.]			3 1½	
Ale for family & friends			2 6	
Coals, between 5 & 6 chaldron per annum, may be estimated at			2 6	
Repairs of Household goods, as Table-linen, bedding, sheets & every utensil for household occasion			1 6	

	Yearly Expense £ s. d.
	£112 10 0
Cloaths of all kinds for the master of the family	16 0 0
Cloaths for Wife, who can't wear much, nor very fine laces with	16 0 0
Extraordinary expense attending every lying-in £10, supposed to be about every, two years	5 0 0
Cloaths for four children, at £7 per annum for each child	28 0 0
Schooling for four children, including every charge thereunto relating, supposed to be equal at least to 10s. per quarter for each child	8 0 0
The Maid's wages may be	4 10 0
Pocket expenses for the master of the Family supposed to be about 4s. per week	10 8 0
For the Mistress of the family & four children to buy fruit, toys, etc. at about 2s. per week	5 4 0
Entertainment in return for such favours from friends & relations	4 0 0
Physic for the whole family, one year with another, & the extra-ordinary expense arising by illness, may exceed	6 0 0

Carried forward

	Yearly Expense		
	£	s.	d.
A Country Lodging sometimes, for the Health & Recreation of the Family; or instead thereof the extraordinary charge of nursing a child abroad, which in such a family is often needful	8	0	0
Shaving, 7s. 6d. per quarter; Cleaning shoes, 2s. 6d. per quarter	2	0	0
Rent & Taxes may be somewhat more or less than	50	0	0
There must be laid up, one year with another, for twenty years in order (with interest) to leave each child & a Widow if there shall be one, £500 a piece	75	0	0
Total	350	0	0

49 Anon., *Apology for Pawnbroking* (1744).

IX

The London Poor

> Something in the natural temper and genius of the nation, generally speaking, they cannot save their money . . . I once paid six or seven men together on a Saturday night, the least 10s. and some 30s. for work, and have seen them go with it directly to the ale-house, lie there til Monday and spend every penny and run into debt to boot, and not give a farthing of it to their families though all of them had wives and children . . .
>
> D. Defoe, *Giving Alms No Charity*, 1704

T H E sort of shops we have been considering in the eighteenth century catered for the 'middling sort' and the well-to-do. But they were not much patronized by the working classes, the general run of semi-skilled manual workers and the unskilled labourers and their families who made up half the population of London, any more than their counterparts in provincial towns served the cottagers and poor working farmers.

In London, most wages at that time seem to us very low compared with the cost of living. In the 1770s, for example, journeymen who had served full apprenticeships to skilled trades earned, with few exceptions, from 15s. to a guinea a week, say £7 10s. to £10 10s. at today's prices; the general run of unskilled workmen received about 10s. for a full week's work, say about £5 today. On these wages they were sometimes accused of indulging in 'a superfluity of luxuries', such as tea, sugar, tobacco, foreign fruit (i.e. oranges), strong beer and printed linens.[1]

---

[1] Anon., *Considerations on Taxes, as they are Supposed to Affect the Price of Labour* (1765).

212

9. Open shops in Bishopsgate, 1736. Before the Fire the butcher's had been a wooden shed on the church wall rented to help the Vicar. Notice the cheesemonger on the right and on the left a grocer and bookshop with the title pages of unbound books on the posts.

10. 'We must have an Elegant, Extensive and Convenient show-room.' Josiah Wedgwood, late eighteenth century.

Saddlemaking, for example, was a fairly 'genteel' trade, but it only earned 15s. a week in 1775 when the saddlers' estimate of the expenses of a man, wife and three children were as follows:

	s.	d.
12 lbs coarse beef @ 3½d	3	6
2½ oz. tea @ 4½d		11¼
1 lb lump sugar @ 7d		7
2 lb coarse sugar @ 5d		10
Salt, pepper		2¼
3 lb salt butter @ 8d	2	0
2 bushels and a half coals @ 14d	3	1
Soap, blue, starch [& presumably candles]	1	0
Lodging	2	6
Bread	4	11
Cheese	1	0
	£1 0	6½[2]

No 'foreign fruit' or printed linens here, and, even more surprising, no beer either. Bread and meat were the chief foods and it is noticeable that bread alone cost twice as much as the rent. This budget was a third as big again as the man's actual wages and, although his wife would be expected to earn a little too, it presumably represented what they thought they deserved rather than what they in fact got. Yet these were among the better-off workmen; for most of the labour force, wages were erratic, meagre and largely mis-spent, and for all their numbers, the poorer half of the population created no mass-demand of the kind to give rise to important developments in retailing except in the case of one commodity—drink.

Beer, as sold in London, was the first consumer commodity to be mass-produced under factory conditions and sold to the public for cash at fixed prices by 'pure' retailers. About one house in fifteen in London in the middle of the century was a public house of some sort, and they tended to be thickest on the ground in the poorer quarters.[3] (By the 'nineties, when licensing had been tightened up, this had dropped to about one in twenty-five.)

[2] Middlesex Sessions Book, April 1777, quoted in Dorothy George, *London Life in the Eighteenth Century* (1925), p. 167.

[3] W. Maitland, *History and Survey of London* (1756), pp. 719, 735.

P

Even allowing for the incredible taste of the times for strong liquor, and the wretched conditions of life that often drove even the soberly inclined to seek the conviviality and warmth of ale-houses, this number of publicans could not have made the barest living if a very large proportion of their neighbours' earnings had not passed, by one means or another, through their hands. An ale-house is not normally thought of nowadays as a shop, but in the working-class parishes of eighteenth-century London the ale-houses were open all round the clock, and were the universal providers for a lot of people.

Many let 'tuppenny lodgings' by the night to the large numbers without settled homes; some kept brothels and thieves' kitchens; some publicans were constables; and others kept small prisons in their public houses. Probably most of London's vast underworld of vice and crime paid some substantial rake-off to the ale-house-keepers. Hawkers peddled old clothes and all sorts of other goods, often of doubtful provenance, among the customers. And there were other, lawful, but socially more harmful ways of augmenting the licensees' profits. Trade unions were illegal, but trade clubs, friendly societies, box clubs and benefit societies of all kinds flourished in ale-houses, spending a good part of the funds on 'entertainment'. Then there were close connections between particular groups of ale-houses and most of the skilled trades, for whom they acted as employment agencies or 'houses of call'. Here the journeyman in effect enrolled with the landlord and sat about waiting to be sent by him to a day's or half-day's work, as different masters sent to the publicans for hands. Employment in most skilled trades was erratic and so in London, the mecca of all journeymen, large numbers of these men spent half their working lives in the house of call, eating and drinking themselves into debt to the landlord, to whom they were then bound in a vicious circle of obligation.[4]

Again, many tradesmen and labourers working by the week at outdoor jobs were paid, for the employer's convenience, at public houses. 'The labourer (otherwise a sober man) waits at an ale-house from 6, 7, 8, 9 to perhaps 10 or 11 o'clock before the master or foreman comes to the pay-table; in course they drink deep, the poor wife and children wait impatiently at

4 George, *op. cit.*, p. 293 *f*.

home for the few shillings the husband is to produce . . .'[5] The vintners and coffee-house men had earlier seen the profit in encouraging all sorts of business to be done on their premises. The ale-house-keepers saw this too, and although their clientele was much poorer, it was the more ignorant and open to exploitation.

The ale-houses also had a large share in selling the great quantities of inferior brandy and later gin, whose consumption by the London poor in the first half of the century—and especially by poor women—wrought such social havoc, as well as helping to curtail more normal expenditure. But during the height of the gin-drinking epidemic 'the great destroyer' was sold by all and sundry. Crude malt spirit was cheap and easy to obtain in quantity and re-distil, and it sold rapidly in penny tots at a high profit. A still was a side-line with most shopkeepers in poor quarters, and the sole stock-in-trade of many. Gin licences were cheap, and until 1751 even these were not enforced on the thousands of dram-sellers who were said to 'sell even in the streets and high-ways, some on bulks set up for that purpose and others in wheel-barrows, and many more who sell privately in garrets, cellars, backrooms and other places . . . All chandlers, many tobacconists, and such who sell fruit or herbs in stalls and wheelbarrows sell geneva, and many inferior tradesmen begin now to keep it in their shops for their customers'.[6] Gin tots, 'on the slate', were sold to men and women at their work by many employers, fore-men and garret masters who thus claimed back part of the wages before they were earned. Only after the Act of 1751 which im-posed a heavy duty and effectively restricted spirit sales to ale-houses, did the government forcibly close up this great drain on the resources of the poor, so that instead of tippling about eight million gallons of gin every year they came down, at the end of the century, to about one million.

Improvidence, debauchery, wastefulness and chronic indebted-ness were generally agreed to be the characteristics of London's working classes in the eighteenth century. Generally agreed, that is, by their betters, who were blind to the many hazards, injustices and deprivations in the lives of the poor which

---

[5] ibid., p. 297, quoting *Public Advertiser*, 9 September 1772.

[6] Report of the Committee of Enquiry into Gin Selling in London, 1735, quoted in J. P. Malcolm, *Anecdotes of the Manners and Customs of London* (1808), p. 80.

combined to beat down even the most admirable among them into a hopeless resignation to the prevailing squalor. It is hard for a sober age to form any conception of the pauperizing effect on the individuals concerned of an era of such excessive drinking, but it is not hard to see how it reduced expenditure on other goods to the barest necessities—bread, cheese, bacon, herrings, second-hand clothes and a slum dwelling were the main purchases of a large part of the inhabitants of the richest city in the country.

The chief suppliers of the poor man's food in cities were the chandlers. These are no longer to be confused with specialist chandlers, such as corn chandlers who did a respectable business in grain, meal, flour and oats for horses, or tallow chandlers of whom there were said to be five hundred in London selling only candles. But the poor man's chandler was an all-sorts shop. To quote Dorothy George's *London Life in the Eighteenth Century*:

> Market women and street sellers went to the chandler's for breakfast when an alehouse was too expensive; provisions were fetched from the chandler's in ha'porth's and farthingsworths, coal by the half pack (say twelve lbs. for 2d) came from the same sources; the link boy went there for his nightly link, the servant maid to fetch soap or sand or candles—and was treated to a dram.

The chandlers were in some respects rather like village shops. Both tended to be gossiping centres where customers lingered and where no business was too petty that would turn a farthing of profit for the proprietor. Both needed a nice judgement, based on personal acquaintance, of how far each of a host of poverty-stricken customers could be allowed to run on the score. 'But if credit is denied,' runs a description of chandlers written in 1764, 'they come a second time to leave a Shift, Cap, Apron or Pocket as a pledge til the Money is paid.'[7] Such a shop was often kept by the wife of a workman; it was the ambition of many a steady couple to save enough to get a roof over their heads by renting a house, letting off most of the rooms and setting up the wife in a shop on the ground floor. The least reputable shops were in cellars: damp, dark holes whose only light and ventilation and means of access was by a flight of unguarded steps from the

[7] Anon., *Low Life* (1764), p. 36.

pavement. Leaving open the flap over this entrance at night to try to admit some air, and admitting instead some unfortunate pedestrian, and possibly breaking his leg in the process, was a constant source of trouble. Cellars (known as kitchens though usually they had no access to the house above and no connection with cooking) were common for cobblers, who 'did up' second-hand shoes and hung them in bunches at the door; for old-clothes-dealers; for 'green shops' that sold roots and firewood and coals; for 'old-iron-dealers' or scrap metal merchants who seem to have abounded in dingy cellars, whose ostensible business defies conjecture although it was alleged to be usually a cover for something illegal; and last but not least for milk retailers.

The milk-cellar was the dwelling and storeroom of a woman who owned a milk-walk or round of customers, although it is probable that little milk was sold in her own neighbourhood. She carried the milk home from one of about thirty dairy farms on the outskirts of the town, left it to stand for several hours in order to sell the cream separately, watered it (sometimes, it was alleged, from the horse trough) and carried it round the houses of her 'walk', either chalking the account on the doorpost or using tallies. Tallies were one of the oldest forms of accounting, now rapidly going out of use. They were simply sticks split lengthways into matching halves; for every pint delivered the two halves of the tally were laid together and a notch cut across both, so that buyer and seller each had a record of the score, and the tallies were broken when the account was paid. They were cumbersome in addition to the heavy churns, but cheap and fool-proof—although a clever milkwoman could sometimes 'cut dead men', or two notches for one, without detection.

In the diet of the working classes, the most important items were bread and cheese and the despised but often necessary herring. Next came meat, and the great day for meat was Sunday. To have no meat for Sunday dinner was to be poor indeed; to have it several days a week meant relative luxury. Most of it was bacon or tripes. The tripe shop sold offal of all kinds, often pickled or ready boiled, and coarse offcuts of meat from the market stalls. It was the bakers' Sunday work, a relatively light task, to bake the dinners of the poor who had few cooking facilities in their crowded lodgings. (Indeed, in some Lincolnshire villages this practice survived within living memory.) We read of 'old gossips in alleys and yards meeting with their dabs of stinking meat fixed upon three bits of stick over dirty pease puddings and carrying them to the bakehouse'.[8]

Another alternative was the cook-shop. Here is the sort of feast that a cheap cook-shop could offer to two young thieves spending their ill-gotten gains:

> So we went to a boiling cooks in Rosemary Lane where we treated ourselves nobly, for we had three pennyworth of boiled beef, two pennyworth of pudding [probably pease or lentil pudding] a penny brick as they called it, or loaf, and a whole pint of strong beer, which was sevenpence in all. N.B. We had each of us a charming mess of beef broth into the bargain.[9]

The cook-shops varied in status; no doubt the 'boiling cook's', lacking an oven, was the lowest of all. In the previous century the better-class cook-shops, generally known as 'ordinaries', had still served all types of customer. Mr and Mrs Pepys called one day at a well-known cook-shop to order a good meal to be sent into the tavern nearby, where they ate it with their wine, and no gentleman then was ashamed to be seen in a good 'ordinary'. But in the eighteenth century we hear little of the respectable ordinaries and the cook-shops were caterers for the poorer classes. Probably they all sold meals on the premises; often their customers stood at the counter or in the street to munch at a hot pie or drink a bowl of broth. But apparently the bulk of their business was to send hot food to the houses round about, and the meal fetched from the cook-shop was the poor man's banquet. Judging by the many references in the book-trade and among authors to the cooks' insatiable demand for old paper, it would seem that they did not always trust their food out on plates, and the customer could assist his digestion by reading parts of someone's unsold sermon or bad poem, much as the modern purchaser of fried fish receives a free copy of last week's newspaper. In many ways in fact, the eighteenth-century cook-shop was the forerunner of the modern fish-and-chip shop, with more variety on the menu and more flexibility in the service.

Clothes were not important items to the working class,

8 *ibid.*, p. 49.
9 D. Defoe, *Colonel Jack* (1722) in *Works* (ed. J. S. Keltie, 1870), p. 214.

except to the few who served in good shops or worked as clerks. As a rule servants' clothes were still part of their wages. People expected to obtain all their clothes and shoes second-hand as a matter of course. The main garments were always of wool or linen and lasted a long time, their lives seldom shortened by washing. A pair of leather stays, a double quilted horse-hair petticoat, a stuff gown and a linen shift would keep the wearer and her fleas warm for several years before they rotted away; 'a Whitechapel beau is one who dresses with a needle and thread and undresses with a knife'.[10] It is curious that the habit of relying on second-hand instead of home-made clothes appears to have developed early even among the country folk of the south, while in the north, right up to the beginning of the nineteenth century, the typical farm-labourer or cottager was clothed from wool and linen spun and often woven at home. No doubt there were fewer good cast-off garments to be had, as there were fewer wealthy people in the pre-industrial northern counties.[11]

In London, Rosemary Lane, known as Rag Fair, near the Tower, and Monmouth Street in Seven Dials, were famous for old-clothes-shops and pawnshops and, as an inevitable consequence, for receivers of stolen goods. (Holywell Street, south of the Strand, held more genteel shops of the same sort.) Here is an authentic account of a poor shoemaker—James Lackington in his penurious youth—shopping in Rag Fair:

> Until this winter I had never found out that I wanted a greatcoat. But now I made that important discovery . . . So that the next half guinea I had to spare away I went to Rosemary Lane and (to my great surprise) was hauled into a shop by a fellow who was walking up and down before the door of a slopseller where I was soon fitted with a greatcoat of the same sort as that of my landlord. I asked the price, but how great was my astonishment when the honest shopman told me that he was so taken with my clean, honest, industrious looks that he would let me have it cheaper than he would his own brother, so, in one word, he would oblige me with it for five-and-twenty shillings, which was the very money that it cost him. On hearing this, I crossed the shop in a trice in order to set off home again, but the door had a fastening

---

[10] Chas. Hindley, *A True History of Tom and Jerry* (1820), p. 216.
[11] Sir F. M. Eden, *The State of the Poor* (1797), p. 108.

to it beyond my comprehension, nor would the good man let me out before I had made him an offer . . . I told him that my landlord had informed me that he had purchased such another coat for ten shillings and sixpence. On which he began to give himself airs, and assured me that, however some people came by their goods, for his part he always paid for his . . . I then told him that I had but ten shillings and sixpence and, of course, could not offer him any more than I had got. I now expected more abuse from him, but instead of that the patient good man told me that as perhaps he might get something by me another time, I should have the coat for my half guinea although it was worth double the money.[12]

This salesman's 'however some people came by their goods' was not an idle remark. London's poorer quarters abounded in second-hand shops, many specializing in clothes or 'translated' shoes, but others in household goods and every conceivable kind of non-perishable article. Much of this second-hand stock was honestly bought from hawkers and old-clothes-men. Much was forfeited at the hundreds of pawnbrokers' shops that drove a thriving business. Much—perhaps most—of it was received from thieves, from pilfering servants and workmen as well as from regular burglars and highway robbers, for although the penalties for theft were savage, the laws against the receiving of stolen property were still virtually ineffective. It was a common saying that 'If there were no receivers there would be no thieves'. But in 1796 a magistrate claimed that there were upwards of three thousand known receivers of stolen goods in London alone, most of them keeping open shop.[13] 'Thieves,' it was said, 'sell good pennyworths.' Here, therefore, in this widespread circulation, both legal and illegal, of second-hand articles of all kinds, is another reason why the numerous incomes of the working classes did so little to stimulate normal retail trade.

More ambitious working people might buy clothes from a 'sales shop'. There existed a much despised class of master-tailors and master-shoemakers who ran a sideline in making up goods to standard patterns, and supplying them to 'salesman-tailors' or 'salesman-shoemakers' whose whole business was in retailing these new ready-made goods. In footwear, the ready-

12 James Lackington, *Memoirs of the First Forty-five Years* (1830), p. 124.
13 P. Colquhoun, *A Treatise on the Police of the Metropolis* (1796), p. 11.

made trade was associated with the export of shoes to the American colonies, where sons of Crispin were still scarce, and the same causes might have accounted for the appearance of ready-made working clothes long before machinery made mass production of these things cheaper than the customer's special order.

Haberdashery and household goods would sometimes be bought from a tallyman who then, as now, supplied goods on credit and called every week for the instalments, usually a penny a week for every thirty pence expended. Some tallymen may have been honest, but the whole race were widely denounced by contemporaries as fraudulent and unscrupulous tricksters, whose real profits were made, not by selling their shoddy goods, but by buying themselves one of the many bailiff's offices at the Whitechapel or Marshalsea Courts so as to be able to arrest their clients for debt; 'and for every arrest, if the debt is not eighteenpence, exacts ten shillings besides other fees'.[14] Imprisonment for debt was common for even the most trifling sums at the beginning of the eighteenth century (and still for £2 and upwards after a reform in 1725).

To lie in a debtors' gaol was at once a great personal danger and a galloping expense; so dreaded was it that some men committed murder to avoid being dragged there. The threat of it, therefore, was a great weapon in the hands of any creditor. It was no uncommon thing for a family to be in debt to an unscrupulous chandler who allowed increasingly short weight at increasingly extortionate prices, so that while they dare not desert his shop, they worked only to enrich him and drive themselves ever more hopelessly into his power.[15] Tradesmen's debts in the case of the rich meant a common convenience which the customer paid for in the high price of his goods. ('The poulterer is purveyor to the rich. If they pay their bills, the nobleman is bit. If they do not, as frequently happens, the poulterer is bit.')[16] Tradesmen's debts were, for the poor, a dreaded aspect of unemployment and sickness, fraught with grave danger and leading to endless weary entanglements.

Another sort of retailer important to the working class was the

[14] T. Baston, *Thoughts on Trade and a Public Spirit* (1716), p. 127.
[15] *Low Life, op. cit.*, pp. 13–14.
[16] R. Campbell, *The London Tradesman* (1747), p. 279.

street-hawker. Street-selling was one of the common occupations of wives of the poorest. A few shillings' worth of fruit, fish or meat purchased at the tail end of the market and cried round the houses could often furnish the money for an evening meal or even for a night's lodging for a needy family. In law, hawkers of fresh fruit and victuals were exempt from the need to take out a pedlar's licence, as were those selling their own home-made goods. There were grades in hawking like everything else. There were respectable women with a little capital who made a steady income, who had a regular walk and regular customers, perhaps trading out of the markets, or hawking their own home-made sausages, hot apple-pies or gingerbread. And at the other end of the scale there was the large army of the fishwives, the match-sellers, the casual class of near-beggars who borrowed five shillings every morning at the ale-house to buy their stock and paid it back with sixpence interest every night, and never looked beyond this. Numbered in their hundreds, if not in thousands, the hawkers sold not only food but every saleable thing that could be carried about. Women predominated, but men had their special trades—the old-clothes-seller, the 'small coale man', the orange-seller who ran halfpenny gambling schools for children at street corners (just as the costard-mongers had done two hundred years earlier). Men often traded their wares in better class neighbourhoods. 'Any Kitchen Stuffe have you Maids?' or 'Maids any Cunny Skins?' was an offer of some tawdry knick-knack in exchange for a half-carved joint of meat from the master's table to sell to a cook-shop, or for rabbit skins to sell to the felt-hat makers. 'Brooms for Old Shoes' was another favourite. And mingled with the hawkers were those offering services. 'Old Chairs to Mend' and 'Sweep, Chimney Sweep' and 'Cully Molly Puffe', which was the cry of a woman offering to do a day's baking. 'Won't you buy my sweet smelling lavender?' sounds plaintively romantic when sung in a drawing-room and looks pretty enough when depicted in a modern cosmetic advertisement. But there can have been little romance or prettiness about the original street-criers of London. Street-selling was a low-grade job entailing desperately hard work for small gains, and every one of these wandering characters depended on a piercing cry, a cry that would rise above the rattle of iron wheels on cobblestones, a cry that would drown the other criers, a cry that would penetrate to every garret and cellar and back room and leave no peace anywhere.

Francis Place, a meticulous observer and recorder of London working-class conditions, said repeatedly that they improved very much in the closing years of the eighteenth century, mainly because less was spent on drink and gambling and more on simple everyday needs. He found, however, so late as in 1830, some isolated parishes still untouched by reformation, still sunk in the squalor that had been so familiar and so general in the days of his youth, with the shops as dirty, ill-stocked and unsavoury as ever.

> Then comes a shop where they sell cats' meat, coal, cow-heels, wood and tripe. And ever and anon a load of coals comes in and black clouds of dust arise as they are emptied into the shop, settling on the cow-heels and the tripe, and the pillars of pudding. Yet these they eat all up, and as one of them once remarked 'the dust does instead of pepper'. From morning till night the pot-boys are ever carrying out beer, from morn till dewy eve it is 'beer', still 'beer'.[17]

It is amusing to find this strictly practical reformer echoing Paradise Lost, but these and other notes made in Place's old age are a sad admission that the chandler's shop still survived in the London slums, reflecting its grim surroundings, and probably continued to do so well into Victoria's reign.

[17] Lock's Fields, c. 1830, as described in Brit. Museum Add. MSS. 27827 (Place MSS.).

X

◇◆◇◆◇◆◇◆◇◆◇◆◇◆◇◆◇◆◇◆◇◆◇◆◇◆◇◆◇◆◇◆

A Household in Buckinghamshire

◇◆◇◆◇◆◇◆◇◆◇◆◇◆◇◆◇◆◇◆◇◆◇◆◇◆◇◆◇◆◇◆

Many families who live in the neighbourhood of small towns purchase half-yearly from London many articles they want, as the cheapest and most economical means of supplying themselves.

Policy of the Tax upon Retailing Considered, Anon., 1786

SOME country towns were fortunate enough to be served by shopkeepers who knew their business and stocked a wide assortment of good-quality wares. Robert Owen, after working for both good and bad provincial shopkeepers, remarked that well-chosen goods would sell themselves—he left little credit for either display or salesmanship. But such towns were probably in a minority, and all the country gentry set great store by shopping bought in London, sometimes because it was cheaper, sometimes because it was of better quality, sometimes because it could be had nowhere else. Visitors to the capital were loaded with commissions to buy for their friends, and despatch home by the carrier's cart, everything from hats to fruit trees, from furniture to dog collars, but above all else, books.

One country household whose records afford some insight into the methods of shopping in the mid-eighteenth century is that of the Purefoys of Shalstone Manor, near Brackly in north Buckinghamshire. A selection of their correspondence, from the letter-books in which copies were kept, was published in 1931 by George Eland, entitled *The Purefoy Letters*. The elderly Mrs Purefoy and her son Henry lived in quiet comfort, seldom away from home; the mother managed the estate with businesslike firmness, the son was a local justice, for some years sheriff of the county, and with interests more scholarly than sporting. They did not mix in fashionable society, but were indefatigable in modernizing their house, improving their grounds, choosing furniture and pictures and clothes with as great concern for quality and style as if they had been living in the public eye. They spent money freely, but watched the pence every bit as carefully as the pounds. They evidently enjoyed a very close understanding about their joint undertakings, but their reciprocal accounting was meticulous to a degree—they even paid by the pint when they drank each other's wine.

The Purefoys cannot be called typical, because that is a word that needs to be used with reserve about such a markedly individualistic age. But at least the parts of their correspondence that dealt with shopping give a very clear picture of how the country gentry used the letter-post and the carrier's cart for this purpose. They also illustrate the common practice of having a London correspondent or agent to do trifles of business (for most country gentry owned estates of some sort which gave rise to innumerable items of small legal business) and relying on him for a miscellany of small purchases. The Purefoys, in fact, had two agents. But above all their letters demonstrate the slow laborious nature of the transactions, the patient 'enquiring out' and 'procuring' of anything not in everyday demand, the great reliance upon friends and connections and personal recommendations.

The basic food for themselves and about six servants they produced at home. They kept several milking cows, some sheep, asses, goats, pigs and poultry, and had a dovecote and three well-stocked fishponds. Henry coursed for hares and had shooting rights in a deer forest. They brewed their own ale and almost certainly baked their own bread. Best clothes were made in London; everyday clothes and the servants' liveries by the tailors in nearby towns. This still left a lot to buy. They lived in the heart of the country, four miles each way from the small towns of Buckingham and Brackley, and London was two days' easy travelling away.

To begin with one of the oldest shopping problems, wine. Here is a typical mixed bag of requests to Henry's wine merchant, and London agent, a personal friend with whom he often exchanged presents of flesh from the country against fish from the city.

Jan 12th 1736

Sir:

I desire your acceptance of a Hare which I this day send you by Mr. Eagles the Buckingham carrier, 'tis sealed at ye knot of the direction as usual with my coat of arms. [i.e. so that the label could not be untied and an inferior hare substituted.] Eagles innes at ye George inne in Smithfield and comes into London on Friday morning. Shall be glad to hear it come safe to hand, and I shall be to hear how you and Mr. Meredith have ended matters. [The vintner was acting for them in a rent dispute.] I desire you will send my mother 8 gallons of Canary in a runlet, she desires of all things it may not be on the fret, for the last you sent was like bottled Cyder and flew all about ye Cellar and broke ye Bottles. Besides ye Physicians say wine on ye fret is very prejudicial to her health. Send it by ye next return of Webster and a letter per post that we may send for it from him.

My mother thinks she may be too much in your debt so hopes to get £10 returned to you by Webster who innes at Warwick house.

Pray in your walks as you go about enquire if an iron chest will secure papers (that may be laid in it) from fire in case a house be fired, if it will, be so good as to enquire the price of one about two foot long and proportionably wide and deep, a second-hand one which is good and strong will be as well for me as a new one. I have had a severe fit of gout in my foot but am now (thank God) able to draw my boot on. My mother and self join in our service to you, and I am, with much esteem, Sir:

Your very humble servant
Henry Purefoy

for Mr. Moulson
   on St. Mary's Hill near Billingsgate
   London

The next consignment of Canary sack was better ('does not fly at all') but fermenting was not the only complaint. Sometimes Mountain wine was too sweet, port was too flat, Hogsheads were leaky, or chocolate (which the vintner made himself from the nuts) was 'so bitter and high dried she can't drink it'. Nevertheless, in spite of frank criticism the connection flourished. Plain speaking is a feature of all their correspondence. Here they are sharing a runlet of Canary with the vicar:

February the 24th 1739

Sir:

The sack came down last Wensday and will be drawn of on Monday morning next at 11 a clock at farthest. I hope one of your family will be there to see it drawn of. With our best services and respects to you all am in hast

Your most Hle. servt.

Henry Purefoy

for the Revd. Mr. Price
    at Whitfield (by hand)

March the 4th 1739

This is to let Mr. Price know that I shall send Mr. Moulson his money for the sack next week. Therefore desire that you will send the money for yours between this and next Saturday.

Your daughter, Mrs. Betty, might have saved yourself and me this trouble but she never mentioned neither the price of the wine, nor to pay for it.

The price is as usual eight shillings a gallon, the vessell of sack was 13 gallons, I should have been glad if Mrs. Betty Price came soon enough to see it drawn of. I had no more than 6 gallons and 1 quart. She had 6 gallons and 1 quart all but a glasse or two in bottles, and 1 quart bottle of yours besides these was broke as soon as it was filled it being crackt first; so there wanted a quart of 13 gallons wch. I suppose I must bear the losse of. Mrs. Betty Price wrangled a little about it but this is the very Truth of the matter. So the money you are to pay comes to £2.10s. and I shall have no more at that price Mr. Moulson sent me word. We would have waited on you ourselves but are very busie on sowing Beans and with our service and respect to you and all am

Your humble servt.

Elizabeth Purefoy

To Mrs. Price senior
    at Whitfield

All their bills were paid with extreme alacrity, which may have been simply good policy when buying at a distance (they were not, after all, titled persons), but at least in part this was a personal eccentricity and characteristic of all their business dealings. When her grocer, 'Mr Wilson at the 3 Sugar Loaves at the West End of St Paulls' sent Mrs Purefoy a receipt not marked 'in full' because he thought she still owed an eight-months'-old debt (which, by the way, he was making no attempt to collect) she promptly turned up the receipt and wrote a scathing and lengthy reply, which ended:

> I admire you do not keep your Books more regular, I suppose if I had lost the receipt and Mr. Robotham had chanced to have dyed—I must have paid the money over again—I always pay you ready money because Mr. Cossins told mee I should be better used for so doing. I am afraid you use mee harder this time, believing me to be in your books, for the pound of Bohea tea is almost all green tea, and the sugar, at 10½d a pound is dearer than anybody else gives. I desire you answer hereto and am
> Your friend to serve you
> Elizabeth Purefoy

She always dealt with Wilson for coffee-berries, teas and the rarer foreign spices and herbs. She also got common things in quantity; for instance, raisins are mentioned by the hundred-weight, powder (i.e. cheap) sugar by the half-hundredweight, and rice and Poland starch by the 'half a quarter of a hundred', i.e. the stone. These big orders every few months were supplemented by smaller orders (a mere half-dozen pounds at a time) from the local grocer at Brackley, who also dealt in cleaning materials and tobacco. Each order was couched in a formal letter sent by hand.

Another frequent purchase was fish, particularly oysters and herrings; both had to be sought in London, and it seemed difficult to find a reliable supplier. Also, by about May of each year as the weather got warmer, the two to three days' journey in the carrier's cart proved to be the undoing of some consignment, and the end of regular supplies for the summer.

> May the 29th 1737
> I was in hope by this time Mr. Fisher could have sent me some mackerell accordingly to my order, but since none are come. The weather is now so exceeding hot that what fish you sent last week stank and could not be eat so I desire you would

The following ARTICLES are Sold Wholesale and Retail at the lowest PRICES, by

LANCELOT SHARPE,

TEA-DEALER,

GROCER and CONFECTIONER,

(No 56.)

FENCHURCH-STREET, LONDON.

ALMONDS, Jordan
Do. Valentia
Do. Barbary
Do. Faro
Anise-Seeds
Blues, Stone
Do. Powder
Barley, French
Do. Pearl
Coffee, Turkey,
Do. Jamaica
Chocolate, plain
Do. Vanilla
Cocoa Shells
Currants
Cinnamon
Cloves
Curry Powder
Carraway Seeds
Coriander Do.

Dates
Figs, Turkey
Do. Faro
Ginger, Race
Do. ground
Hartshorn Shavings
Do. Burnt
Isinglass, whole
Do. beat
Mace
Millet Seed
Morilles
Mustard, Durham Flour
Nutmegs
Nuts, Pistachia
Pepper, Chian
Do. white
Do. long
Do. Jamaica
Do. ground

Plums, French
Prunes
Prunellas
Rice, whole
Do. ground
Raisins of all Sorts
SUGARS of all Sorts
Sago
Salloop
Starch, Poland
Do. common
Soap, white
Do. mottled
Do. brown
Senna
Salt-petre
TEAS of all Sorts
Truffles
Vermicelli

C O N F E C T I O N A R Y.

PRESERV'D FRUITS OF DIFFERENT SORTS.

Currant Jelly
Ratberry Jam
Quince Marmalade
Madeira Citron

Orange and Lemon Chips
Do.   Do. Peal
Lemon Juice
Bottled Fruit for Tarts

Gooseberries
Currants
Damsens
White Plums

11. Stock of an eighteenth-century grocer.

12. Near Billingsgate. Early nineteenth century.

not send any more fish until further orders, let me have a letter
what they come to and will order you payment, and Am

Your humble servant

Elizabeth Purefoy

for Mr. James Fisher
a fishmonger in
Newgate Market, London

Or another year in a letter to a friend in March:

> We also rec'd your kind present of a codling and oysters; the
> codling was very good but the oysters, half of them were as black
> as ink and the other half was poisoned with the stench for they
> were all of a froth and your fish-monger should give you your
> money again. Wee return you hearty thanks for them . . .

Mrs Purefoy tried many fishmongers, some recommended by
friends, but without satisfaction, and was eventually driven at the
beginning of the 1748 season to answering an advertisement
for Colchester oysters from a shop near the Mansion House. It
was becoming quite common for dealers in seasonal foods to
advertise the arrival of their first stocks in the press, usually in
wordy notices of great length. One such advertisement for
Colchester oysters contains the following paragraph:

> And that all persons in City or Country who send for them may
> no ways be deceived of having the right sort, the prices are all
> branded on the side of the Cask. Note, they are all branded at the
> Pits where they are pickt, so that if there be any cheat it must
> be the Oyster Men which hath so often been practised to my Loss
> and their shameful Gain . . .[1]

Professional copywriters had not yet appeared to advise the
fishmonger to stick to his slab. But the professional tailor was
accepted as the authority on fashion by those not near enough
fashionable society to observe for themselves:

> May the 5th 1736
> This desires Mr. Boyce to lett me have a letter of what Cloaths
> are most fashionable together with some patterns of superfine
> Cloath, and whether they button their Cloaths with silver or
> gold buttons or continue to wear laced Wastcoats of silk or cloath
> and whether dressed Coats or undressed Coats . . .

[1] John Ashton, *Social Life in the Reign of Queen Anne* (1882), p. 146.

The answer, whatever it was, was prompt, for a week later:

May the 11th 1736

I rec'd Mr. Boys's letter of ye 6th inst. and have sent you enclosed the pattern of cloath that I will have my coat and Breetches of, with Buttons and Trimmings of the same colour, the coat to be lined with a shagreen silk and to be half trimmed, and but one pair of Breetches which I desire may be made the same size as ye Breetches sent with pockets on each side but no flap to the codpiece. The wastcoat to be a very good unwatered Tabby [silk] the same green as ye pattern trimmed with silver buttons and silver lace about the breadth of the gold lace I had last year on my wastcoat, and to have pockets to it. I would not bestow anything extra-ordinary in the ounce for the making the lace, but let it be a showy lace of the common price by the ounce.

The Gold laced wastcoat you made me last year has done you no credit in the making, it gapes so intolerably before at the bottom, when I button it at the wastbone of my breetches and stand upright it gapes at the bottom beyond my breetches and everybody takes notice of it. As to my size I am partly the same bignesse as I was when in Town last but you made the last Cloaths a little too streight.

Pray let this be all done perfectly well and send mee some coat and wastcoat and breetches buttons and mohair and a nail [2¼"] of cloath the same as ye coat and a quarter of a yard of silk the same to ye wastcoat for I han't a bitt left to ye last Wastcoat—if I had ye gaping might be rectified ...

The tailor supplied the cloth and trimmings (as well as some dress material for Mrs Purefoy). It is noticeable that quality matters more than fit, for in all this lengthy instruction Henry Purefoy never once gave an actual measurement, but relied on his tailor's remembering how big he was last year—when he had underestimated his size. Small wonder that when these clothes arrived, though they were said to 'fit tolerable' they were nevertheless too short in the breeches, and too long in the coat and the sleeves. But the serious complaint was 'the green wastcoat is a very poor silk and my mother has bought better for 4s. I doubt your man did something to it for sure yourself would not put such a silk in any wastcoat. I have sent you a bit of my wastcoat and a piece of the 4s. silk . . .' This practical reproof was made merely to relieve Henry's feelings, for he sent the full payment (£13 15s., a very modest price then) by the carrier. Breeches too short, hats too big, boots too tight; Henry has all these troubles. Wigs from the Buckingham barber were not always right either; 'The new periwigg you made mee has some hair on the top of the crown that don't curl and when I put on my Hat or the Wind blows it stares and rises all up'.

The Purefoys were evidently fond of buying up-to-date furniture to suit the 'modern' fireplaces and decorations they installed with much trouble and expense in Shalstone Manor. They often attended auction sales in the vicinity, and 'picked up' all sorts of oddments, like quilts, a tablecloth, a pair of sconces, a tea-tray and so forth, as well as bigger items like a bureau or a chimney-glass or a chest of drawers. Though appearances may be deceptive, their purchases at sales do not look particularly cheap, and when it is remembered that the Purefoys were not interested in antiques but only in the latest fashions, and that they were not short of money to order new articles for themselves, their willingness to take second-hand furniture can only be explained in terms of the pleasure they felt in actually seeing, for a change, what they were buying. It must have been a rare treat to buy 'two pictures' or 'six wrought workt chairs' on impulse because they had taken their fancy, instead of always ordering things to be made and having to wait and accept what turned up, like this:

February 8th 1743

This desires Mr. Belchier to send mee a round neat light maho-gany folding table with four legs, two of them to draw out to hold up the folds. It must be four foot two inches wide. Send it (with the price thereof) by Mr. Zachary Meads the Bucks carrier who sets out of London on Monday nights and Friday nights. This will oblige

Your humble servant
Elizabeth Purefoy

P.S. My son's service waits on you. Pray a letter by post when you send it.
for Mr. Belchier
A cabinet maker at the Sun. The
South Side of St. Paul's in St. Paul's
Churchyard, London.

This table, when it arrived, cost £2 7s. plus 6d. for carrier's charges. Multiply this by, say, ten, and it affords a good example of how Georgian furniture—the same furniture now prized so highly by collectors of antiques—was a fairly cheap commodity in its day compared with other things. Compare it, for example, with Henry's coat and breeches mentioned above for £13 15s. Who today would sit down to dinner in a suit costing nearly six times as much as the dining-table? This is not because tailoring skill was dear and cabinet-making cheap in the eighteenth century—indeed, the reverse was the case. Fashions, of course, were very elaborate, but even more important, it was the materials that made clothes dear; hand-spun, hand-woven, hand-finished, hand-dyed cloth and silk, not to mention silver lace and buttons. Consider, for example, this bill, dated 1745.[2]

A MASTER TAYLOR'S BILL AS IT STANDS COMMONLY CHARGED TO THE NOBILITY AND GENTRY OF THIS KINGDOM.

	£	s.	d.
Making a velvet suit of cloaths		1.10.	0
Materials			
12 yards of velvet @ £1.4s per yard		14. 8.	0
11 yards of silk serge @ 5s. per yard		2.15.	0
2½ yards dimmity to line body of waistcoat		3.	1½
Pockets to coat and waistcoat		2.	0
4½ doz. gold wire buttons @ 9s. per doz.		2. 0.	6
4½ doz. small buttons @ 4s. 6d. per doz.		1. 0.	3
Silk and silk twist		5.	0
Buckram and canvas		4.	0
Hair cloth, covering and wadding		5.	0
Breeches linings and pockets		5.	0
Puffs and French garters		3.	0
Total		23. 0.	10½

Mechanization has since revolutionized the price of textiles and consequently our whole attitude towards clothes, but it has done little to hasten the growing and seasoning and handcarving of timber for fine furniture.

Glass was still dear by our standards, its laborious manufacture still untouched by machinery. Here is a piece from

[2] F. W. Galton & B. Webb, *Select Documents Illustrating the History of Trade Unionism: The Tailoring Trades*, I (1923), p. 40.

another letter to the same Mr Belchier ordering a chimney-glass
for the Purefoys.

> You say you must have £3.16. for a glasse in a gold frame three
> foot and eleven inches and a half long by twenty-four inches, the
> middle glasse to be thirty one inches long. I do leave it to you
> if you must have so much. Do it at your liesure, but pray let ye
> glasse be true, and you shall have your money so soon as I have
> ye glasse.

And finally, here are four short letters out of the Purefoys'
shopping correspondence that have an unmistakable eighteenth-
century flavour:

> March 1st 1747
>
> Mr. Sayer
>   I desire you will make me so many pounds of candles as you
> have had pounds of fatt of me, and make them the same size as the
> pattern, which will oblige
>   Your servant
>   Elizabeth Purefoy
> for Mr. Sayer, a Chandler
>   at Buckingham

The next, to Mrs Purefoy's London agent, concerns a small
rent like a peppercorn rent. Such old spice rents still existed here
and there, not commuted into money.

> May the 1st 1737
> I am forced to give Mr. Robotham this trouble, having been
> called upon for some Quit Rent which is to be paid in Cummin
> seed—so pray send me seven pounds of Cummin seed done up
> in single pounds; you are to have it at the Drugsters [i.e. import
> merchants dealing in drugs]. Send it with the rest of the things
> and let us know the newest fashioned hats the ladies wear. My son
> and self join in our service to you and Mrs. Robotham and I am
>   Your humble friend
>   Elizabeth Purefoy
> for Mr. Robotham at
>   the King's Head at
>   Islington near London

The nature of the next order suggests that like many other people they had been buying brandy from dubious sources.

May 27th 1738

Sir

When you send for the stuff that distinguished ye French brandy from the other that is not French pray send for 2 bottles thereof such as you showed mee here for mee which will oblige
Your hle. servt.
Henry Purefoy

P.S. My mother's and my service herewith yr. self and family.

for Mr. Wallbank
    surgeon at Buckingham

And finally to a doctor friend in Buckingham.

February 14th 1746

Sir

I send you enclosed the Proposals for Printing by subscription Mrs. Leapor's Poeticall works. If you like to subscribe thereto I will either bring or send you a receipt next Saturday for the money. My mother desires you'll buy a Sirloin of Beef with the Sewet on of 20 or 25 or 30 pounds in weight. If you can't have it without you may buy a boiling piece with it. The Bearer has orders to pay you for it. Wee both join in compliments to you all and I am, Sir,
Your very humble servant
Henry Purefoy

for Mr. Passelow
    at Buckingham

Both the Purefoys wrote scores of 'shopping' letters every year to shopkeepers in town and country, to friends and acquaintances, to craftsmen in nearby villages, to their London agents. Often they must have been disappointed; sometimes they complained; they refused and returned goods (carriage paid) very occasionally. Although they were probably less self-sufficient overall than their grandparents had been a century before, the differences was not that they provided less for themselves—indeed the housekeeping routines of the country gentry seem to have changed very slowly over the years. But things that had been rarities to one generation were becoming commonplace to another; luxuries were passing into the category of necessities, and nearly all this extra consumption came from outside the home and meant more shopping to make life comfortable and satisfying.

XI

<><><><><><><><><><><><><><><><><><><><><><><><><><>

The Man with a Pack

<><><><><><><><><><><><><><><><><><><><><><><><><><>

For they carry their shops on their backs and do sell that way more
than many shopkeepers do in their shops. Which is not only a
prejudice unto them, but if suffered, will in time be the utter
ruine of all the Cities and Market Townes in England . . .
                                    N.H., *The Compleat Tradesman*, 1684

With mobile shops operating on the hawking principle just prior
to the weekend, the normal butcher was losing revenue . . . It was
not fair that the normal butcher had to pay such high taxes and
rates when the mobile shop dealer got off practically free . . .
        *Report. The Annual Conference of The National Federation
                of Meat Traders' Associations*, 1959

Among so many obscurities and uncertainties in the history
of retail trade, nothing is so obscure and uncertain as the role
of the pedlar. He must have played a considerable part over a
long period in the distribution of consumer goods, yet almost
nothing is known about him. Few pedlars could write, let alone
record their experiences, and as a class they have, as Mr Hoskins
remarks of the poor in general, 'no annals, not even a tax assess-
ment, that sad passport to immortality'.

Up to a point, of course, everyone knows what pedlars were
like. They are enshrined in legend and ballad, carved in parish
churches, part of our folklore. The pedlar is always a jolly old
rascal, with a ragged coat, and a nimble tongue, and thieving
fingers; his open pack discloses a bewitching assortment of

pretty things to tempt simple country folk and trick them out of their money; he brings news of great events, tales of far places, begs his dinner, steals a kiss and is off over the hill. Every child knows about pedlars. But the very vividness of this popular image makes it harder to guess what really lay behind it. What did they sell? How much and to whom? Where did they get it and how far did they carry it? Who were they and what did they earn? Few people seem to have been curious about their business or troubled to describe them.

Yet there have been pedlars since at least the fourteenth century, when a handbook for merchants reminded them that 'Men as march with foot-packs owe to buy all manner of penny ware, also purses, knives, girdles, glasses, hats, and other penny ware, also farthing ware'[1]—a sort of travelling Woolworth's in fact. The pedlar of those days was often a good customer of the merchant both in London and at the fairs, where he came to replenish his pack. He often tried to linger in towns after the fairs were over to sell a quick pennyworth where there were plenty of people, until the town authorities moved him on; no doubt they reminded him that theirs was a respectable town with a market-day and a market-place and outside these limits heaven help any stranger who tried to take the bread out of the mouths of the local tradesmen. The moving-on process was more difficult in London, of course, where pedlars were arriving to buy goods in all seasons, and there were perennial grumbles from the City's freemen about the pedlars who sold at ale-houses and inn-yards and street-corners. In fact, from the fourteenth to the nineteenth century, the streams of protest in London are almost unchanged about the country pedlars who invade the capital and ruin its retail trade.

Once on his travels, however, the medieval pedlar probably did not lack customers, for he called everywhere, from cottage to castle, on his devious route to the next big fair. But he probably found that cash was scarcer than customers, and no doubt often accepted food instead, or bartered his goods for some other saleable article, especially with poorer folk. 'Come, cheap for love or buy for money!' is a cry familiar in ballads of various periods and a writer of 1561 says 'a pedlar procureth of the

---

[1] *The Noumbre of Weyghtes*, quoted in E. Power & M. M. Postan, *English Trade in the Fifteenth Century* (1933), p. 394.

children or servants a fleece of wool or the worth of twelvepence of some other thing, for a pennyworth of his wares'.[2]

His choice of goods would be small, of course, and medieval pedlars would themselves be few and far between, for not many of the poor would have the resources or the knowledge to step out of the rut into this arduous life. We hear of the occasional lucky one making enough money to turn merchant or settle down; what happened to the rest we can only guess. But there is no doubt that they had a status of a sort in medieval society. Dwellers in benighted cottages or remote castles welcomed and appreciated the pedlar in the long intervals between local fairs, and he did not figure as an automatic member of the rogues' gallery, as did town bakers and butchers.

A change came in the pedlar's reputation when the big upheavals of Tudor society threw so many unemployed on the road and the pedlars were joined by large numbers of homeless wanderers and beggars. Respectable society was appalled and intimidated by the numbers of idle vagabonds wandering the countryside, most of whom carried some sort of pack if only to hold what they could steal, and called themselves 'tinker' or 'pedlar'. Tudor legislation lumped together indiscriminately pedlars, beggars and wandering thieves, although an Act of 1553 did allow the more respectable ones to be licensed by two justices—that is, it allowed them to buy themselves off the harsh whippings and removals that normally followed when vagrants were picked up by town constables.

'These swadders or pedlars be not all evil,' wrote a J.P. in 1566, 'but of an indifferent behaviour. These stand in great awe of the "upright men" for they often have both wares and money of them.'[3] ('Upright men' were the notorious bullies or leaders of wandering bands of thieves.) The pedlars tended to become merged with the general vagabondia of the roads, and it was not for nothing that Shakespeare made his pedlar in *A Winter's Tale* steal linen off the hedges and purses from his customers and boast he was 'a snapper-up of unconsidered trifles'. This was what his audience expected of pedlars.

But just when the term 'pedlar' was becoming synonymous with 'rogue', genuine trading opportunities were opening up

[2] A. V. Judges, *The Elizabethan Underworld* (1930), p. 54.
[3] *ibid.*, p. 93.

for the more enterprising members of this calling. For one thing, there were more suitable goods to sell. Hitherto the pigskin bundle had held in the main four types of haberdashery. There were small leather items, purses, gloves, girdles and especially points for tying clothes; then there were metal goods, particularly pins and needles and knives; narrow woven goods such as laces, ribbons and tape; and lastly 'toys' such as an odd mirror, fan or pens for adults and wooden 'babies' for children. From Elizabethan times onward there were far more of all these things to be had, while new items with even readier sales were becoming available. Tobacco, and especially cheap contraband tobacco, was a favourite early in the seventeenth century. Almanacks, broadsheets and ballads ('very true and but a month old') had a glad reception in the countryside. And ready-made trifles of dress in silk or linen were to be had in town shops and were light to carry.

> Lawn as white as driven snow, Cyprus black as ere was crow,
> Gloves as sweet as damask roses, masks for faces and for noses,
> Bugle-bracelet, neckless-amber, perfume for my lady's chamber,
> Golden quoifs and stomachers for my lads to give their dears,
> Pins and poking sticks of steel, what maids lack from head to heel . . .[4]

There is not much doubt that Autolycus's famous pack owed more to the licence of the poet than of any genuine pedlar. Compare it with an authentic pedlar's pack that was seized for debt (admittedly in the poor north country) not so many years after *A Winter's Tale* was written.

Sept. 14th, 1657. Goods arreasted of Jo. Wilson, pedler, for [debts to] Geo. Scot of Cockermouth.
    Impr. 3 hankes and 4 Cutts [of yarn],
      jii 1. of tobacco
        A Candlesticke
        A little measure for drinking hot waters in.
            (probably a scotch whisky-cup)
        An old Pistell
Prised by Geo Milner, Edw. Brisco and Par. Johnson.
All, vj. shillings. Turned out with the full consent of Jos. Wilson, pedler.[5]

[4] W. Shakespeare, *A Winter's Tale*, IV, iv.
[5] James Jackson, *The Diary of a Cumberland Farmer 1650–83* (Trans. Cumberland & Westmorland Antiq. Soc., n. s., XXI), p. 109.

Had he taken the yarn in trade for tobacco, the spinning of some busy housewife at a wayside cottage? And had he got his tobacco (cheap, plentiful and often smuggled through west-coast ports about this date)[6] from a shopkeeper in Cockermouth? We know too little about pedlars even to guess. But one thing he had not got, although it was probably more characteristic of pedlars in the south and midlands than so far north, and that was rabbit skins. Felt hats were replacing the older fashion for knitted caps from Elizabeth's reign onward, and felt was made of fur, which fetched a good price. The rabbit or the hare went into the countryman's pot and the skin was saved up for the pedlar.

> What lack you? What buy you? Any good pinnes?
> Come let us bargain! Bring forth your coney-skins![7]

In ballads about pedlars in the sixteenth and seventeenth centuries, 'coney skins' rhymes with 'points and pinnes' with a wearisome monotony. But although this trade was then at its height, it was evidently an old one, as witness the lines in *Piers Plowmans*:

> I have as much pity on poor men as a pedlar has on cats
> Who would kill them if he could catch them, coveting their skins.[8]

When it ceased is hard to determine, but it was probably killed by the cheap imports of American beaver after the Restoration. Even in Victorian times, however, travelling salesmen in country districts often accepted skins in payment for small wares because there was still a regular market for them in London.

As trade of all kinds was increasing all through the seventeenth century, the pedlars took their share. 'For of late,' wrote an alarmist pamphleteer in 1684, 'there is not any commodity to be named that can be in any way ported but that the Pedlar doth carry it all about the countrey to sell, that People (after a while) will have little or no occasion to come to the Cities or Market Townes for anything.'[9] So the shopkeepers as a class

[6] R. Davis, English Foreign Trade 1660–1700 *Econ. Hist. Rev.*, VII (1954), pp. 150–66.

[7] *The Pedlar's Prophecie* (1595), Malone Society Reprints (1914), line 650 f.

[8] N. Coghill, *The Vision of Piers Plowman* (1949), p. 40.

[9] N.H., *The Compleat Tradesman* (1684).

were now numerous enough to raise their voice not only against pedlars lingering in towns to steal their trade, but against the volume of business being done in the open country. It is tempting to see this and the many similar complaints that followed, as evidence not so much of the prosperity of the pedlars as of the difficulties of the people who had rushed into shopkeeping in the small towns and villages in the freer commercial atmosphere of the times, only to find that there was more to making a living than merely sitting behind a counter with a small stock.

As we have already seen, the great difficulties of country shop-keepers were getting stock and getting in debts. Pedlars, on the other hand, had the best reasons for refusing all credit,[10] while their constant travelling made it easier for them to replenish and diversify their stock. Moreover, they had no shop-rent, and were not limited to the sprinkling of customers within a radius of five miles or so of a village shop. It is not altogether sur-prising, therefore, that in the seventeenth century many pros-pered, like the one in the ballad.

> And when his sins had made his pack too heavy for
> his shoulder
> In th' aforesaid place he eased his back and turned
> a staid householder.

In 1698 it was thought financially worth while to resume the taxing of pedlars which had lapsed since Commonwealth days. Four pounds a year was the cost of a licence and as much again for a horse, though sellers of their own or their employers' pro-ducts were exempt. Armed with a licence signed by two justices, the pedlars outfaced local by-laws and invaded the towns with impunity and the wrath of the shopkeepers broke forth in ever-increasing screams of protest: 'The Shopkeeper has the Milk where the Pedlar has the Cream; the Shopkeeper has the Gleanings where the Pedlar has the Harvest',[11] and so on. And as the next century progressed, the burden of the complaints took on a different note. Pedlars had long been accused of dealing in defective and stolen goods; now it began to be contraband that they were blamed for selling. 'Foreign silks, linens, Indian

---

[10] Anon., *The Case of the Fair Trader* (early 18th C.).
[11] Anon., *Brief State of the Inland and Home Trade* (1730).

Handkerchiefs and other prohibited Goods.'[12] And indeed, so many foreign goods were prohibited or heavily taxed in the eighteenth century, and smuggling was such a lively trade that it is easy to believe this widespread notion was true. Probably many genuine pedlars found contraband a profitable sideline, and probably many country justices exchanged bad licences for good French brandy. And since smuggling after all was but a venial offence in many people's eyes at that time, the shopkeepers would sometimes damn them for *not* smuggling.

> They harangue their customers with the long journeys that they make and the pains they are at and the hazards they run to get those goods at the sea-side and out of the ships that bring them over, though in fact they never came there and have that part done to their hands. By these fine stories they delude ignorant people and persuade them to believe the goods foreign when they are not and cheap when they are dear.[13]

There were, however, some pedlars who were even above the taint of smuggling, who prospered and won through to respectability and solid citizenship. One such is the famous Mr McGuffog, an early master of Robert Owen's in the drapery trade. In the 1770s he had a handsome and prosperous shop in Stamford out of which he made a considerable fortune. 'The articles dealt with were the best, finest, and most choice qualities that could be procured from all the markets of the world.'[14] Owen says that the shop 'became the rendezvous of the higher class nobility' of the district, with sometimes six or seven carriages waiting outside, and that most of the day's business was confined to the elegant shopping hours of ten till four. The singular success of this shop was evidently unusual and due to the exceptional talents of the popular Mr McGuffog, but that man had started life as a pedlar, tramping the villages with his humble pack and serving cottage and manor-house, farm and country mansion like any other.

But new forces were at work in the eighteenth century which set quite a new kind of salesman to tramp the country lanes

[12] *Journals of the House of Commons*, XL, 1107, 1109; J. Stow, *Survey of London* (ed. J. Strype, 1755), II, 560.
[13] Anon., *Brief State of the Inland and Home Trade* (1730).
[14] R. Owen, *Life of Robert Owen* (1879), p. 16.

alongside the traditional pedlar. The first stirrings of the industrial revolution in the midlands and north began producing a spate of consumer goods, and manufacturers began to look around for new outlets for their wares that would be quicker and wider than the annual fairs and the distant London merchants. One answer was provided by wholesale travelling dealers who carried goods from the new factories to offer direct to shop-keepers up and down the country. Their trains of heavily laden packhorses brought to the retailer's doorstep a tempting choice of cheap new goods that he could examine and buy on the spot, often for credit, and their services gradually transformed the resources of the provincial shops, especially in towns remote from London. 'The shopkeepers in country towns do not buy an eighth part in London now that they did,' wrote an indignant London wholesale merchant (though with some exaggeration) at a very early stage of this process.[15] In the course of the eighteenth century the country shopkeepers were beginning, if only in a small way, to be at last wooed by 'the traveller'.

These itinerant wholesalers, or Manchester Men as they were called, were not pedlars, though sometimes stigmatized as such,[16] and they affected the consumer only indirectly through giving new life to country shops. But though some of them were substantial merchants who set out from the mills and factories with stocks valued in thousands of pounds on the backs of a string of several dozen horses, and returned home with saddle-bags heavy with gold, they were not all like that.[17] They came in all sizes down to the modest one-horse operator who dealt whole-sale where he could but at a pinch was not above getting rid of his remainders by opening his pack in a local market, or auction-ing them at some country inn to all comers at knock-down prices;[18] such salesmen were often popularly confused with pedlars, though their true business was wholesaling.

But there was also a new kind of genuine retailer who came on the scene at this time to specialize in selling the cheap textiles

---

[15] Anon., *The Trade of England Revived and the Abuses thereof Rectified* (1681).

[16] *Journals of the House of Commons*, XIV, 498, 504.

[17] D. Defoe, *Tour through the Whole Island of Great Britain* (1727), III, 119 ff.; G. W. Daniels, *The Early History of the English Cotton Industry* (1920), p. 61.

[18] Anon., *The Trade of England Revived and the Abuses thereof Rectified* (1681); F. M. T. Lamb, ed., *The Diary of Thomas Turner, 1754–65* (1925), p. 89.

the new mills were producing. He was known as a 'Scotch Draper', and was a sort of half-pedlar, half-tally-man. He travelled on foot, calling from house to house, but unlike the ordinary pedlar he sold on credit and always concentrated on a well-defined area so that he could call on his customers every week for instalments of his money. By the end of the eighteenth century the Scotch Drapers were numbered in thousands, and they got their goods from certain wholesale dealers who had started up especially to supply this type of trade. Some Scotch Drapers obtained their stock on credit from these specialist suppliers; they owed, and were owed in their turn, large sums.[19] Others were the paid employees of firms or 'societies' with ten or more agents on the road. 'The Scotch Hawkers,' we are told, 'travelled slowly and laboriously from town to town . . . conveying huge and weighty packs on their backs some four feet in length and two or more in depth, stored with hosiery, drapery and other necessary articles.'[20]

This new gentleman of the road established himself very rapidly as the industrial revolution gathered momentum, because he met the needs of the new communities of wage-earners growing up around factories in remote situations. His typical customers were families of factory hands with whom he established a position of trust. It was the rule for whole families to work in mill or factory or mine. They had little time for shopping or visiting market-towns; they lived from hand to mouth on the weekly or fortnightly wage. The Scotch Draper brought to their door just the kind of goods they needed, was content to settle for a small weekly sum, and as one gown or jacket or blanket was paid off was ready with the next article. If it was truly the Scots who first invented this trade (for by the time it became well known it was Scotch only in name) they seem to have conferred a great blessing on the working people of their day.

Superficially, there is some resemblance between the London tally-man, and the Scotch Draper of the provinces. Today both survive, and their methods are virtually indistinguishable. In the eighteenth and early nineteenth century, however, they were very different. The London tally-man had an evil reputation as a

19 *Journals of the House of Commons*, XL, 1017–18, 1020, 1026.
20 Samuel Bamford, *Early Days* (1849), quoted in A. P. Wadsworth & J. de L. Mann, *The Cotton Trade and Industrial Lancashire* (1931), p. 240.

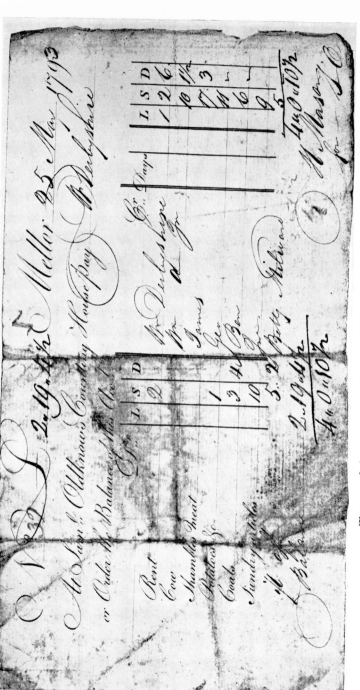

13. Two weeks' wages for a family paid by truck note, with deductions. The back shows it exchanged for bread, butter, cheese, meal, flour and linen, and old debt of 4s. 11d. and a new one of 3s. 5½d.

14. A Pedlar. Early nineteenth century.

money-lender whose shoddy goods were primarily a bait for clients and who made more money out of exorbitant interest and (so long as imprisonment for small debts was in force) out of defaults, than out of honest trading. No doubt this widespread condemnation was too sweeping, but this kind of charge was not made in the eighteenth century against Scotch Drapers, although the latter shared in the abuse that their enemies the shopkeepers heaped upon pedlars in general.

How important was the Scotch Draper's trade? There is no way of measuring it, and since its practitioners did not serve the gentry, they operated out of the 'public' eye; they do not figure as do London shopkeepers, for example, in eighteenth-century novels. Nevertheless, for a trade that has attracted so little attention, indirect evidence suggests that it was surprisingly great. In the 1780s a greedy Exchequer hit upon a Shops Tax as a means of easy revenue, and at the same time, to sweeten the pill to the shopkeepers, it brought in a Bill to make all peddling illegal. At the last minute, this arbitrary sentence of death was revoked. This was not out of pity for pedlars; what the pedlars thought about it was of no account.[21] Nor for their customers, for by then only the poorer classes were sufficiently dependent on their services to miss them. But storms of protest had arisen from an unexpected quarter to which even Members of Parliament were obliged to listen. The pedlars' champions were no less than the manufacturers of linen, wool and cotton, the mill-owners of Glasgow and Lancashire and Yorkshire, many of whom objected that they would be driven to close down their mills without pedlars—and in particular Scotch Drapers—to market their goods. From Manchester came several petitions, one asserting among other things that

> The Quantity of Goods purchased by that Class of Dealers is much more considerable than may have been apprehended . . .[22]

A petition from Whitehaven was especially eloquent.

> Many great and important Advantages are derived from the said useful and industrious Class of Tradesmen, the Quantity of goods

[21] *Journals of the House of Commons*, XL, 1007.
[22] *ibid.*, p. 1001.

bought and disposed of by them being considerably more extensive than has been generally conceived, and the Mode of Sale which is wholly confined to small Villages and Places remote from general Markets tends very greatly to diffuse the Manufactures of the Kingdom in general and is a source of great convenience to those Inhabitants who live at a Distance from the principal Towns, great Quantities of goods of almost every Description being vended in detail, which the remote Inhabitants could not find Leisure to seek and when Necessity might compel him to go from Home, the Expence of his Journey would frequently be as great as the Object of his Purchase.[23]

Or again, from Paisley manufacturers:

The Hawkers and Pedlars have carried on their trade in which they have employed considerable Sums of Money and by their Industry and Perseverance have contributed greatly to the Extension of many of the Manufactures of both England and Scotland by introducing them into Parts of the Country where they could not otherwise have been sold . . .[24]

Another one alleged that the Scotch Drapers in the neighbourhood of Halifax were owed about £40,000 by 'labouring mechanics and manufacturers' in the mill-villages of the West Riding.[25] These and many other petitions addressed to the House of Commons in defence of the pedlars, and particularly the Scotch Drapers, even if some overstatement is allowed for, are strong evidence of the important part played by them in developing new markets among the working classes.

In spite of licensing, it is hard to know how many pedlars there were on the roads. During the eighteenth century, when they were probably at the height of their importance as retail traders, the number of licences each year was roughly 2,000, but many of these would be taken out by well known street-hawkers in London and the big cities, who could not avoid it. How many country pedlars dodged the plate it is impossible to imagine. Justices tended to ignore them unless they got into trouble, and even then it was well known that a pedlar always knew where he could borrow a licence if called upon to produce one, for in

23 *ibid.*, p. 1072.
24 *ibid.*, p. 1054.
25 *ibid.*, p. 1026.

the days before signatures and photographs who was to say which licence was whose? Even the Census returns of the nineteenth century fail to bring the peddling fraternity out of its obscurity; they declare some 30,000 odd pedlars in 1851, but by then we know that all sorts of vagrant characters, from quack-doctors to 'hanky-panky' conjurers were finding a pedlar's licence useful in dealing with those new busybodies, the police. True pedlars were probably diminishing rather than growing in number in Victoria's reign, for at last their old enemies the shopkeepers had usurped their function in even the remotest places. The shadowy figure of the pedlar still persisted, however, and still persists, but only as a curiosity on the fringe of retail trade and no longer an integral part of it.

MODERN TIMES

XII

The Climax of Traditional Retailing

◇◇

Six or eight years ago, the epidemic began to display itself among the linen drapers and haberdashers. The primary symptoms were an inordinate love of plate-glass, and a passion for gas-lights and gilding. The disease gradually progressed, and at last attained a fearful height. Quiet, dusty old shops in different parts of town were pulled down; spacious premises with stuccoed fronts and gold letters were erected instead; Floors were covered with Turkey carpets, roofs supported by massive pillars; doors knocked into windows; a dozen squares of glass into one; one shopman into a dozen; and there is no knowing what would have been done if it had not been fortunately discovered, just in time, that the Commissioners of Bankruptcy were as competent to decide such cases as the Commissioners of Lunacy and that a little confinement and gentle examination did wonders. The disease abated. It died away. A year or two of comparative tranquillity ensued. Suddenly it burst out again amongst the chemists; the symptoms were the same, with the addition of a strong desire to stick the royal arms over the shop door, and a great rage of mahogany, varnish, and expensive floor-cloth. Then the hosiers were infected, and began to pull down their shop fronts with frantic recklessness. The mania died away again, and the public began to congratulate themselves upon its entire disappearance, when it burst forth with ten-fold violence among the publicans and keepers of 'wine-vaults'. From that moment it has spread among them with unprecedented rapidity, exhibiting a concatenation of all the previous symptoms; onward it has rushed to every part of the town, knocking down all the old public-houses, and depositing

splendid mansions, stone balustrades, rosewood fittings, immense
lamps and illuminated clocks at the corner of every street.

Charles Dickens, *Sketches by Boz*

In the nineteenth century industrial development gathered
momentum and transformed the face of Britain, but retail trade
was for a long while allowed to jog along in its traditional
grooves. Until at least halfway through the century the size of
shops, the kind of people who ran them and their methods of
buying and selling were all very much as they had been a
hundred years before. Shopkeepers prospered with the prosperity around them, but they were content to be borne by the
tide and struck out no new courses for themselves. Even the
successful beginnings of Consumer Co-operation in those years
were made not by shopkeepers but by amateurs interested in
social theories rather than in retail trade. Indeed, it seems as
though so much of the nation's energy and imagination was
being drawn into industry and foreign commerce that none was
left to fertilize the retail trades with new ideas. Perhaps a dull
calling attracted dull recruits. Certainly there is plenty of
evidence that the prestige of retailing as a career was at a lower
ebb in the first half of the last century than at any time before or
since. 'It would be next to impossible,' it was said in 1843, 'to
apply to a well-dressed man in the street a more offensive
appelation than "shopman".'[1]

But shopkeepers were complacent enough as a class. When
they discussed retail business in the press or before parliamentary
committees of inquiry, they talked of the big improvements on
all sides since the days before the Napoleonic Wars; they con-
gratulated themselves on their better premises, their more
varied stocks, their quicker turnover and their sounder book-
keeping.[2] They showed no signs of realizing that the industrial
and social changes they saw going on all around them would
soon convulse their own little world and transform it too; that
the traditional shop was no more secure against change and
progress than any other business. Let us, therefore, take a last
look at the old form at its height after two and a half centuries of

---

[1] Edward Flower, *Hours of Business* (1843), p. 27.
[2] *Report of Select Committee on Manufactures and Trade* (1833), Q. 1338, 1421.

steady, slow development since the days of Elizabeth, and then see how the old methods broke down in face of the needs of the new industrial populations growing up in the Midlands and North.

To begin with, there was still a very real distinction between 'marketing' and 'shopping'; between buying perishable food which was an arduous chore delegated wherever possible to a servant, and the implied leisureliness of sitting down inside a shop and having goods brought out and displayed by a shop assistant. Markets were still of the first importance to the housewife until nearly the end of the century. Even in cities there was an immediate connection, now quite lost sight of, between the food on the table and the surrounding countryside. Every-where outside London, dairy-stuff as well as poultry and eggs were local produce brought into towns for sale straight from the nearby farms, closely reflecting not only local geography but also the weather and the seasons. Fruit and vegetables too—especially potatoes—were all getting more popular, yet even in London they had made little headway into fixed shops, while elsewhere greengrocers' shops were practically unknown. For all these things the customer went to one of the stalls in the market and dealt with the farmer or one of his household—only rarely, outside London, with the stall-holding middleman of later times. Meat and fish-sales were divided, as they had always been, between market-stalls and fixed shops, but markets were the great selling places for ready-cooked food, such as sausages, pies, gingerbread and so forth, which were literally 'home-made' by the hawkers who sold them.

The importance of markets little over a hundred years ago can perhaps best be realized by the fact that today over half the shops in Great Britain are food-shops, while at that time most of the food sold passed through the markets. In the south, these markets were much as they had always been, but in the industrial districts it was a different story. Liverpool led the way in providing a covered municipal market-hall for this business, a fine spacious building, gas-lit, and supplied with fresh water, a building still in use today, and eloquent of the importance of the market-trade at the time it was built, in 1822, to serve only about 150,000 people. But Liverpool was exceptional. Municipal control of markets did not become general until the very end of the century, and by that time most of the market-trade had already moved into fixed shops. Meanwhile, during most of the century, growing numbers in many of the manufacturing towns continued to crowd into the ancient markets, usually some particular group of streets and narrow lanes, where a private individual owned or leased a legal monopoly to hold the only market within five miles. Overcrowded, insanitary, inconvenient and even disorderly, these relics of a rural past often yielded a considerable private profit to their owners, in exorbitant rents and perquisites.[3] Just as perishable commodities had been the first to spill out from the crowded London markets of the seventeenth century into the hawking trade, so now, in the growing northern cities, farmers' carts and hawkers with their barrows and baskets roamed the streets in great numbers doing a casual trade.

In any large town, especially in the manufacturing districts, the market reached its peak of activity on Saturday nights after people had drawn their week's wages. Then the farmers gave way to the street-traders and hawkers, and the poorer classes came thronging in to buy their Sunday dinners. Here is part of a contemporary's impression of late Saturday night in the New Cut, Lambeth, in 1861, a scene that was no doubt being re-enacted in towns all over the country at the same time:

There are hundreds of stalls and every stall has one or two lights; either it is illuminated by the intense white lamp of the new self-generating gas-lamp, or else it is brightened by the red smoky flame of the old grease lamp. One man shows off his yellow haddock with a candle stuck in a bundle of firewood, another makes a candlestick of a huge turnip and the tallow gutters over its sides, while the boy shouting 'Eight a Penny, stunning pears!' has rolled his dip in a thick coat of brown paper that flares away with the candle. . . . These with the sparkling round-glass globes of the tea-dealers' shops and the butchers' gas-lights streaming and fluttering in the wind like flags of flame, pour forth such a flood of light that at a distance the atmosphere immediately above the spot is as lurid as if the street were on fire. . . . Then the tumult of the thousand different cries of the eager dealers all shouting at the tops of their voices at one and the same time, are almost bewildering. 'So-old again' roars one.

[3] *Report of Royal Commission on Market Rights and Tolls* (1891), p. 84.

'Chestnuts all 'ot, a penny a score' bawls another. 'An 'apenny a skin, blacking' squeaks a boy, 'Buy, buy, buy, buy, bu-u-uy' cries the butcher. 'Half quire of paper for a penny' bellows the street stationer. 'An 'apenny a lot, ing-uns', 'Two pence a pound grapes', 'Three a penny Yarmouth Bloaters', 'Who'll buy a bonnet for fourpence?' 'Pick 'em out cheap here, three pairs for a halfpenny, bootlaces'. 'Now's your time, beautiful whelks, a penny a lot'. 'Here's ha'porths' shouts the perambulating confectioner. 'Come and look at 'em! Here's toasters' bellows one with a Yarmouth bloater stuck on a toasting fork. 'Penny a lot, fine russets' calls the apple woman. And so the babel goes on . . .

This stall is green and white with bunches or turnips, that red with apples, the next yellow with onions, and another purple with pickling cabbages. . . . . Each salesman tries his utmost to sell his wares, tempting the passers by with his bargains. The boy with his stock of herbs offers 'A double handful of fine parsley for a penny' and the man with a donkey cart filled with turnips has three lads to shout for him to their utmost with their 'Ho! Ho! Hi-i-i! What d'you think of this here? A Penny a Bunch— hurrah for free trade! Here's your turnips!' Such indeed is the riot, the struggle and scramble for a living that the confusion and uproar of the New Cut on a Saturday night have a bewildering and saddening effect on the thoughtful mind.[4]

And so the outward appearance of the mid-nineteenth-century markets would not have been wholly unfamiliar to the modern shopper; like a modern fair-ground on Saturday night, like any modern country town's bi-weekly market by day. The only essential difference was that they were in every way more important in the scheme of things, as well as more tumultuous, more urgent, more disorderly, more often a battle of elbows as well as a battle of wits.

When we come to the shops themselves, however, the differences from the present day are much more striking. In the first place, they were still almost invariably small, independent shops, owned and run by the shopkeeper on the spot. Department stores, chain and multiple shops, national or even regional 'big names', these things as we understand them were quite unknown before mid-century. One master, one shop was the rule, and although a successful shopkeeper occasionally opened a branch, it was a rarity to do so. Shopkeepers were regarded as

[4] Henry Mayhew, *London Labour and the London Poor* (1861), II, 9.

skilled men—skilled, that is, in their particular trade and no other. Like craftsmen they served an apprenticeship, and in all the leading trades there was much to learn. Where to buy, from wholesalers or manufacturers or individual craftsmen, how to bargain with them for the right purchase and mix (or 'sort up' as they called it) a stock suitable to their particular custom—these formed, as always, the most important and the most difficult part of their skill in any trade. Goods were not of standard quality, not even textiles. Every consignment had to be expertly valued and priced, both for buying and for selling again in the shop. A typical butcher had to judge and bargain for his meat 'on the hoof' and know how to slaughter and dress it in his own shed, a practice now surviving only in a few country towns. In London there were an increasing number of 'carcass' butchers who supplied shops wholesale, but even as late as 1873 there remained 1,500 private slaughterhouses in the metropolitan area alone.[5] Grocers had to understand how to choose, blend and grind as well as weigh and package much of their stock. Even haberdashers bought cotton and thread by the pound and disentangled it and folded it into hanks for sale and cut coloured sewing silks into single lengths which the customer could draw out one at a time from a big multi-coloured bundle, for even the humble cotton-reel was still not familiar. Every trade needed its own knowledge and skill.

Untrained shopkeepers there were, of course, but usually we hear of them trying to make a living with a general shop, or as a poor man's chandler in a country town; a widow, for example, was often set up in a shop in a small place by her friends who patronized her out of sentiment. Miss Mattie in *Cranford* followed a well-trodden path. But good-sized shops doing a busy trade needed a professional hand, and as the century progressed and competition between shopkeepers took the form of keener prices, it became increasingly essential to know the tricks of the trade to stay in business in any fair-sized town.

The wholesale trade was becoming more highly organized, employing travelling salesmen to supply country shops. A sober Bristol draper of the 1820s 'made a practice of declining going to the inns the commercial men stayed at, it being the custom in those days for the drapers or their buyers (very few buyers were

---

[5] Charles Booth, *Survey of London Life and Labour* (1897), VII, 202.

then kept, the draper generally buying his own goods) to go and drink a glass of wine at the expense of the sellers'.[6] Wholesaling was especially well developed in all branches of the so-called 'drapery' trades. Drapery now embraced not only dress materials and household piece-goods but hosiery, gloves, 'fancy goods' or haberdashery—all the trades, that is to say, where machinery and mass-production had been first in the field and where they were constantly bringing forward cheaper, better and more varied merchandise. Apart from these and a few major food trades, however, only goods that entered largely into foreign commerce enjoyed any efficient wholesaling organization.

But in all trades many substantial shopkeepers, both in London and out of it, still aspired to develop a sideline in selling whole-sale to their lesser brethren; looked forward to being able to call their shop a 'warehouse' and perhaps even put up a sign saying 'Retail, Wholesale and Exportation'. In the past, when substantial shops had been fewer and the consumer had bought bigger quantities at a time, sales to other tradesmen had been an indistinguishable part of the business of the leading shops in any town, and especially of course in London. But now that true, full-time wholesalers were appearing, holding really big stocks from a wide variety of sources and selling them to the trade by travellers, at keen prices for large quantities, there was less room for retailers to dabble in this as a sideline. And yet they seem to have been all the keener to do it. It was, after all, one way of growing; indeed, the only way most of them knew.

Here is the same Bristol draper of the 1820s, as his business improved:

We often attracted a new customer in the shape of a hawker or a small shopkeeper who would come in and ask if we would sell them goods at a lower rate than our usual retail price, for them to sell again. This we were quite willing to do. . . . This was the commencement of a small wholesale trade, and when it became generally known that we made an allowance to the trade a good many small shopkeepers began to come to us and in order to prevent the other customers hearing the prices that were quoted we made a point of serving all this kind of people at the bottom of the shop, as we got into trouble on one or two occasions, a bystander having overheard the price quoted. We felt at times as

[6] W. H. Ablett (ed.), *Reminiscences of an Old Draper* (1876), p. 166.

if we were committing an act of injustice, almost, by making such a distinction, although now (1870's) it is clearly understood and expected that a difference should be made betwixt the wholesale and retail prices. [7]

The most successful retailer passed over to the wholesaling side altogether, trying to lose the shopkeeper in the merchant, to 'get the creases of the apron strings out of his coat'. Again, this was particularly so in the drapery trade, but there were plenty of other examples, some of them well known like Twinings the tea firm (although their original retail shop still survives), and Allen and Hanbury the chemists.

But there was another way for the shop to grow, and this was demonstrated by a few drapers who did a cheap class of trade in London. It was summed up in a new saying: small profits and quick returns. It meant ceasing to rely on the loyalty of regular customers and appealing to the passer-by; it meant resorting to advertising, which was a matter of pushing handbills through letter boxes;[8] it meant display and cheapness, and it therefore involved strictly cash sales and the rather vulgar practice of price tickets in the windows. Price tickets were not at all genteel, as will be remembered by readers of Arnold Bennett's *The Old Wives' Tale*. A Parliamentary Committee was told in 1833, 'It is not a practice that would be resorted to by those who would seek their custom from the higher class of the community . . . it is much more resorted to where they seek principally customers among the lower and middling classes of people.'[9] This sort of business, since it made its appeal by cheapness, also involved fixing prices, and so the price tickets in the window were usually accompanied by a notice saying 'No Second Price' or 'No Abatement'.

There was one thing I remember I used to dislike cleaning very much, it was the words *No Abatement* set in brass letters on a black velvet ground and enclosed in a heavy frame, and one of these was always hung up in a prominent place in each window . . . ours being a pushing and ticketing shop.[10]

[7] *ibid.*, pp. 147–8.
[8] *ibid.*, p. 206.
[9] *Report of Select Committee on Manufactures and Trade* (1833), Q. 1425.
[10] Ablett, *op. cit.*, p. 6.

This kind of shop made no effort to hold large and comprehensive stocks, as did the more conventional shops in order to be able to meet any conceivable demand of their customers. Instead it aimed at selling quickly, turning over the entire stock in a couple of months; any lines that hung fire were reduced and 'pushed', and bonuses or 'tinges' offered to the assistants to get them off; and if that did not work, goods would often be discreetly singed at the edges and soaked in water and offered as 'salvaged stock'.

Such shops sometimes prospered and grew big. We hear in 1821 of £500 a day taken in a linen draper's shop over long periods; it had twenty or thirty assistants whose salaries did not amount to £40 per annum plus board.[11] These were the allegations of a rival shopkeeper. Very few shops were this big (if, in truth, any at all were before mid-century). A shop half this size would have been called a big store then. But all the same, they caused a good deal of alarm among ordinary shopkeepers; there was even a proposal, which came to nothing, to get shops over a certain size forbidden by law. These pushful methods were not very common in the first half of the century, but gradually they affected all drapers' shops and to some extent set an example to other trades. There are many testimonies to the all-round tightening up of business methods. 'By increased skill,' wrote a shopkeeper in 1851, 'the same amount of capital is made to do a greater quantity of work than before. In fact the substitution of quick for slow sales is precisely like an improvement in machinery which cheapens the cost of production.'[12] The author of this somewhat sophisticated comparison was, of course, away ahead of his time, but this sort of rational analysis of the shopkeeper's trade was to become commonplace in the next fifty years. So was another of his remarkable insights. Big 'pushing' shops, he declared, did not get all their trade at the expense of their small rivals, but actually created demand. 'But for their establishment [i.e. large shops] and the mode of dealing they have introduced, a great part of that business would have had no existence . . . there have been improvements in the habits of the people, leading them to consume clothes and articles of ornament instead of ardent spirits.'

11 Anon., *The Book of Trades* (1821).
12 W. N. Hancock, *Competition between Large and Small Shops* (1851).

One important result of bigger drapers' shops was the bad effect on the assistants. These were nearly all young men; women assistants only appeared in drapers' shops after mid-century and were not common until the 'eighties and 'nineties. In most shops the old apprenticeship system still lingered in a feeble form; premiums were virtually unknown now in the commonplace trades, but juniors as a rule served several years for nothing except their board and lodging to learn the trade. But all the assistants, whether apprentices or not, usually lived and worked with the master as part of his family. In most cases, where there were only two or three assistants who ate their meals with the proprietor, this produced something like a family life for them. But in the big shops where there were a score or more of them, living-in was coming to mean regimented slavery, their quarters a shared bed in a crowded attic, the food skimped, the discipline super-abundant. The living-in system was retained 'for motives of economy, convenience and discipline', and it went hand-in-hand with very long hours of opening. These twin evils were commonest in the drapery and grocery trades.

In the north of England, it was commoner for assistants in even the biggest shops to live at home, and for hours of opening to be a little more reasonable. But in the south of England, in all but the very highest class of trade, long hours and compulsory living-in persisted until the very end of the century.

It was usual for the staff to rise at 6 a.m. to clean the shop and set out the stock before breakfast. In drapers' shops at least, windows were dressed every day. In the eighteenth century the shopkeeper and his assistants in 'polite' trades had needed the daily attentions of a hairdresser for their long hair, but although men's hair was now short, they had still to spend much time and much of their scanty wages in achieving a smart appearance if they wanted to keep their place. 'The shopmen,' as Dickens described them, 'in their white neckerchiefs and spruce coats look as if they could not clean a window if their lives depended on it.' Up to now the difficulties of moving about the streets after dark and the unsatisfactoriness of doing business by candle-light had combined to restrict evening trade; but the invention of gaslight—cheap, bright, and exhausting to the indoor

15. Early Victorian milk shop in Golden Lane, London.

16. Early morning in the New Cut, Lambeth.

atmosphere—was no blessing to the shop assistant whose hours of work, and often his busiest hours of the day, were advanced by artificial light into the late evening. Ten o'clock at night on weekdays and midnight on Saturdays were the common closing hours, after which all the goods on display had to be taken down and put away. Later in the century, weeknight closing became a little earlier in high-class trade, and Saturday closing shortened to eight or nine, but the opposition to half-holidays and earlier hours came in the main from the medium and cheap class of drapers and food-shops who did their briskest trade after seven o'clock in the evening. Shop assistants had a long and bitter fight to secure the enforcement of early-closing hours and their grievance might be summed up in the words of one of them who, as late as 1892, was able to say that 'during four years he had never had the opportunity of putting on his coat or his hat, except on Sundays'.[13]

The most important group of retail trades, after the food trades, has always been as it is now connected with clothing and footwear. In the nineteenth century, the continued prominence of drapers and haberdashers reflected the large amount of home-sewing of dresses and shirts, underwear and nightwear, to say nothing of household linen, that was still taken for granted. But when it came to suits and cloaks and coats and boots and shoes, these had to be bought from the tailors and shoe-shops. And since the sewing-machine and the shoe-making machine had not yet arrived, the consumer still came in contact in this important branch of his shopping with the craftsman-retailer still selling his own hand-made product direct. Tailoring and footwear were the last trades of any size where the direct link between producer and consumer was still the rule. And even here, of course, there were exceptions. At the upper end of the social scale, the fashionable tailor or shoemaker had long forgotten, if he ever knew, how to cut a coat or close a shoe. He employed journeymen outworkers, and a skilled fitter on the premises, to do this work for him. Francis Place was a successful tailor at the beginning of the century who had only learned, himself, to sew leather breeches, but in spite of this he gained a fashionable connection for his shop by having a good business head, being tactful to customers and employing good workmen.

[13] *Shop Life and its Reform*, Fabian Tract No. 80.

Again, at the lower end of the scale the working man's rig already consisted of cheap ready-made clothes and shoes that were hand-made in a sweat shop, or of second-hand made-over articles, and visits to a bespoke shoemaker or tailor were rarities reserved for special occasions like weddings and funerals; a best suit lasted a great many years.

There were also, of course, a host of minor trades—far more than now—where the craftsman-retailer persisted. Milk, for example, was sold in cities by dairymen who kept their cows in cellars or at the backs of their shops, often in appallingly dirty and primitive conditions. There were about 700 licensed cow-houses in the metropolitan area in the 1880s, before 'railway milk' began to push them out of business. Craftsmen-retailers ranged all the way, in fact, from the exclusive to the disreputable; from the sculptor or jeweller or instrument maker—gentlemen who served gentlemen—to the humble fashioner in his home of brooms or baskets, or dog-collars or mousetraps who hawked his own products in the city streets or country markets in preference to selling them to shopkeepers. There was a growing demand as income increased for innumerable kinds of small manufactured articles that had still to be made by hand, and there was a great readiness among all classes to buy things casually in the street. Mayhew in mid-century estimated that upwards of 13,000 hawkers earned a living on the streets of London.[14] ('Do you know the Muffin Man?, is a nonsense-rhyme to the modern child who would make more sense of the question, 'Do you know the Baker's Telephone Number?' But it was a sensible song to his grandparents. Like so many nursery jingles it contains a tiny relic of our past fossilized in the timeless world of children, along with 'Simple Simon met a Pieman' and 'Half a Pound of Twopenny Rice' and the even older 'Malt that Lay in the House that Jack Built'.)

Another characteristic of shopping in this period was that it differed very much between regions and even between localities. In cities and big towns, shops in some streets still catered only for the upper and growing middle classes. The only working-class customers to cross their thresholds were street hawkers coming to replenish their baskets and usually relegated to the side-door. The working classes had shops to go to but they were

[14] Mayhew, *op. cit.*, I, 4.

few, meagrely stocked and struggling to counterbalance bad debts by high prices. 'Few small shopkeepers,' it was said, 'have the knowledge or the courage to introduce cash payments',[15] and this applied with special force to the poorer quarters. But the poor in cities did most of their shopping of every kind in the street.

The country dwellers and those in small towns still shopped much as their grandparents had done. Only the rich could send frequently to shops in big cities, and the middle-class country dweller still relied heavily on weekly markets for other things besides food, and on the annual or semi-annual fair for larger purchases and general 'stocking up'. The biggest of the old fairs had declined a good deal in importance; they were no longer national events, and many changed their character to become wholesale markets in particular commodities. But there was still plenty of life left in the innumerable small local fairs in country towns. 'The cottager goes to it for his store pig, the agricultural labourer for his linen gaberdine—the good old garment of his Saxon forefathers—and for his leathern gaiters, and the shepherd for his bells.'[16]

An autobiography that casts a good deal of light on this aspect of country shopping is *The Life and Adventures of a Cheap Jack*, written in old age by a prosperous tradesman who had started in life in the 1820s travelling the markets and fairs all over England with a horse and cart. He describes in lively terms the varied characters and atmospheres of these rural occasions, the workmanlike bustle of the markets, the holiday atmosphere of the local fairs where, nevertheless, much serious shopping was done with money long saved for the purpose. Many traders made, as he did at one time, a regular round of the markets and fairs in one region.

> I used to go out with a lot of goods on the Wednesday to Romford Market, on Thursday to Bishop Stortford, Friday to Chelmsford, Saturday to Colchester, Monday to Hadleigh, Wednesday to Bury St. Edmunds, Thursday to Diss, and on the Saturday to Norwich; that is, on the market days as they fell to each of the above places . . .

[15] Hancock, *op. cit.*
[16] John Page (Felix Folio), *The Story of the Manchester Fairs* (1887), p. 20.

The best fairs are those held in the autumn, as Peterboro, Canterbury, Maidstone, Maldon, Colchester, etc.[17]

Cheapjacks at that time sold what was roughly termed 'hardware', but the name comprised all sorts of small manufactures outside the drapery line. Not only pots and pans, but crockery, tools, guns, saddlery, watches, and almost anything else they could get. In spite of their name they often did a better business than many small shopkeepers. He mentions a colleague who fell on hard times and had to take a small shop in a country town and who struggled for years to save or borrow enough capital to get back on the road with a horse and cart and stock:

> A man that travells as a cheap jack is thought nothing of as a master unless he has at least £100 of goods of his own—literally his own by reason of their being bought and paid for—a good horse and a good carriage. . . .[18]

The practice was to stand on the tailboard of the cart (which served not only as stall but as transport and sleeping quarters as well) and to attract a crowd by a stream of comic patter much as itinerant pot-sellers do in country markets to this day. 'Who'll give me ten shillings for this? Half a crown then? Two Shillings? Come, two shillings only! I'll take no more nor I'll take no less, sell it or never sell it! Buy my last one and I'll give you two! So-old! Sold again, to the pretty young lady. Cheapest goods in all England!'

The goods they sold were the kind that did not yet find their way into the village or small town shops in any quantity.

> At Country fairs everything sells, bridles, saddles, whips, guns, padlocks, saws, etc. etc., all goods of amounts varying from one shilling to three pounds and upwards.[19]

The wholesale handling and distribution of this kind of thing seems to have been chaotic, but the cheapjohns, who dealt always in cash, often knew where to get goods direct from the makers; in their widespread travels they could collect many of the goods themselves. For example, 'At Wolverhampton the ordinary curry combs of the shops were being made by families for nine-

---

[17] Charles Hindley (ed.), *The Life and Adventures of a Cheap Jack* (1876), p. 33.
[18] *ibid.*, p. 2.
[19] *ibid.*, p. 26.

pence a dozen, the rivets being clenched and the teeth cut by mere infants.' Cheapjohns took advantage of this sort of thing while it lasted, but after mid-century their trade gradually died away as rail transport enabled the sort of goods they had dealt in to become part of the stock of permanent shops in every country town.

Apart from the salesmen who only appeared on market-days every small town had by now its handful of permanent tradesmen. The commonest single trade of all was the shoemaker's, for people used a lot more shoe-leather in the days before public transport, and the making of boots and shoes by hand took a lot of labour. Then even the smallest town would have its grocers and drapers and bakers (although in the north there were still noticeably fewer bakers per head of population than in the south where the habit of domestic bread-making died out much sooner). Most towns would have at least one coal or timber dealer, a cornchandler who dealt partly in retail, and the services of a tailor, barber, joiner and blacksmith, perhaps an old dame who sold home-made boiled sweets and of course several beer- and spirit-sellers. In very small towns there was a certain arbitrariness about the way tradesmen described themselves for they often fulfilled several roles at once, but even so they boasted a surprising variety of services in early Victorian times.

Take, for example, Aldeburgh, the little fishing village on the Suffolk coast with a population of 1,300 in the 1830s (half its present size).[20] It held markets on Wednesdays and Saturdays, fairs in March and May, had eight inns and public houses and not a single butcher or fishmonger or greengrocer living in the town. But it had no fewer than six shoemakers, four grocer-cum-drapers, two haberdashers, three bakers and two chemists and the services of four tailors, three milliners, five blacksmiths and a saddler, a coach-maker and a hairdresser, and a carrier two days a week to nearby Ipswich.

Compare this with Thirsk, with a population of 5,000 at the accession of Queen Victoria.[21] It had only one weekly market-day (when, however, there was 'fish from the coast in great perfection') but six fairs a year. It supported thirty public houses but no special wine-merchant. Twelve butchers made a living

20 *Pigot's National and Commercial Directory* (1840).
21 *White's Gazeteer of the East and North Ridings of Yorkshire* (1840).

there and two fishmongers, but no greengrocer and only four bakers. It had twenty-five boot-and-shoe shops, twelve grocers and eighteen 'general shopkeepers'. It had three confectioners (presumably sweet-boilers), four chemists and two tallow chandlers. Appearances were kept up by the aid of fifteen tailors, eight drapers, nine milliners, five hairdressers, four hatters and two clog-makers, and the miscellaneous trades included two china-shops, four booksellers, three ironmongers, four watch- and clock-makers, six cabinet-makers, 3 blacksmiths and a coal-dealer.

A village which was big enough to have a shop at all would have a shoemaker and a public house and either a grocer who kept a sideline in drapery or a draper with a sideline in grocery. The little hamlet of Sand Hutton, some three miles away from the considerable facilities just enumerated at Thirsk and containing at the same date 275 souls, was fortunate to possess three shoemakers, four public houses, and two general shopkeepers, besides a butcher (who probably practised his trade in Thirsk), a blacksmith, and a parish clerk who claimed to do some tailoring.[22]

Among pure retailers, the role of the very general shop is obviously predominant in all these and many other examples. Something of the flavour of a village general shop may be gained from a recommended inventory for country shopkeepers which appeared in a handbook for retailers published in 1853. This, so obviously not an exhaustive list, at least suggests a marked advance on the dreary, amateurish village shops of a century before. It makes an interesting comparison with the inventory of a present-day small general shop.

The author of this nineteenth-century guide, who was preaching the need for up-to-date methods and good service, advocated making up many of these goods only on demand, so that they would be sold fresh, but to save keeping the customer waiting longer than was absolutely necessary, he suggests that wrapping-paper may be conveniently kept ready-cut to handy sizes. Verdigris on the scales and pans is a bad thing, as it has been known to contaminate food, and polishing the counter with the apron may give an untidy appearance, while 'such filthy

[22] *ibid.*

practices as chewing a cork before use or blowing into a bottle to remove dust, *must* be abstained from'.[23]

STOCK OF THE SMALL GENERAL SHOP, THEN AND NOW

1853

Grocery. Tea, coffee, cocoa, chocolate, chicory, spices, barley, patent flour, semolina, sauces, pepper, mustard, bird-seed, scent.

Chandlery. Black-lead, paste-blacking, starch, grits (prepared), night-lights, German paste, twine, cord, rottenstone, emery, whiting, putty-powder, oxalic acid, sweet-oil, soda, sandpaper, bath-brick, Fullers' earth, congreve matches, soap, blue, gum, etc.

Hardware. Nails, tools, cutlery, tinware, toys, turnery (i.e. brushes, clothes pegs and other cheap wooden items), garden seeds, stationery.

Drapery. Cheap cotton and woollen piece-goods, needles, threads, wool, beads, etc.

1958

Foodstuffs. Butter, margarine and other fats, cheese, sugar, cakes, sweets, chocolate, biscuits, rice, sago, tapioca and similar goods, bacon, cooked ham, breakfast foods such as cereals (all the popular ones), oatmeal and porridge oats, rusks, flour, bread, teacakes or muffins (occasionally), currants, sultanas, raisins, dates, figs, glacé cherries, candied peel and other dried fruits, eggs, jams, frozen food and vegetables, custard powders, blancmange, jellies, fish and meat paste, etc.

Tinned foods. Meat, fish, peas, carrots, fruit of all kinds, syrup, Russian salad, sandwich spread and similar goods, tinned milk and vegetables for babies, tinned skim milk, full cream condensed milk, soup (also in packets).

Spices and Flavourings. Salad cream, salt, pepper, mustard, vinegar (bottled and loose), mixed spice, ground almonds, vanilla and other essences or flavourings, sauces (horse-radish, tomato, etc.), pickles, pickled cabbage, chutney, Marmite.

Drinks Tinned ground coffee, proprietary brands of coffee compound, liquid coffee extract, tea, cocoa, drinking chocolate, mineral waters, fruit squashes, Lucozade, syphons of soda water, Bovril, Oxo.

Greengrocery. Potatoes, carrots, cabbages, tomatoes, other vegetables in season (peas, beans, cauliflower, etc.), oranges, lemons, apples, salad greens.

[23] Anon., *The Shopkeeper's Guide* (1853).

STOCK OF THE SMALL GENERAL SHOP, THEN AND NOW

(1853 cont.)

(1958 cont.)

Drugs. (To be compounded by the shopkeeper) purgatives (black-draughts from senna, ginger, etc.), siedlitz powders, adhesive plaster, ginger beer (stone bottles from the Potteries at 10s. a gross), soda-water powders, sherbert powders, ginger-beer powders, baldness pomades, tooth-powders, hair-dyes, phosphorus paste for rats, inks, bug-poison.

from *The Shopkeeper's Guide* (Anon.), 1863

Hardware. Scrubbing brushes, clothes lines and pegs, fly and insect sprays, pan-cleaners, steel wool or similar, toilet rolls, firelighters.

Fancy goods. Pins, needles, knitting needles, cotton, some silks, darning wool, silk, rayon and ladies' nylon stockings, children's socks, birthday cards, doylies, cake-cases, writing paper and envelopes, buttons, hair-nets, combs, hairpins.

Cleaning materials. Soap (washing and toilet) soap powders and grease-solvents, shampoos, synthetic detergents in bewildering variety, disinfectants, W.C. cleaner, shoe-polish, floor-polish, dyes, window cleaning materials, Brasso, Silvo.

Toilet requisites. Shaving soap, face cream, powder (baby, talcum and face), lipstick, hand cream and certain other cosmetics, brilliantine hair cream, setting lotion, health salts of various kinds, cough medicine, toothpaste, aspirin, baby's comforter, cotton wool, sanitary towels, liniment, olive oil.

Other goods. Cigarettes, pipe tobacco, matches, small cigars, drawing pins, stamps, electric light bulbs, drinking straws, ice-cream, lollies.

from W. Burns, *British Shopping Centres*, 1959

These were the old small-scale retailing methods, not wholly unfamiliar to us, for even today relics of all these features can be found still surviving. But before the 1850s they existed everywhere and there were still no signs of large-scale organization, big capital investment or forward planning. Shopkeeping was still patterned on the needs of a pre-industrial society, and seemed unaware of the challenge of a growing class of weekly wage-earners and an increasingly affluent lower middle class. In part, of course, this was due to the geographical shift of population. New industrial communities were growing in the Midlands, in Lancashire and Yorkshire and in South Wales, where shopkeeping was slow to follow. Although plenty of money was being earned and spent in those places by a new class of consumer, in the distressful 'thirties and 'forties prosperity was irregular and jobs were short-lived. Spells of steady wages alternated with spells of near-destitution. It was said in 1842 by someone in the meat trade:

> From some recent statistical enquiries in the manufacturing districts of the north, it has been found, on a comparison of a period of prosperity with one of stagnation and embarrassment, that the consumption of meat fell off by one fourth or even one half. [24]

These were not attractive conditions for the typical small shop-keeper with limited resources. Also, there was a good deal of ignorance on the part of tradesmen in other places about the opportunities in the rapidly growing industrial districts. For example, Merthyr Tydfil in the midst of the coal and iron revolution in the 1820s, is described as a place where the local shopkeepers continued in the desultory habits suitable to traders in a minor country town, while all around them the new mining and iron-manufacturing workers clamoured for goods of every sort.

> Looking back, I am struck by the fact that no draper at that time had sufficient business energy to take advantage of the opportunities that presented themselves for establishing a large and flourishing business which might have been so easily done. If the truth must be told, men were not so eager for trade as they are now, and were in the habit of taking things very quietly indeed. The primitive sort of way in which business was conducted often amused me. Then again, I apprehend, as an adverse cause in its early stage of rising prosperity as an iron district, it was such a wretched place to live in. [25]

[24] Charles Knight (ed.), *London* (1842), II, 325; article by J. C. Platt on Smithfield.
[25] Ablett, *op. cit.*, p. 132.

For in spite of bad wages, long hours and intermittent unemployment, the standards of living of the poorer classes were rising. Rising, that is, in the important sense that they were setting their sights higher and demanding more. Population was rising, consumption per head was rising faster, and notions of what constituted a decent minimum living standard were rising fastest of all. Drink was no longer the almost universal waste and scourge that it had been. Observers spoke of the 'great increase in the consumption of all those articles which form the comforts of those a few steps above the indigent class. Thus within the last twelve years the increased use of soap, candles, leather, sugar, and other articles . . . in that class of society who are not compelled to live on the lowest description of food.'[26] Of which, Francis Place remarked, 'People thus improved will struggle hard still further to improve their condition and harder still to prevent degradation.' And struggle they did, on many levels, and not least, as we shall consider in a moment, to get what wages they were entitled to be paid in full in cash and at the proper times. But meagre though their wages and their spending were, the powerful spiral of rising consumption and rising production had achieved its mysterious take-off and was now well under way.

One feature of the growth of working-class expenditure was the growth of credit in all its less desirable forms. As in so many things, London had led the way and the provinces followed many years later; London's 'respectable poor' in the previous century had had a constant struggle against becoming enmeshed in tradesmen's debts; the new wage-earners in the industrial districts found themselves trusted from one pay-day to the next to an extent the rural poor had never been. 'Credit shops' swindled them notoriously; pawnbrokers and Scotch Drapers flourished; the beginnings of the clothing-check trade appeared. All the sorry entanglement of petty debts can be illustrated in the replies of a working-class man called as a witness before the House of Commons Select Committee on Manufactures in 1833. This witness lived in Stockport, at that time one of the most prosperous and fast growing of the new industrial towns. A town where both houses and shops were increasing 'not only in

[26] British Museum, Add. MSS. 27827, f. 93 (Place MSS., quoting House of Commons Report of 1828).

multitude but likewise in magnitude and splendour'; where a population of about fifty thousand shared 263 public houses; and where, although there was a substratum of destitution and many were dissolute and ignorant, yet he could claim 'there is a more marked distinction among the working classes than there used to be'. It was of this hopeful, go-ahead place that he proceeded to say:

> With respect to the credit system, I will state how it is carried on as to clothing. The clothing is generally bought from Scotchmen who travel. They call upon the families once in three weeks and I should think that one half of the population get their clothing in that way. There are some families that will deal with three or four or five of these men. I know one firm of this description in Manchester which employs five travellers. One traveller has in Stockport 360 customers and in Manchester 1100, and I believe the others are doing an equal amount of business, and I believe there are in Manchester upwards of 20 such firms as these, besides others of a subordinate character, and the receipts average half a crown every three weeks from each family. They range from two shillings to seven shillings or eight shillings. And from this you will be able to form an idea of the magnitude of the credit system among the people.
>
> If I were to give an order to a Scotchman when he called, he would, upon the following Saturday, send it to me, and the next day he calls. Afterwards I begin to pay from 2s. to 10s. at a time according to the amount of the order . . . Their goods are very much dearer than those from shops. I have it from undoubted authority that the lowest percentage they put on is 50% and some go as high as 100%.[27]

Asked why people bought clothes in this way, he attributed it to 'An anxiety to indulge in finery and things of that kind before they have the money to pay for it'. This has a familiar ring about it, but the typical instalment-buying of today is a model of hard-headed prudence compared with the muddled helplessness of many of the early industrial wage-earners. For instance, this witness went on to say how the number of pawn-brokers in the town had increased fourfold in twenty-five years, and each of them threefold in magnitude. 'There are, I think, not less than one-fourth of the population of Stockport who make a

[27] *Report of Select Committee on Manufactures and Trade* (1833), Q. 10572 ff.

practice of going to the pawnbroker weekly and taking almost all the clothing they have on a Monday morning and fetching it away on Saturday night.' The evidence continued as follows:

Q. What are the habits of the people dealing at the retail shops? Do they deal mostly for ready money or upon credit?

A. I should think that one half of the commodities purchased by the labouring people of Stockport for domestic purposes of every kind are purchased on credit.

Q. What length of credit?

A. With the retail shopmen of the town who sell food, it is generally from week to week.

Q. Is there any difference in price between cash and tick?

A. Yes. From 2s. to 4s. in the pound. But I estimate it in more ways than by the money paid. When a person begins with a huckster he is generally more inclined to consume above his income than when he has to pay ready money. He generally gets bound to the huckster, and when it is so, he cannot always insist upon having the weight or an article of the proper quality, and it is always higher in price besides, 2d. or 3d. for a dozen of flour, and about a penny a pound for sugar, and so on.

Q. Is not irregular work the reason for getting into debt to shop-keepers?

A. I think there are more persons who continue it for want of a little prudence than what are compelled to it by necessity. Those who are actually poor are more induced to go to a ready money shop on account of having more commodities for the little money they have to spend.

Q. Is there a distinction between ready money shops and shops giving credit?

A. Yes. Some ready money shops refuse all credit to the labouring population.[28]

This witness may not have been entirely accurate in all his estimates, but his other answers show that he was generally sympathetic to the difficulties of the working class and so not likely to exaggerate their shortcomings out of prejudice. Even allowing for this, however, two strong impressions emerge from this picture. One is the widespread ignorance and gullibility that made it hard for workers above the barest subsistence level to manage even regular wages and get good value out of them.

[28] *ibid.*, Q. 10566-71.

When we remember how meagre those wages actually were, and how painfully subject to interruption, the handicaps to wise spending must have been very great. The other impression that jars on modern sensibilities is the virtually unhampered freedom of rogues to take advantage of these weaknesses.

Stockport claimed at this time, that is in 1833, to be free of the evils of truck. This applied to most of the textile districts and it was no light blessing. But among the more scattered population in the coal and iron trade, and in domestic industries like hosiery-knitting, or hand-nail-making many workers were still getting their wages partly in goods instead of money right up to the 1870s. As a miner remarked in Disraeli's *Sybil*, 'The question is . . . what *is* wages? I say, 'taynt sugar, 'taynt tea, 'taynt bacon. I don't think 'tis candles. But of this I be sure, 'taynt waistcoats!' Truck was an old complaint already well known among the cottage outworkers of the eighteenth century,[29] but it was certainly at its worst in the first half of Victoria's reign. Masters kept shops for their workpeople for different reasons in different industries, and employees dealt at these shops either because there was nowhere else to go, or because they were paid in tickets or 'tommy-books' which could only be used at the employer's shop, but chiefly because they were under some threat of losing their jobs if they did not. If a workman was bold enough to demand money for his wages there was a short answer, and a powerful one—'If you don't want tommy you don't want work'.

Not all truck-shops were intended to defraud workpeople. When spinning mills were first set up beside the sources of water power in remote districts, or collieries or ironworks were started in open country, there were often no shops anywhere near, and a 'company' shop was a necessity. Moreover, cash was still scarce, particularly small coin, and it was expensive to fetch a lot of weekly cash up a country valley. It was simpler, and also saved a lot of working capital, to pay wages at fortnightly or monthly intervals and in the meantime to advance some sort of credit-note or tally or 'tommy-book' that the workers could redeem at the firm's shop, leaving little, if any, cash to be handled on settlement day. Some large firms ran respectable truck-shops, selling sound goods at full weight for

[29] *The Miseries of the Wiltshire Manufacturers, by a Gentleman of Wilts.* (1739).

little if anything above current prices. Many, of course, did not. Again, some employers kept their workers to their own shops in an honest endeavour to see their wages spent on groceries rather than on beer. But this was hard on the sober ones, and anyway there were never wanting publicans who would let a man get drunk any time on a pound of truck-shop tobacco or a length of truck-shop cloth.

The famous pioneer factory-spinner, Samuel Oldknow, ran a truck-shop at the beginning of the century, and paid his hands in paper money. About one-fifth of his total wages bill was settled by deductions for rent, milk, coals, meat and potatoes already supplied by him, and the balance of his tickets were mostly spent at his truck shop (known as 'Mr Downs's'). Here is what one of Oldknow's employees thought of it who was already in debt to the firm for some reason:

> Mr. Oldknow
> Sir,
>   This is to let you know that I am Extortiant in buying Mr Downs' shop goods every Article his a penny a pound dearer than I can buy at Marpor Bridge, and a menny of the Artles three hapence and 2d. worse. Sir, I should be greatley oblige to you if you'll give me a note to go to Marpor Bridge it would save me 4s. a payment and then I can pay you 4s. a payment to wards the ould monny if I ceep trading at Mr Downses I can never pay you for I can hardly gett vittles.
>   From your humble servant,
>   Thos. Austin[30]

This was a 'good' truck-shop. The worst ones were run by small masters short of money, who used the excess profits of the shop to depress wages and bolster up a shaky business. At one such shop in the Staffordshire mining district in the 1830s for example, flour cost 3s. 4d. a stone when it was 2s. 8d. elsewhere, bacon cost 9d. instead of 6d. and so on for all the basic groceries that formed the stock; it was generally reckoned in that district that being obliged to get all their goods at truck shops cost the miners four or five shillings in the pound, not counting adulteration and false weight which were very common.[31] Pay-

---

[30] G. Unwin, *Samuel Oldknow and the Arkwrights* (1924), p. 185.
[31] G. W. Hilton, *The Truck System* (1960), pp. 25–6.

days in any industrial district were famous days for all concerned, but in areas where truck was common the 'tommy-shops' would be besieged on these occasions by pathetic queues of women bringing their husbands' books to claim a week's groceries, sometimes waiting all night in the rain to get the best food out of a poor choice or to get what they wanted before stocks ran out. The lurid scene in a 'tommy-shop', the women fighting and fainting, the manager cheating and bullying, as described by Disraeli in *Sybil*, was based on evidence given before a Royal Commission on truck, and thirty years afterwards it was amply confirmed before another one that the scenes in that novel were not exaggerated.[32]

It is probable that even the ordinary markets and shops in these tough new towns would be little if any more attractive or honest or orderly, but at least their worst features were gradually eliminated by competition. What was most degrading, and indeed most sinister, about the truck system was not its more spectacular hardships, bad though these were, but its element of monopoly and compulsion. Indeed, it may be claimed that truck was not really a retailing phenomenon at all but simply a feature of the employment system. It remains, however, a flagrant example of a problem that in one form or another is always with us; that is, the chronic difficulty of establishing a free choice of consumption at a known level for all paid workers. Employers have always tended for various reasons of self-interest to interfere with consumption, from the days of livery-board-and-maintenance for servants and journeymen to the modern business executive's expense allowances and other fringe benefits. The Victorian 'tommy-shop' had very deep roots indeed, and those roots are still bearing.

[32] *ibid.*, pp. 24–5, quoting *Report of the Royal Commission on the Truck System* (1871).

XIII

<hr/>

The Second Retailing Revolution

<hr/>

The absence of concentration, of monopoly, and the existence of
a vast number of individual entrepreneurs mean that changes and
developments in retailing are not so much the result of a new
process, of years of research in the laboratories of giant firms, as
the outcome of separate decisions and actions of millions of
individual retailers. Retailing . . . is still a very small scale and
human occupation.

J. B. Jefferys and D. Knee, *Retailing in Europe*, 1961

So much has happened in retail business in the last hundred
years that to describe it in any sort of detail would require not
one chapter, but another large volume. Moreover, both the
changing social climate and some of the prominent features of
shopkeeping in this period are already familiar to the general
reader either at first- or second-hand. This last chapter, therefore, is in the nature of an epilogue. All that is attempted here
is to point out the general lines of retailing's evolution in this
period, and to speculate where it may lead us in the near future,
and the reader must provide for himself the illustrations and
examples from his own memories or from those passed on to
him by his elders.

If we compare present-day shops with those described in
previous chapters, it is evident that development has not just
continued along the old lines. It is not only a matter of there
being more and better and cheaper things to buy, or even of
there being grander and cleaner and pleasanter places in which
to buy them. The changes have been so great in the last hundred

276

years that shopping is now further removed from what it was in mid-Victorian days than it was then from the days of Elizabeth. The industrial revolution has set off a revolution in distribution which is still working itself out. Indeed, it may turn out to be a revolution that is only just beginning.

In the past hundred years, changes have occurred in two directions that seem at first sight to be rather contradictory; the process of retail selling has grown immensely simpler and less skilled, while at the same time the organization of retail trade has become much more complicated. These two trends are, of course, closely connected. Many of the most difficult things shopkeepers once had to do have been taken over by the manufacturers. The shopkeeper as a rule no longer has to find and judge and price goods and invite his customers to trust him for the result, because so many of the makers of consumer goods now regard the advertising and selling of them as very much their own concern. It is as if, in an age of mass-production, retailing has become too important to be left entirely to the retailers. Many chains of shops sell only one manufacturer's goods, such as shoes or sweets or sewing-machines or suits. An even greater number of shopkeepers do most of their business in branded commodities which advertising has already 'sold' to the customer in all but the physical handing over, and they are frankly ignorant about the contents of the sealed tins and packages for which they take the customer's money. A century ago a shopkeeper could say with conviction, 'This is a sound article,' where his descendant today only dares to say, 'We get asked for a lot of these.'

On the other hand, shopkeeping has become big business. Instead of shops consisting entirely of small private personal units, they have come increasingly into the hands of large impersonal organizations whose names are household words from one end of the country to the other, where the customer no longer deals with an independent tradesman but with a manager, a salaried employee. Only about one in five of the actual shops in the country are owned by these big concerns, but they do over half the total trade (a bigger proportion than in any other country in the world) and, what is even more important, they are still expanding, they occupy the best sites in the main shopping streets, and they set the pace, the style, the standard for all the rest.

The new shopkeeping organizations have taken a number of forms, co-operatives, multiple stores, department stores, bazaar-type stores, each with its own story of origin and development, but all stemming basically from changing social conditions, the growth in numbers and prosperity of the English people and the widening variety and increasing standardization of the available merchandise. It remains to glance briefly at the development of each of these four new forms of retailing, and then to consider how the independent shop has so far managed to keep an important place among them.

During the second half of the nineteenth century, the total number of consumers roughly doubled. Not only this, but instead of being scattered for the most part in small villages, they moved closer together into towns. And most important of all, there was a dramatic rise in the standard of living; real income per head (that is, when allowance has been made for changes in prices) is just about two and a half times as great now as it was a century ago. Up to the end of the last century the biggest effect on shopkeeping of these changes was that a real working-class demand emerged that was worth catering for: big, stable, and important for the first time. It meant a steady call for a gradually widening range of what were regarded as basic necessities from millions of households, whose weekly wages poured regularly over the shop counters in the crowded industrial areas. And if, for a long while, the individual wages were still not very big, this meant that from the shopkeepers' point of view they tended to be spent pretty much to a pattern; a changing pattern, but the change was very slow. At least up to 1914, the demands of the working class for food, clothes, furniture, smokes, newspapers, were homogeneous, predictable, concentrated, and, in the mass, enormous.

These were the conditions in which the early co-operative societies, after so many false starts, struck such firm roots and made such phenomenal growth in the second half of the nineteenth century. They did not serve—they did not try to serve—the poor who wanted credit for their half-loaves and penn'orth's of 'butterine', their ounces of tea and sugar. Such people, as Sir John Clapham remarks, 'could not afford to pay a round price for a sound article and then wait six months for a 'divi' like the substantial wage-earners and small salaried people who determined co-operative policy. . . .'[1] Co-operatives flourished best in the industrial north, and especially in the small one-industry towns, the close-knit communities round the pithead or textile mill, where by the end of the century they often almost monopolized the trade of the district. In the big commercial cities on the other hand, in places like London or Liverpool or even Manchester, not only did they have far more competition from the very beginning, but they never generated quite the same degree of earnest loyalty. Even though, in this century, the London societies grew very big, the proportion of the local wage-earners that they attracted was small compared with that of the successful pioneer societies, while even the members who did build the giant metropolitan co-operatives still spent much of their money elsewhere. This was also true, and even more curious, in industrial areas where the work was of a mixed character, or where the small employer predominated, such as the Birmingham-Coventry area or in Sheffield. And in rural districts, of course, co-operatives have always been relatively weak. So it was not a difference of class, or of earnings, or even of regions that mapped out the strong and weak spots of the co-operative movement. It was a difference of communal feeling and solidarity. 'The birth and growth of a successful co-operative store was no more determined by brazen economic laws than was the growth of an eminent private retail firm,'[2] says Clapham, but the conditions that favoured such growth were clearly distinguishable and have affected the pattern of the movement to this day.

Sir John Clapham accounts thus very clearly for the distinctive local pattern of co-operative societies, but from the point of view of retail trade as a whole, the question remains: why did shops, because they were run on co-operative lines, not merely keep going and pay their way like other shops, but rocket to such sudden and dizzy success under the leadership of the Rochdale Pioneers after 1844? Some part of the answer lies, of course, not in the realm of economics but in the history of nineteenth-century thought and the ethical appeal of the co-operative principle. But this alone is not enough to explain commercial success; high principles do not, by themselves, bring

[1] J. H. Clapham, *Economic History of Modern Britain* (1951), III, 250.
[2] *ibid.*, p. 246.

in hard cash. Moreover, the famous shop of the Pioneers in 't'owd lane' Rochdale was at first not significantly different from the scores, possibly hundreds, of others that had already tried to make a go of the same thing; the Pioneers did not invent dividends on purchases or cash payments or open membership or any other of the distinctive rules of co-operative trading.[3] But they were exceptional men, for they stumbled, more or less by accident, on two brilliant new ideas which had nothing to do with co-operation, namely vertical integration and the branch system. These two new inventions, for that is, in effect, what they were, brought them such overwhelming commercial success that they turned not only their own society but the whole co-operative movement away from its earlier preoccupation with utopian, self-supporting communities towards a concentration upon retail trading.

These two innovations, both the work of the Pioneers, were nothing less than the keys to large-scale trading, and yet it is ironical and perhaps even significant for our own day, that they came at the hands of men who were not seeking to build commercial empires. The first societies experimented with the opening of branch shops at a time when multiple-shop trading was still unknown and even single branch shops were still distrusted as unsound business. It was not profits, or even dividends, that they had in mind. The reason why they took the risk of operating branches was simply to suit the convenience of members who were already loyal customers. 'A numerously signed memorial from the members on the Castleton side of the town was presented to the Quarterly Meeting. . . . The prayer of the memorialists was granted.'[4] Here, in the words of one of the original Pioneers, was the quixotic reason why the Toad Lane store embarked on its first branch in 1856. It was soon found, apparently with some surprise, that the 'branch system' was not only a help to certain customers but a genuinely profitable business. Other societies soon followed their example and the system of widespread branches became characteristic of co-operation while it was still unknown to commercial retailers.

In a similar fashion, the Rochdale Pioneers experimented with vertical integration of the wholesale and retail functions for the

---

[3] G. D. H. Cole, *A Century of Co-operation* (1944), p. 63 ff.
[4] G. J. Holyoake, *The Rochdale Pioneers* (1857), p. 143.

benefit of the retail side of the business. In 1855 they started the Wholesale Society (known at first simply as the 'wholesale department') with their own capital and as a branch of their own business, 'with a view to supply the co-operative stores of Lancashire and Yorkshire whose small capitals do not enable them to buy in the best markets nor command the services of . . . a good buyer who knows the markets'. [5] The Wholesale Society ran at a loss for a number of years, and the Pioneers got tired of carrying other societies on their back and voted to wind it up, but were finally persuaded to persevere. Here again, they were motives of philanthropy, or at least of social principle, and not commercial foresight which were responsible for a stroke of business genius that soon proved the biggest asset of the whole co-operative movement.

In these two instances, the development of multiple branch organization and the large-scale integration made possible by the two Wholesale Societies (as well as in other less spectacular ways), the co-operative movement was the first in the field with modern methods of distribution. And this was not because it was run by keen business men. Rather the reverse. It was because it was run by people who, for reasons which had nothing to do with business, were prepared to take a completely fresh look at the consumer, to assess his changing needs and take bold and, if necessary, unconventional steps to meet them. In time, of course, the ordinary commercial traders beat the co-operative movement at this game. The co-operatives began to put profits—in the shape of dividends—before service, while their rivals have had the advantage of increasingly professional study of consumer needs.

There is not much evidence that co-operative methods in these two respects were admired or deliberately copied by other traders. But the transformation of retail trade really began when businessmen also adopted large-scale organizations for retailing. For example, during the 1870s the grocery trade began to change. Late Victorian prosperity for working people meant, first and foremost, eating more food: plain, basic groceries such as flour, tea and sugar and perishable provisions like bacon, butter, cheese and eggs, which could now all be imported cheaply from abroad. Only the co-operatives, being

[5] *ibid.*, p. 34.

progressive, sold all these under one roof, for the old-style grocer generally held aloof from handling perishable provisions which until recently had been local produce, sold like green-grocery in the local markets or occasionally, in big towns, by special provision merchants. The grocer thought of himself as a supplier of delicacies to the well-to-do.

It took a new type of retailer, prepared to operate chain-stores on a large scale, to realize the opportunities for importing the new cheap foreign provisions and selling them in the working-class districts. The new concerns just concentrated on the handful of basic foods and on selling them as cheaply as possible. They took small shops and gave to each one the same standard appearance, the same stock, the same policy. The staff had little to do but sell, for the central headquarters saw to the wholesale side, and even blended the tea, ground up and bagged the sugar, and weighed up goods into the little pound and half and quarter packages that working people wanted. Everything was sold for cash; the staff had no bills to get in, no orders to deliver, no customers' books to keep. They were free to concentrate on pushing sales by every available means, by advertisement and bargain lines and often by having a 'barker' on the pavement outside. This is how a modern writer has described them:

> The typical multiple-branch shop unit on the provisions side of the trade was not so much a shop as a simple structure for dis-tributing a limited number of articles to the public in a limited time and space. Physically, the unit was small, with one counter as the only fitting, and the main display of goods was in the open shop fronts and hanging from rails outside the shop. Most of the trade was undertaken in the evenings, the shop being open till ten or eleven p.m. and often to midnight on Saturdays, and the hissing fish-tail gas-jets or oil lamps lit up the heaped piles of eggs, the mountains of butter and margarine, the bacon, sugar and tea that customers were invited to purchase. The staff num-bered two or three, and the 'outside' man in his white serving coat would be shouting the price, value and quality of the goods, enticing and attending to customers, and handing or throwing purchases or money back to the counter for weighing, wrapping or putting in the till. . . . The mass-distribution methods certainly lacked refinement, and consumer choice and service was kept to an absolute minimum. But thanks to these organizations, and to

other representatives of the new race of retailers, commodities such as butter, eggs, tea and bacon ceased to be special luxuries on the working class table, and could be and were purchased by the working class cheaply, easily and regularly.[6]

The formula worked like a charm. Thomas Lipton started a one-man grocery shop in Glasgow in 1872; within eighteen years he had seventy branches in London, and eight years later still they had shot up to 245 all over the kingdom. He called them 'Lipton's Markets' to emphasize their character as sellers of cheaper food to the poorer sections of the community. The Home and Colonial Stores did even better with 200 branches by its tenth birthday. In the late 1880s, Lipton's alone were handling over 10 per cent of the national sales of tea. By 1913, the Maypole Dairy Company was selling about one-third of all the margarine in the country. All the big chains floated public companies to raise capital for these nation-wide operations. Some began to grow their own tea, own their own butter-creameries or manufacture their own margarine, reaching back from retailing into production to keep their shops economically supplied. Similar multiple-branch shops started up on the Continent, but in most countries the clamour of the small shopkeepers was successful in getting them suppressed by law.

The grocery trade could not stay divided for long between the old-style individual grocer serving the better-off customers and the new multiples selling a few cheap lines to the rest. The traditional grocer was soon obliged to broaden his ideas and accept fresh provisions as part of his stock-in-trade, and he gradually passed from farmhouse butter and home-cured bacon to include the imported articles in his stock as well. At the same time, the big multiple organizations were obliged to cater increasingly for the widening tastes of their working-class customers. Up to the time of the First World War, the big multiples spread at a great pace, eating up their competitors in every part of the country, but after 1918 their growth slowed down a good deal, for by then not only had the country passed the peak of the sudden growths of population and spending power, but the multiples had come up against the hard core of

[6] J. B. Jefferys, *Retail Trading in Great Britain, 1850–1950* (1954), p. 146.

the competition: the best and most business-like and most wide-awake of the small shopkeepers.

What finally brought all sorts of grocer on to common ground —and, incidentally, saved the lives of many small dealers—was the appearance of an entirely new style of commodity in the form of manufactured foods. Jars of pickles and sauces and jams, tinned goods of all kinds, packets of powder that could be turned like magic into custards and puddings and gravies and substitutes for porridge were all being made in factories. Housewives whose mothers had laid in sugar and spice and vinegar for preserving, cured their own hams, bottled their own fruit, now found that these things could be had ready-made, as good and sometimes better than the products of their own kitchens. Once again, the poorer sections of the community led the way and the fashion spread upwards. Those who had never enjoyed, because they had never been able to afford, home-preserved food, were glad enough of the crude efforts of the early food-manufacturers, while the better-off, with well-staffed and well-equipped kitchens, continued for a long while to distrust ready-processed food. The prejudice has died hard, and even today 'shop jam' is generally assumed to be inferior to any amateur effort, while tinned salmon and bottled sauce have entered into our class mythology as plebeian tastes.

In spite of this, however, by the end of the last century the qualities and varieties of manufactured and semi-prepared foods improved so fast that all the grocers were being asked for them and had to make room for them in their shops. The big jars of loose syrup and treacle, the open sacks of flour and sugar and oatmeal, the barrels of currants, the canisters of loose coffee-beans, the chests of tea, disappeared, one by one, from the saw-dusted floor of the traditional grocer and were replaced by shelves upon shelves of branded pre-packaged articles that neither mouse nor dust could corrupt nor dogs walk in and defile. For class differences nowadays, whatever may be happening to them in other contexts, are rapidly ceasing to have any meaning for the bulk of the food trades—or, indeed, for retail trade generally. The vast majority of consumers of all income groups drink the same brands of tea, and smoke the same cigarettes, and their children eat the same cornflakes just as they wear the same clothes and watch the same television sets. People with higher incomes spend more money outside shops altogether, and on different proportions of the things in them, but over a surprisingly large sector of retail trade, the goods themselves that all classes buy are becoming increasingly alike, and nowhere is this clearer than in grocery.

Of all the groceries sold in this country at present about one quarter are sold by the big multiples (that is, firms with upwards of ten branches). The co-operatives account for about another quarter. Of the remaining half, some is sold in supermarkets, department stores, dairies and so forth and the rest is the share of the independent grocer, a share which is tending to decline. The small grocer's share would almost certainly have declined still further, probably by now to insignificance, if the free play of competition had allowed the big retail organizations to go on cutting prices. But the older grocery trade as the nineteenth century understood it has now been swamped by the sale of manufactured foods, and the producers of these foods wanted as many outlets for their own brands as possible. Resale price maintenance was therefore enforced to protect the high-cost small grocer from being priced out of business by his big brothers. There are signs, moreover, that habits of voluntary resale price maintenance may prove surprisingly long lived. Never the less, big organizations will almost certainly take over much more of the field. But there is another side to the manufacturer's eagerness to get his goods onto as many shop counters as possible; while the independent grocer has in the past benefited from price control, he has also found that high-pressure advertisement and salesmanship by the makers is forcing many of the best-selling grocery goods into all sorts of other trades, into the chemist's, the greengrocer's, the dairyman's, the baker's, and of course into the department store and the supermarket.

Originally one of the minor food trades, grocery has overtaken all the others in importance, and now accounts for the same value of sales as do all the others (meat, fish, greengrocery, bakery and dairy-produce) put together. As we have seen, there have been two phases in its development. The first was the response to the rise of a mass demand, and took the form of organizing big networks of specialist shops. But before these multiples could swallow up the whole trade, the first phase came to an end; there were no new classes of consumer to conquer but instead there were increasingly different sorts of commodity to handle. In the first phase it had been a race to sell the traditional goods (imported, it is true, in hitherto undreamed-of quantities, but still familiar goods) to new kinds of customer. But in the second, the present, phase it is predominantly a competition to sell new kinds of manufactured, branded goods to the same body of customers. And here the multiple grocers derive fewer special advantages from their centralized organization. No longer is the small independent grocer their only competitor; they too are noticing that their trade is being invaded by non-grocers, some of whom are very big organizations indeed and who can dispose of prepacked, standard articles in great quantities in supermarkets or variety chain stores.

There is a tendency nowadays, widespread even among independent shopkeepers, to think of themselves as general businessmen, rather than as specialist traders and it is especially noticeable in the food trades. There is a growing tendency now, which was rare before the Second World War, to take on sidelines from half a dozen different trades. The grocer who sells wrapped bread and nylons and cigarettes; the baker who sells sweets and cooked ham and butter and cigarettes; the greengrocer who sells paraffin and tinned fruit and tinned beer and cigarettes; the dairy that sells fresh fruit and groceries and aspirins and has a cigarette and a nylons machine outside on the pavement. And increasingly the bigger ones are realizing that it is uneconomic to pay assistants to wait on customers who can very easily wait on themselves. Where it is simply a question of handing over standard articles at standard prices they are looking for ways to simplify the process of selling with self-service layouts or 'self-selection' fixtures, or automatic machines. 'Retail productivity' is the present fashionable name for cheap labour-saving methods of selling. Its possibilities are endless, and in England as yet it has scarcely begun.

And it is surely not fanciful to see all the other food trades eventually following grocery in this second form of development. In all food distribution the trend is unmistakably in the direction of some form of factory processing of the commodities to make them less perishable, more standardized, more easily handled, branded and pre-priced. The canning industry is improving the quality and variety of its goods every year. Cheap polythene has revolutionized the packing and semi-preservation of many fresh foods, from ready-cut joints of meat and ready-sliced half-pounds of bacon, to branded cakes, kippers, ground coffee and small cheeses. All these things are on sale in all sorts of shops, big and little. Compulsory pasteurization has already prolonged the life of fresh milk and so increased the outlets for it, and non-returnable paper cartons may soon put the milk-roundsman along with the bread-roundsman among the vanishing figures that once rendered consumer services. Sliced, wrapped bread from nationally advertised factories is such an astonishing post-war success that not only is it on sale everywhere but it has even crept on to the shelves of the little home-bakery alongside hot loaves straight from the oven—and often beats them into the shopping baskets.

All these new ways of buying food are familiar already, but the really great changes are only just beginning with new methods of dehydration on the one hand and the spread of refrigeration on the other. Already some sort of refrigeration unit is a commonplace in most food-shops. The back-street greengrocer in the town, for example, or the village shop, or Woolworth's, are already stocking in the 'cabinet' such diverse goods as cakes, fish, fruit, vegetables, meat, poultry, butter and made-up dishes. And as the proportion of households with refrigerators grows, the impetus to expand, and so cheapen and improve and so further expand, frozen foods will obviously be great. One is almost tempted to say that the process will snowball.

If the trend now gathering way towards more and more processing, standardizing and branding of all kinds of food is continued into the future, the purpose of specialized food-retailing will diminish. When more and more food manufacturers are mass-producing and packing and advertising more and more goods which demand no skill except the skill of quick salesman-ship from any shop that handles them, then the only way for shops largely dependent on such goods to increase their own profits will be to cut their operating costs. And the easiest way to do this is to have a big shop that sells everything and specializes in nothing except how to get the largest number of sales with the fewest assistants per cubic foot of space. Already in the United States approximately 90 per cent of all food is sold in general food-shops, and the small specialist shops have been rapidly vanishing. In this country it has been estimated that by 1970, if present trends continue, one shop in twenty will be a self-service shop of some kind, and that these will account for (among other commodities) about half our total food sales.

There are, of course, many people who deplore this tendency, people who prefer their food uncanned, uncooked, unfrozen and undried, who like their butcher to provide them personally with peculiar cuts of meat, their baker to pick them out a loaf with a burnt crust, who want to taste the cheese or pinch the lettuce before buying. But the tide of progress is set against them, and they are likely in the long run to become a dwindling minority who must pay increasingly dearly for personal idiosyncrasy.

So much for the large-scale retailing of food. In the non-food trades the story has many similarities and one big difference. On the one hand, there has been from the 'eighties onward the same quick spread of nation-wide multiple networks, each selling a limited range of cheaply priced goods to the working classes. On the other hand, there has been the birth of that most interesting of all modern retailing phenomena, the department store.

Multiple shop organizations were exceptionally successful in the nineteenth century in footwear, men's clothes, chemists' goods and sewing-machines, all of them trades where the manufacturers were making great strides in mass-production and found that it paid to control their own shops, to ensure a steady outlet for their enormous, planned production. At the same time other chains of shops were appearing whose owners were concerned only with distribution, in newspapers, for instance, and hardware and tobacco; in fact in any trade where bulk-buying and centralized organization could reduce costs. The multiple shops have gone on growing ever since and extending into one trade after another. But it is only since the First World War that they have made big strides into the last, and perhaps the most important, non-food trade, that of women's fashions, and to understand why this came so late in the day, it is necessary to consider first the rise of the department stores.

Just as the multiples may be said to be a British idea, so the department store was a French invention. The Bon Marché and the Louvre were taking shape in Paris in the 1860s when nothing of the sort was to be seen here. In London during the next two decades, the honours were divided in the race to blossom into a full department store between several existing drapers (including among others Debenham's, Swan and Edgar's, Dickens and Jones', Harvey's, Marshall and Snelgrove's and Schoolbred's), one existing grocer (Harrod's), and a handful of new arrivals like Whiteley's, the Civil Service Stores and the Army and Navy. And as was to be expected in the nineteenth century, the industrial north was well to the fore in the early days with Lewis's of Liverpool, Kendal Milne's of Manchester, and John Anderson's of Glasgow.

Each of them started as a small shop and grew larger at the hands of an enterprising individual who seized some particular chance to extend, improvised, and felt his way forward step by step. So the history of department stores is a collection of highly personal success stories. In the nineteenth century the pioneers were not conforming to any particular pattern, for there were no precedents, but once an enterprising shopkeeper reached a certain size and could see from the example of others that the supposed evils of mixing various trades under one roof could in fact be turned into positive advantages, then it was inevitable that the best and most daring of them should rush headlong to explore the possibilities of size and yet more size. Once the breakthrough was made they laid department upon department as fast as they could buy and build space, until there was nothing else they thought they could sell. 'Everything from a pin to an elephant' as William Whiteley used to boast. Not until the twentieth century did they pause to compare themselves with one another, to realize that giant must compete with giant and that they must watch one another for points. Then they began to draw nearer to a common formula, the modern Big Store, closely concerned with public relations and projecting its own image, actually employing fewer people to sell goods than to wait on customers as liftmen, doormen, vanmen, accounts staff and so forth.

There were obviously certain underlying conditions that enabled department stores to grow up when they did. Before these conditions were ripe, any number of Whiteleys or Harrods must have lived and died small struggling shopkeepers. And now these same conditions impose a certain similarity on them all, in spite of their carefully preserved personalities. From the start they all catered for middle-class customers and set out to convey to them an air of luxury, or at least of solid comfort; 'the subdued and disciplined atmosphere of a gentleman's mansion',[7] as Gordon Selfridge described it when he first came from America. Of necessity, they all arose in central positions where large numbers could reach them easily by the new means of public transport then coming into use. Physically, they grew up in an era of big technical developments in building so that not only could they afford multi-storey palaces (that would have cost a fortune only a few decades before), but they could have enormous plate-glass windows for display, and gas-lighting and novelties like lifts and cash tubes. But above all the department stores rose with the rise of the Victorian white-collar workers, the small business and salaried and professional men whose womenfolk had money to spare for a few luxuries and were gradually switching the emphasis of their housekeeping expenditure from food to other kinds of things.

Most stores started their big expansions with a popular custom attracted by genuine bargains of sound quality, and went on gradually to improve their 'tone'—though never too far or too fast. They drew enough customers to fill their huge shops by offering two new things. One was the new manufactures, particularly dress goods and accessories, and household furnishings and equipment of all kinds that were coming out of the factories in increasing quantity. The specialist shops stocked these too, of course, but the department stores always made a point of being the first in the field if they could with any novelty in any line. And the other special thing they offered the middle-class shoppers, many of whom were but newly affluent and a little inexperienced in luxury shopping, was a lavish display and a wide choice of these goods.

Suppose a newly promoted railway clerk and his wife wanted to celebrate their fresh prosperity by moving for the first time to a house with a drawing-room. They could go to a cabinet-maker and expose their ignorance and their strictly limited means, and to an upholsterer and do the same, and perhaps to a print-seller and a china-shop and an ironmonger and so forth, and wrestle with the unfamiliar problems of furnishing for them-

[7] Reginald Pound, *Selfridge* (1960), p. 29.

selves. Or they could walk round a department store and inspect the displays of many grades of chairs, carpets, curtains, find out what was the stylish thing, all clearly labelled and priced, while at the same time the sight of all sorts of other items, ornaments, pictures, mirrors, aspidistras, would suggest ideas they had never thought of, tempt them to a diversity of semi-luxuries, educate them in the pleasantest manner imaginable into wanting a higher standard of living. And department stores made the great retailing discovery that if a woman went to buy an umbrella in an umbrella shop she went home thinking about umbrellas, but if she bought it in a department store, she went home with several other 'impulse' purchases, and probably thinking about the new type of gas-lamp or clothes-wringer that she had seen.

It has often been alleged that department stores owed much of their early success to their practice of having fixed prices for goods in place of the bargaining still in vogue elsewhere. But this is not so; it implies, in any case, a transition from old to new too abrupt to be credible. In fact, fixed prices in the non-food trades came into use in respectable shops during the Napoleonic wars. This was one of the hard truths that the author of *Reminiscences of an Old Draper* had to learn when, as an expert chafferer from Whitechapel, he came into a good-class draper's in the City and found his talents wasted. He is referring to his youth before the Battle of Waterloo when he says, 'This method of business of only having one price was just then coming into vogue and all the best houses had adopted it, many of them preferring to let customers go away unserved rather than break through the rule.'[8] Haggling must have been pretty well done away with in ordinary business by mid-century. According to Valerie Pirie, *A Frenchman Sees the English in the Fifties*, a visiting Frenchman remarked that if a customer offered to bargain in London, the shop-assistant 'thinks at first that you have misunderstood him but when he understands what you are driving at, he stiffens visibly like a man of honour to whom one has made a shady proposal'.[9]

What the department stores did do, however, was to introduce into a respectable class of trade the vulgar practice of openly

---

[8] W. H. Ablett, ed. *Reminiscences of an Old Draper* (1876), p. 73.

[9] Valerie Pirie, *The Frenchman Sees the English in the Fifties*, quoted in R. S. Lambert, *The Universal Provider* (1938), p. 26.

marking or ticketing goods with their price—a practice that has not even yet penetrated to shops with pretensions to being really exclusive. But the department stores as a rule made a virtue not only of displaying their wares as openly as possible but of boldly pricing them for all to see. Their large-scale purchases enabled them to sell cheaply and they were not ashamed in their early days to make price one of their selling points. 'Store prices' were a by-word for cheapness.

The lines they concentrated on were fashion goods, things that shoppers were prepared to come some distance for and to take some time and trouble in choosing. Ideas of fashion or style were only beginning in Victoria's reign to mean something to middle-class people; hitherto, 'fashionable' society had meant a very small *élite*. Stout quality and long wear were the virtues that even well-to-do people most admired in clothes and furniture and indeed in all their possessions, so that popular styles hardly changed from one decade to another. The department stores were at least partly responsible for the way the middle classes gradually became fashion conscious. They helped to create the demands for which they catered with their ever-changing windows and shop-displays emphasizing 'novelty' and 'up-to-dateness' and 'the latest from the manufacturers'. In a sense they were pulling themselves up by their own boot-straps, for the palatial surroundings, the high degree of service, the sheer quantity and variety of merchandise were all somewhat better than the prices seemed to warrant or than the customers were altogether used to. They were awed and flattered and before they knew it they were influenced and persuaded. Long before the cinema or broadcasting existed, the department stores were helping to mould the tastes of the rising middle class. And they began also to guide people's steps towards the important new concept of obsolescence; they were the first preachers of the modern creed that goods ought to be replaced when they are outdated rather than when they are outworn.

It has always been the role of department stores to try to cultivate a characteristic atmosphere, even a certain glamour; they have been able to afford carpeted floors and rest-rooms, live Father Christmases in winter, roof gardens in summer. They offer the customer more than mere goods and the customer has been willing to pay the price. 'You know why they come here?' remarked Gordon Selfridge watching the crowds trooping into his store. 'It's so much brighter than their own homes. This is not a shop—it's a community centre.'[10] Selfridge was proud of this, but a more far-sighted man might have noticed the same thing with misgiving, for profits, after all, are made out of business not out of social institutions. Between the wars the era of department store expansion came to an end, and it is now many years since any big newcomer joined their ranks. The advantages of sheer size on a single site seemed to have reached a limit. Stores strove even harder to attract more customers on to the premises where they would be tempted to buy. The advertising, the store-decorations, the sales events, became extravagantly costly. But the days of their supremacy were over, for new and powerful rivals were appearing.

Up to the time of the First World War, women's and children's clothes were still mostly home-made or dressmaker-made. The department stores had taken the lead in introducing ready-made goods, and because of their size they had been able to place big orders with the makers and so buy cheaply, or even to manufacture for themselves in their own workrooms. For many years the small draper could not attempt to compete with them in fashion goods. But gradually, the difficulties were solved of manufacturing women's clothing on mass-production lines and yet in the latest styles and with plenty of variety. The 'rag-trade' arose—a modern soubriquet for a modern industry—and at the same time, the taste for bigger wardrobes more frequently renewed was spreading to all classes of society. At last the conditions were ripe for the spread of cheap fashion multiples; they began between the two World Wars and since 1945 have gone ahead at a tremendous pace.

Some of these new multiple networks began by specializing in underwear and accessories and others in selling outer garments, but soon most of them were selling both. In their chosen lines their branches can carry nearly as big a selection of up-to-date goods as the corresponding department of a big store. They concentrate on the popular standard lines, ordered in quantity by highly paid experts in fashion trends. Anything likely to hang fire in the shops such as odd sizes, goods outside the

[10] Pound, *op. cit.*, p. 107.

U

popular price range or for minority tastes are rigidly avoided. And while they enjoy the advantages of large-scale organization, their small shops are a good deal less costly to run than a huge store. They need no doormen, or lift-men, no nurses or store detectives on their payroll.

The development of really efficient large-scale multiples in the fashion trade, and perhaps to a lesser extent in the furnishing trades, has hit the department stores in the most vital place, for clothes account for roughly half the business of the average store, and durable household goods for another quarter. At present the customer is getting the benefit of the fairly intense competition between these two kinds of big organization in catering for women's fashions, but the rivalry takes place largely out of sight in the buying departments. Now that mass-production has at last come to the fashion trades, the buying sphere is all important to the big organizations.

At the beginning of this century, the department store was a big concern, a colossus. It is so no longer, for ideas of scale have changed. In its heyday, it was a big buyer *vis-à-vis* its suppliers; it gained heavy discounts on its big orders, could exact good terms for the privilege of its custom, and could suggest or even dictate details of finish and style to suit its own customers. In 1886, for instance, Lewis's of Liverpool bought direct from the makers a quarter of a million felt hats in a year and sold them at 3s. 11d. instead of the usual 6s. 6d. The Hat and Cap Traders Association threatened to boycott Lewis's and have all their supplies of hats cut off but, 'Lewis's sell more hats in a week than most middlemen can buy in a month, and the Manufacturers know too well who are their best Customers to allow themselves to be dictated to in that manner'.[11] Things are different now. The manufacturers have themselves grown bigger, the wholesalers have grown bigger, the stores' rivals in the fashion trade, the multiple shop organizations, have grown bigger even faster. The once proud department store, unless it merges its valuable identity in a group, is no longer cock of the walk in the buying sphere. 'In fact, the average department store,' says Mr Pasdermadjian, 'is not, as regards buying, a large-scale establishment, but a collection of selling departments

[11] Asa Briggs, *Friends of the People* (1956), pp. 45–6.

in each of which retailing is carried out on a relatively small scale.'[12]

In tracing the recent development of food retailing just now we saw that the rapid growth of nation-wide multiple networks, each selling particular foods, was now halted, but that a new-comer on the scene, still young but with a promising future, was a food retailer whose specialism was not any particular kind of food but a way of selling it, that is self-service. In the non-food trades there is, of course, a corresponding trend, but already much further developed and gaining ground even faster, and that is the bazaar type of shop, or, as it is sometimes called, the variety chain store. This new departure stems originally from the radical experiment of F. W. Woolworth and his Five-and Ten-Cent stores which need no describing. His lead was soon followed in this country by Marks and Spencer's Penny Bazaars and others, and today his followers include a handful of very big organizations indeed.

There are about 1,500 variety chain stores in the United Kingdom, and they all have three things in common with the original Woolworth's. One is, they stock many kinds of mer-chandise, that is to say they rely on variety as one of their main attractions, but confine their stock to quick-selling goods which need the minimum of fitting or explanation or any knd of sales-service. (How quickly goods can move into this category may be instanced by the fact that Woolworth's now sell radios, men's trousers, garden plants.) The second is, they avoided when necessary, brands subject to resale price mainten-ance, preferring to buy, or if necessary even to make, alternatives that could be sold cheaper. The third is, they lay open and price every article so that the customer can inspect it, handle it, and do for himself the work of finding and comparing without calling on the assistants' time for anything but wrapping and taking money. The variety chain store aims to be the complete anti-thesis of the old-fashioned upper-class shop that competes on service but not on price.

These bazaar shops have been carefully designed to cut the element of personal service to a minimum; credit and delivery services are not offered. On the other hand, busy customers often

[12] H. Pasdermadjian, *The Department Store* (1954), p. 152.

find that for routine purchases the bazaar type of shop is quicker and more efficient. Many people enjoy the strictly impersonal atmosphere which, even more than that of a department store, enables them to inspect goods and not buy them, without explanation or embarrassment. The success of the variety chain stores has been very marked since the last war; in the 1957 Census of Distribution it was shown that people in the United Kingdom did 5·8 per cent of all their shopping in department stores, and nearly as much, 5·4 per cent, in variety chain stores. And it is interesting to notice that as much as a further 3 per cent is now done through the newest form of shopping, by post through the big mail-order houses. The modern mail-order business resembles the variety chain store in many ways. One firm at least, Littlewoods, runs both. They have the same cheap, popular, varied stocks and they offer the same freedom to choose at leisure without the attentions of a salesman. As one of the spokesmen for the mail-order business remarked, 'We are, after all, a portable Marks and Spencer's.'

In the United States, where price competition between shopkeepers is much freer, the so-called discount houses sell a wide range of household goods such as radios, washing-machines, beds, as well as innumerable less expensive items in big, bazaar-like premises where the customer inspects and selects for himself from the stock on show with the minimum of service from the assistants. These stores depend on small profit-margins and a high turnover. They have been called 'warehouses with pay-check exits'—that is, places not deserving the name of shop—and this is not a bad description. It also reminds one that they need a great deal of space. Groups of these stores with similar selling techniques form extensive shopping centres on the outskirts of towns and a largely car-borne consuming public find such locations and the spacious layouts that they permit, a positive convenience.

Attempts to copy the discount store in this country met with fierce opposition for many years from the interests favouring resale price maintenance, especially the manufacturers of expensive durable goods. And there are other reasons—lack of space, for example—why thorough-going self-service methods will not progress nearly so far or so fast in Britain. But in many lines there are approximations to it, variously called 'preselection' or 'semi-self-service', based on the principle of pricing and arranging goods in such a way that the customers can help themselves and save the time and wages of shop assistants. Some multiple shoe-shops, for instance, expect women customers to select a style and price that suits them, from a big display, and only approach the sales staff for a fitting in a particular number. Other shoe-shops have tried giving the customers a free run of innumerable left-hand shoes and only when the customer has found a suitable price, style and fitting for herself, accepted her money and supplied her with a matching shoe. In C. & A. Modes, customers take gowns from open racks, try them on themselves in fitting-rooms and then either return them to the racks or to the wrapping and payment counter. The same trends towards simplified selling are apparent on all sides. Not all attempts to introduce such methods are skilful enough to be successful, but the shopkeepers and the public are learning fast.

Here, then, are the outstanding features of the past hundred years of rapid change in shopkeeping. But all this leaves a big question mark. What about the small independent retailers who run most of our shops; how have they stood out so long and so well against their big competitors who have still captured little more than half of the total trade? Out of every twenty shops in Britain today, approximately three belong to the big organizations, another three to local firms with several branches, and the remaining fourteen are all independent small single shops (including no fewer than six with a vestigial turnover of less than £100 a week). This seems an astonishingly high proportion of independent shops to anyone who thinks of the appearance of the typical local High Street where the big names predominate. But many single shops are not in the busy thoroughfares; they are scattered among the houses in the side-streets and residential suburbs so that their great numbers are seldom realized. Some are busy and efficient establishments in good positions whose owners hold their own against their big competitors by taking intelligent advantage of the chance to meet the peculiar needs of their own locality, for their stock and trading policy can be much more personal and flexible than those of a branch manager, and some of the more enterprising small shopkeepers are now taking advantage of bulk-buying by joining together in buying groups set up for the purpose. Other owners of single shops sell very special goods, cameras, for instance, or pictures, or antiques, or electrical goods, and rely for their success on their own skill and reputation as specialists. This is the oldest shopkeeping style of all, of course, and it is noticeable that it is reserved nowadays for the sale of goods that have come onto the market—or come onto it in any numbers —fairly recently.

But many other single shops, perhaps even a majority, are not efficient in either of these senses. They are often the ones where a family lives over a shop and all the members help to run it, where the family's rent and food bills are muddled into the shop's accounting and where father often fits in a part-time job to help out the total income. In such shops profitability, in the businessman's sense, has no meaning, although when the motives that lead their owners to work very long hours for small returns are viewed as a whole, they are seen to be reasonable enough. In the past it was possible for anyone to open a shop wherever he wished, and in all the older parts of towns, wherever there are closely built-up streets of terrace houses, innumerable isolated shops have at some past time been started in someone's front parlour or built out over the front garden. Small shops, these, with a limited but regular custom from the surrounding houses, and offering great convenience to people who want things frequently or in a hurry. Food-shops and tobacconist-newsagents predominate, with the occasional draper or chandlery-hardware dealer, but a very large number style themselves 'general' shops and stock a variety of day-to-day needs that would do credit to a village shop in the heart of the country.

This scatter of little shops among the houses was not allowed on the new housing estates built after 1918. Here small shops were built along with the houses in parades of half a dozen or so, of uniform size and each rented as a rule to a different trade. Often they are a long way from the nearest real shopping centre, and each shop has therefore very little competition. The big multiples secured some of them from the start, but most are private single shops doing well for their owners and tending to stay in their hands.

The survival of all these various kinds of small shops dotted about in residential areas, many of them doing a ludicrously small business, often inefficient and wasteful by modern standards, suggests that there is more to retail trade than the survival of the fittest. Dr F. D. Klingender discovered when he made a close study of a hundred independent shopkeepers in Hull, that three-quarters of them worked upwards of a 64-hour week for very meagre rewards; indeed, their motives for starting to keep shops were extremely varied and their rewards seem to have included almost everything except money.[13] But even though so many of them compete with the big efficient retailers by exploiting themselves and their families, the results are not cheap for the consumer. How, then, do they survive?

As has already been said, the practice of resale price maintenance at levels which give a bigger margin of retail profit than the efficient retailer requires has had the effect of helping to prop up the wasteful and inefficient shops, and this alone has helped many to survive. Yet even when there is no question of fixed sale prices of branded goods, the small man often gives the customer something she badly needs and can get only from him, and that is service on, or at least near, her own doorstep.

A hundred years ago, housewives or their servants thought little of walking a few miles for even their basic household shopping. They bought fewer varieties of things, and in bigger quantities. They would have been ashamed of a kitchen cabinet so small that it needed replenishing several times a week, and the attitude of 'slipping out to the shops' for each day's needs would have been taken as the mark of disgraceful improvidence. But the habit of frequent small purchases has, like so many other habits of the poor, gone up the social scale, and now a majority— probably a large majority—of housewives shop for small things nearly every day, while their husbands buy papers and cigarettes daily and their children visit the sweet-shop even oftener. For branded, mass-produced goods the best shop is usually the most convenient one, as it is for many other things wanted at short intervals.

'Economists may argue as to the exact reasons which determine price policies and may help us to understand why differences arise, but the simple fact which strikes the consumer is that the

13 F. D. Klingender, *The Little Shop* Bureau of Current Affairs (1951).

price charged in the corner shop is often just that little bit more than the price charged in the centre of town. While the housewife may constantly grumble about it she is not sufficiently irritated to forego the convenience of the corner shop for the coppers that may be saved by travelling further afield.[14]

In times gone by, when an enterprising couple in a back street took down their curtains, filled their parlour window with goods, opened their front door and called themselves a shop, they were offering the public in their immediate neighbourhood as valuable a service in their way as Messrs Whiteley or Woolworth or the Rochdale Pioneers did in theirs.

The pattern of retailing that has grown up in this country is enormously varied and flexible, almost certainly more so than anywhere else. Government interference with the activities of shopkeepers, as distinct from control over the quality of the goods they sell, has up to now been minimal. (The Shop Acts which confuse hours of work with hours of opening are an unhappy exception.) Consequently the chief controls that shop-keepers have felt have been those imposed by their suppliers, often arbitrary and undesirable but not, in their total effect, restrictive. The present abundance of shops and of different kinds of shops benefits everyone, for virtually everyone is a shopper of some sort. What streamlined, rational system of distribution would put a sweet-shop in the path of nearly every schoolchild in the early morning, or enable so large a proportion of the working class to buy fish and chips a few yards from their doorstep in the late evening, still less put a street market beside Waterloo Bridge to serve the office workers of the South Bank in their lunch-hour?

But the present variety and multiplicity of shops is an anachronism. It will not be allowed to last and it is not desirable that it should. The conveniences that we all enjoy from having so many shops are paid for heavily in other ways, not always willingly or knowingly and not always in the price of goods. The ending of resale price maintenance will inevitably weed out many of the least efficient (though not necessarily the smallest) shopkeepers, and the process of competitive elimination, once begun, can be expected to go on for a great many years. But in the long run, a more decisive influence on the shape of retail

[14] Wilfred Burns, *British Shopping Centres* (1959), p. 22.

trade is likely to be that of the town-planning authorities, for today people can no longer please themselves where they will set up a shop. Even between the wars there grew up a strong resistance in new residential areas to the untidy, old-style 'corner shop' and to the conversion of houses into retail premises, and nowadays local town-planning authorities have complete control over the position of all new shops and very often control over their size, car-access and parking facilities and hence over the general nature of their business as well. They can also, through zoning schemes and compulsory purchase orders, sometimes end the lives of existing shops, although they seldom do it.

Trade, however, is never channelled into new directions without causing a good deal of personal hardship, and deliberate reforms as acts of public policy are bound to proceed slowly. So it will be a long time before planners can re-site, for example, the many badly-placed shopping centres in the inner suburbs of big towns. Many of these have survived great changes in the districts they originally served, but having acquired a life and reputation of their own, they now draw customers from far afield into congested areas where there are no proper facilities for either private or public transport where pedestrians overflow from the pavements, endangering their own necks as persistently as they obstruct fast-moving traffic, where there is no room to build the large modern stores of today. Such focal points of retail trade, especially if viewed on a busy Saturday afternoon, may look too firmly embedded in the city's life to be given marching orders. Probably they are. But trade, even retail trade, never stands still, and although the powers of the planners are largely negative, the cumulative effect of thousands of small planning decisions to permit or to refuse proposed new shops to be built, is bound in the end to have very great effect indeed.

And what will the planning authorities use as a yardstick? They will probably have to pronounce life or death on the eccentric proposals of some Whiteley or Woolworth of the future. Will they always recognize a genius when he comes asking to put up an unorthodox building in an unconventional place? Almost certainly not, but mistakes are inevitably the price of progress in town planning as in any other field. What is not inevitable, however, is that such important and perhaps far-reaching decisions should have to be taken in the dark. Shopping habits and needs are highly complex, bound up as they are with technical and traditional and domestic situations and changing along with them. But town planners are obliged to rely too much on their personal guesses about consumers, instead of on facts.

How far do different sorts of people travel now to buy a camera or a cabbage or a carpet? Even more important, why do they choose to shop where they do? How much importance do they attach to price or choice or service or convenience, and how far are they consistent or merely habit-ridden in these supposed motives? How far are all our ideas on these questions irrational, out of date, and capable of being formed along more constructive lines if only we could hear any voice above the special pleading of the advertiser? There is an almost total absence of reliable information or of informed public opinion about what we want from our shops today, and about how they should be shaping for the future.

Select Bibliography

ANON. *The Charitable Physician* (1639).

ANON. *Sea-cole, Cher-cole* (1644).

ANON. *The Ladies' Cabinet* (1667).

ANON. *Reasons Humbly Offered by Trading Housekeepers* . . (1675).

ANON. *The Trade of England Revived and the Abuses thereof Rectified* (1681).

ANON. *General Considerations Relating to Trade* (1694).

ANON. *Further Reasons for Suppressing all Pedlars and Hawkers* (late 17th cent.)

ANON. *The Case of the Fair Trader* (early 18th cent.)

ANON. *An Essay to Prove that Regrators, Engrossers and Forestallers* . . . (1718).

ANON. *An Act to Punish Pedlars* (1725).

ANON. *Brief State of the Inland or Home Trade* (1730).

ANON. *The Case of the Shopkeepers etc. Against Hawkers and Pedlars* (1730).

ANON. *The Pleasant Art of Money Catching* (1737).

ANON. *The Miseries of the Wiltshire Manufacturers, by a Gentleman of Wiltshire* (1739).

ANON. *The Hard Case of the Retail Traders Invaded by Hawkers* (1741).

ANON. *Frauds and Abuses of the Coal Dealers* (1743).

ANON. *Apology for Pawnbroking* (1744).

ANON. *The General Shop Book* (1753).

ANON. *Considerations in the Case of the Bakers* (1757).

ANON. *The Tradesman's Director* (1757).

ANON. *Poison Detected* (1757).

ANON. *Low Life; or, One Half of the World Knows Not How the Other Half Lives* (1764).

ANON. *Considerations on Taxes as They are Supposed to Affect the Price of Labour* (1765).

ANON. *The Book of Trades* (1821).

ANON. *The Shopkeeper's Guide* (1853).

ANON. *A Handy Guide for the Draper and Haberdasher* (1864).

ANON. 'Old English Cookery' (*Quarterly Review*, 1894).

W. H. ABLETT (ed.) *Reminiscences of an Old Draper* (1876).

W. ADDISON *English Fairs and Markets* (1953).

W. J. ASHLEY *The Bread of Our Forefathers* (1928).

J. ASHTON *Social Life in the Reign of Queen Anne* (1882).
—— *Old Times* (1885).

G. AYLMER 'The Last Years of Purveyance' (*Econ. Hist. Rev.*, new series X, 1959–60).

F. E. BALDWIN *Sumptuary Legislation and Personal Regulation in England* (1926).

S. BAMFORD *Early Days* (1849).

J. N. BARTLETT 'Some Aspects of the Economy of York in the Late Middle Ages' (unpublished London Ph.D thesis, 1958).

T. BASTON *Thoughts on Trade and a Public Spirit* (1716).

T. BECON *The Jewel of Joy* (1564).

N. CURTIS-BENNETT *The Food of the People* (1949).

M. W. BERESFORD 'The Common Informer, the Penal Statutes, and Economic Regulation' (*Econ. Hist. Rev.*, new series, X, 1958).

W. BESANT *London in the Time of the Tudors* (1903).

W. BEVERIDGE *Prices and Wages in England* (1940).

Beverley Town Manuscripts, Historical Manuscripts Commission (1900).

J. BICKERDYKE *The Curiosities of Ale and Beer* (1886).

J. BLACKMAN 'The Food Supply of an Industrial Town' (*Business History*, V, 1963).

R. W. BLENCOWE *Household Accounts of Timothy Burrell of Cuckfield 1683–1711* (Sussex Archeol. Collections, 1850).

M. E. BOHANNON 'A London Bookseller's Bill' (*The Library*, 4th ser., XVIII, 1938).

CHARLES BOOTH *Life and Labour of the People of London, series 2, Vol. III—Industry* (1902).

NICHOLAS BRETON *Fantastickes* (1626).

ASA BRIGGS *Friends of the People* (1956).

BUCKINGHAM. 'Household Accounts of the Duke of Buckingham, 1507–08' (*Archeolægia*, XXV, 1834).

R. BULKELEY 'A Seventeenth Century Diary' (*Trans. Anglesey Antiq. Soc.*, 1930).

J. H. BURN *A Descriptive Catalogue of Tradesmen's Tokens* (1853).

W. BURNS *British Shopping Centres* (1959).

R. CAMPBELL *The London Tradesman* (1747).

R. W. CHAMBERS & M. DAUNT *A Book of London English, 1384–1425* (1931).

A. CLARK *The Life and Times of Anthony Wood* (1891).

G. D. H. COLE *A Century of Co-operation* (1944).

P. COLQUHOUN *A Treatise on the Police of the Metropolis* (1796).

COSIN *Bishop Cosin's Correspondence* (ed. G. Ornsby, Surtees Society, 1870).

G. G. COULTON *Social Life in Britain from the Conquest to the Reformation* (1918).

—— *The Medieval Village* (1925).

—— *Medieval Panorama* (1938).

J. M. COWPER (ed.) *The Diary of Thomas Cocks, Cathedral Auditor* (1901).

H. CURWEN *History of Booksellers* (1873).

G. W. DANIELS *Early History of the English Cotton Industry* (1920).

M. G. DAVIES *The Enforcement of English Apprenticeship 1563-1642* (1956).

J. DAVIS 'London Goldsmiths in the Sixteenth Century' (*History*, XVI, 1932).

J. DAW *A Sketch of the History of the Worshipful Company of Butchers* (1869).

D. DEFOE *The Review*, 8th and 31st January 1713.

—— *Colonel Jack* (1722).

—— *Tour through the Whole Island of Great Britain* (1724–7).

—— *The Complete English Tradesman* (1727).

THOMAS DEKKER *The Gull's Hornbook* (1609).

J. DRUMMOND & A. WILBRAHAM *The Englishman's Food* (1939).

E. GORDON DUFF *Account Book of Jas. Wilding, an Undergraduate 1682-88* (Oxford Hist. Soc. Collectanea, 1885).

O. J. DUNLOP *English Apprenticeship and Child Labour* (1912)

JOHN DUNTON *Life and Errors of John Dunton* (1705).

JOHN EARLE *Microcosmographie* (1628).

F. M. EDEN *The State of the Poor* (1797).

G. ELAND *The Purefoy Letters* (1931).

H. ELLIS (ed.) *The Obituary of Richard Smyth* (Camden Society, 1849).

F. G. EMMISON *Jacobean Household Inventories* (Bedford Hist. Record Soc., 1938).

PETER ERONDELL *The French Garden* (1605).

Fabian Tract No. 80: Shop Life and its Reform (1897).

F. W. FAIRHOLT *On Tobacco* (1859).

CELIA FIENNES *Through England on a Sidesaddle* (1888).

F. J. FISHER 'The Development of the London Food Market, 1540–1640' (*Econ. Hist. Rev.*, V, 1935).

—— 'The Development of London as a Centre of Conspicuous Consumption' (*Trans. Royal Hist. Soc.*, 4th ser., XXX, 1948).

E. FLOWER *Hours of Business* (1843).

FELIX FOLIO (J. PAGE) *Hawkers and Street Traders of Manchester and the North* (1858).

—— *The Story of the Manchester Fairs* (1887).

G. E. FUSSELL 'London Cheesemongers in the Eighteenth Century' (*Economic History*, 1928).

—— *The English Rural Labourer* (1949).

F. W. GALTON & B. WEBB *The Tailoring Trades* (1923).

JOHN GAY 'Trivia' (*Poetical Works*, ed. John Underhill, 1893).

D. M. GEORGE *London Life in the Eighteenth Century* (1925).

W. H. GODFREY *Colsoni's Guide de Londres*, 1693 (1951).

A. W. GOULD *History of the Fruiterers' Company* (1912).

N. S. B. GRAS *The Evolution of the English Corn Market* (1915).

J. GRAY *The Policy of the Tax on Retailers Considered* (1786).

N.H. *The Compleat Tradesman* (1684).

HALIFAX Household Expenses of Lord Halifax (Public Record Office, SP 9–48).

W. N. HANCOCK *Competition between Large and Small Shops* (1851).

J. HARLAND (ed.) *The Autobiography of William Stout of Lancaster* (1851).

M. DORMER HARRIS (ed.) *The Coventry Leet Book* (Early English Text Society, 1907).

W. HARRISON *Description of England* (ed. Fl. J. Furnivall, 1877).

EDWARD HATTON *A New View of London* (1708).

AMBROSE HEAL *London Tradesmen's Cards of the Eighteenth Century* (1925).

—— *The Signboards of Old London Shops* (1947).

—— *London Furniture Makers from the Restoration to the Victorian Era* (1953).

W. HERBERT *History of the Twelve Great Livery Companies* (1836–37).

G. W. HILTON *The Truck System, 1465–1960* (1960).

C. HINDLEY *The Life and Adventures of a Cheap Jack* (1876).

—— *The Life and Times of James Catnach* (1878).

—— *The History of the Cries of London* (1884).

P. C. HOFFMAN *They Also Serve: the Story of the Shopworkers* (1949).

CLAUDE HOLLYBANDE *The French Lyttelton* (1573).

G. J. HOLYOAKE *The Rochdale Pioneers* (1857).

W. HONNYWELL 'Diary, 1596–1614' (*The Antiquary*, XXVI, 1892).

House of Commons Journals, XXV, XL, XLI, XLIV, LVIII.

HOWARD. *Household Book of Lord William Howard* (ed. G. Ornsby: Surtees Society, 1877).

J. HOWELL *Londonopolis* (1657).

P. HUDSON *On Trade* (1761).

E. HUGHES *North Country Life in the Eighteenth Century* (1952).

W. HUTTON *The Life of William Hutton* (1816).

C. JACKSON (ed.) *Yorkshire Diaries* (Surtees Society, 1875).

JAMES JACKSON 'The Diary of a Cumberland Farmer, 1650–1683' (*Trans. Cumb. & Westm. Antiq. Soc., New Series*, XXI, 1921)

JAMES I, KING *Counterblast to Tobacco* (1604).

N. J. BRETT-JAMES *The Growth of Stuart London* (1935).

M. JAMES *Social Problems and Policy during the Puritan Revolution* (1930).

J. B. JEFFERYS *Retail Trading in Britain, 1850–1950* (1954).

—— and D. KNEE *Retailing in Europe* (1961).

A. H. JOHNSON *The History of the Worshipful Company of Drapers* (1914–1922).

ERASMUS JONES *Luxury, Pride and Vanity, the Bane of the British Nation* (1750).

A. V. JUDGES (ed.) *The Elizabethan Underworld* (1930).

J. R. KELLETT 'The Breakdown of Gild and Corporation Control over the Handicraft and Retail Trades of London' (*Econ. Hist. Rev.*, X, 1958).

Kenyon Manuscripts, Historical Manuscripts Comm. (1894).

F. D. KLINGENDER *The Little Shop* (1951).

CHARLES KNIGHT (ed.) *London* (1842).

JAMES LACKINGTON *Memoirs of the First Forty-Five Years* (1830).

F. M. T. LAMB (ed.) *Diary of Thomas Turner, 1754–1765* (1925).

G. LAMBERT *History of the Barbers Company* (1881).

J. M. LAMBERT *Two Thousand Years of Gild Life* (1891).

R. S. LAMBERT *The Universal Provider: The Story of Whiteley's* (1938).

MERITON LATROON *The English Rogue* (1668–69).

J. LAWLER 'Book Auctioneers and Auctions in the 17th Century' (*The Antiquary*, XIX, 1889).

J. LARWOOD & J. C. HOTTEN *A History of Signboards* (1866).

W. W. LEMPRIERE (ed.) *John Howes Manuscript, 1582* (1904).

E. M. LEONARD *The Early History of English Poor Relief* (1900).

M. LETTS *As the Foreigner Saw Us* (1935).

H. LEVY *The Shops of Britain* (1948).

H. LONG *The Oglander Memoirs* (1888).

D. LUPTON 'London and the Country Carbonadoed' (*Harleian Miscellany*, Vol. IX, 1812).

P. V. MCGRATH 'The Marketing of Food in London in the 17th Century' (unpublished London M.A. thesis, 1948).

N. MCKENDRICK 'Josiah Wedgwood: an Eighteenth Century Entrepreneur in Salesmanship and Marketing Techniques' (*Econ. Hist. Rev.*, XII, 1959–60).

J. H. MACMICHAEL *The History of Charing Cross* (1906).

W. MAITLAND *A History and Survey of London* (1756).

J. P. MALCOLM *Anecdotes of the Manners and Customs of London in the 18th Century* (1808).

DR. MANNING *The Nature of Bread* (1758).

GERVASE MARKHAM *The English Housewife* (1631).

—— *The Way to Get Wealth* (1638).

DOROTHY MARSHALL *English People in the Eighteenth Century* (1956).

P. MATHIAS *English Trade Tokens* (1962).

H. J. MATTHEW *Shops or Stores* (1879).

HENRY MAYHEW *London Labour and the London Poor* (1861).
—— *Shops and Companies of London, and Trades and Manufactures of Great Britain* (1865).
C. MERRETT *The Frauds and Abuses of the Apothecaries* (1670).
C. MIEGE *The Present State of Great Britain* (1707).
LADY GRACE MILDMAY 'An Elizabethan Journal' (*Quarterly Review*, 1911).
R. J. MITCHELL & M. D. R. LEYS *A History of London Life* (1958).
GILES MOORE 'Diary of the Rev. Giles Moore, 1665–1679' (*Sussex Arch. Soc. Trans.*, 1848).
H. MORLEY *Memoirs of Bartholomew Fair* (1874).
FYNES MORISON *Itinerary Containing Ten Years Travels'* (1907).
F. A. MUMBY *The Romance of Bookselling* (1910).
THOMAS NASHE *Works* (ed. R. B. McKerrow, 1903-10).
L. NEAL *Retailing and the Public* (1932).
J. U. NEF *The Rise of the British Coal Industry* (1932).
H. NEVILLE *Newes from the New Exchange* (1650).
P. K. NEWMAN 'The Early London Clothing Trades' (*Oxford Economic Papers*, new series, IV, 1952).
J. NICHOLS *Illustrations of the Manners and Expenses of Antient Times in England* (1797).
ROGER NORTH *Lives of the Norths* (1826).
W. H. OVERALL *Analytical Index to the Remembrancia of the City of London* (1878).
ROBERT OWEN *The Life of Robert Owen, by Himself* (ed. M. Beer, 1920).
Parliamentary Papers: Select Committee on Manufactures and Trade (1833).
—— *Royal Commission on Market Rights and Tolls* (1891).
H. PASDERMADJIAN *The Department Store* (1954).
PASTON *The Paston Letters* (ed. J. Gairdner, 1900).
H. PEACHAM 'The Art of Living in London', 1642 (*Harleian Miscellany*, Vol. IX, 1812).
A. PEARCE *History of the Butchers' Company* (1929).
N. PENNEY (ed.) *The Household Account Book of Sarah Fell, 1673–1678* (1921).
S. PEPYS *Diary* (ed. H. Wheatley, 1923–29).
THOMAS PERCY (ed.) *The Northumberland Household Book* (1905)
'Petition to the Lord Mayor of London', 1689 (Brit. Mus. 816.1.43)
The Vision of Piers Plowman (ed. N. Coghill, 1949).
FRANCIS PLACE Place MSS., British Museum.
THOMAS PLATTER *Travels in England, 1599* (ed. C. H. Williams, 1937).
R. POUND *Selfridge* (1960).
C. POVEY *A Discovery of Indirect Practices in the Coal Trade* (1700).
—— *The Unhappiness of England as to its Trade* (1701).

E. POWER & M. M. POSTAN (eds.) *English Trade in the Fifteenth Century* (1933).

R. HILTON PRICE 'Signs of Old London' (*London Topographical Record*, 1907).

W. H. PRIOR *Notes on the Weights and Measures of Medieval England* (1924).

W. H. QUARREL & M. MARE *London in 1710* (1934).

T. F. REDDAWAY *The Rebuilding of London after the Great Fire* (1940).

H. T. RILEY (ed.) *Liber Albus* (Rolls Series, 1859).

—— *Memorials of London and London Life in the 13th, 14th and 15th Centuries* (1868).

W. ROBERTS *The Early History of Bookselling* (1890).

A. B. ROBERTSON 'The Open Market in the City of London' (*East London Papers*, I, 1958).

—— 'The Suburban Food Markets in 18th Century London' (*East London Papers*, II, 1959).

C. B. ROBINSON (ed.) *Best's Farming Book, 1641* (Surtees Society, 1857).

E. F. ROBINSON *The Early History of Coffee Houses in England* (1893).

S. VON LA ROCHE *Sophie in London* (1786).

J. E. THOROLD ROGERS *A History of Agriculture and Prices in England* (1866–82).

—— *Six Centuries of Work and Wages* (1912).

K. ROGERS *Old London: Cheapside and Poultry* (1931).

—— *Old London: Cornhill and Around* (1935).

S. ROWLANDS *The Letting of Humour's Blood in the Head Vaine* (1600).

Roxburghe Ballads (ed. W. Chappell, 1871).

R. RUDING *Annals of the Coinage of Great Britain* (1900).

Rutland Manuscripts, Historical Manuscripts Commission, IV (1905).

W. B. RYE *England as Seen by Foreigners in the Reigns of Elizabeth and James I* (1865).

E.S. *The Compleat Housewife* (1729).

W. L. SACHSE (ed.) *Diary of Roger Lowe, 1663–74* (1938).

L. F. SALZMAN *English Life in the Middle Ages* (1927).

—— *English Trade in the Middle Ages* (1931).

A. L. SIMON *History of the Wine Trade in England* (1906).

—— *Bottlescrew Days* (1926).

J. T. SMITH *Etchings of Remarkable Beggars* (1815).

—— *The Cries of London* (1839).

—— *A Ramble through the Streets of London* (1849).

—— *Vagabondia* (1874).

T. SMOLLETT *The Expedition of Humphry Clinker* (1775).

C. A. SNEYD (ed.) *The Italian Relation of England* (Camden Society, 1846).

L. STONE 'Inigo Jones and the New Exchange' (*Archæological Jnl.*, CXIV, 1957).

STONOR *The Stonor Letters and Papers* (ed. C. L. Kingsford; Camden Society, 1919).

J. STOW *A Survey of London* (1598).

—— *A Survey of London* (ed. W. Strype, 1755).

British Museum, Stowe MSS., 326–29.

P. STUBBES *Anatomie of Abuses* (ed. F. J. Furnivall, 1877).

SWINFIELD *The Roll of the Household Expenses of Richard de Swinfield, Bishop of Hereford* (ed. J. Webb: Camden Society, 1853–55).

G. SCOTT THOMSON *Life in a Noble Household* (1937).

—— *The Russells in Bloomsbury* (1940).

RICHARD THOMSON *Chronicles of Old London Bridge* (1839).

S. THRUPP *Short History of the Worshipful Company of Bakers* (1933).

R. TRAPPES-LOMAX (ed.) *Diary and Letterbooks of the Rev. Thomas Brockbank, 1671–1709* (Chetham Society, 1930).

R. TROW-SMITH *A History of British Livestock Husbandry to 1700* (1957).

R. TRUSLER *The Honours of the Table* (1788).

G. H. TUPLING 'Early Lancashire Markets and their Tolls' (*Trans. Lancs. & Chesh. Antiq. Soc.*, L, 1935).

—— 'An Alphabetical List of the Markets and Fairs of Lancashire Recorded before the Year 1701' (*Trans. Lancs. & Chesh. Antiq. Soc.*, LI, 1936).

S. H. TWINING *The House of Twining* (1956).

G. UNWIN *Industrial Organisation in the 16th and 17th Centuries* (1904).

—— *Gilds and Companies of London* (1908).

—— *Samuel Oldknow and the Arkwrights* (1924).

C. WALFORD 'Early Laws and Customs of Great Britain Regarding Food' (*Trans. Royal Hist. Soc.*, VIII, 1880).

—— *Fairs Past and Present* (1883).

G. WALLAS *The Life of Francis Place* (1898).

T. WALLER *A General Description of All Trades* (1747).

E. WARD *The London Spy* (1698).

—— *A Step to Stirbitch Fair* (1700).

A. WAUGH *The Lipton Story* (1951).

S. & B. WEBB 'The Assize of Bread' (*Economic Jnl.*, XIV, 1904).

R. B. WESTERFIELD *Middlemen in English Business, 1660–1760* (1915).

H. B. WHEATLEY & W. CUNNINGHAM *London Past and Present* (1891).

N. J. WILLIAMS (ed.) *Tradesmen in Early Stuart Wiltshire* (1960).

G. C. WILLIAMSON 'Tradesmen's Tokens' (*The Antiquary*, XX, 1889).

J. DOVER WILSON *Life in Shakespeare's England* (1926).

BARBARA WINCHESTER *Tudor Family Portrait* (1955).

C. WRIGHT & C. E. FAYLE *History of Lloyds* (1928).

Index

Abacus, 45
Ablett, W. H., fixed prices, 258, 291
industrial areas, 269, travellers, 257
Advertising, manufacturers, 277, 285, retailers, 229, 258
Aldeburgh, 265
Ale and Beer, med., 10–12, 17th C.,73, 95–6, 118, bottled, 145, free gifts, 168, home brewed, 134, transported, 134, 18th C., adulterated, 206, consumption, 203, cookshop, 218, mass prod., and fixed price ret., 213, 19th C., chandlers, 223, truck, 274
Alehouses, 17th C., 95–6, 18th C., benefit societies and houses of call, 214, numbers, 213, universal providers, 214, 19th C., country towns, 265–6
Allen and Hanbury, chemists, 258
Almanacks, 177, 239
Almonds, 26
Alum, in bread, 208
Anderson, John, Glasgow, 289
Apothecaries and Chemists, 37, 94, 103, 203, 265–6, 285, 288
Apprentices; see also Shop Assistants. med., 31, 61–2, 17th C., girl, 106, London, 81, 101–26 passim, premiums, 103, provinces, 149–55, 18th C., 182, 183, 196, cabinet making, 197, 19th C., 256, drapery, 261
Armour, 18, 26, 36, 59, 105, 112, 115, 140
Army and Navy Stores, 289
Arrows, 50
Arsenic, 93
Assize of Bread, med., 10–12, 29, 17th C., 82–3, 18th C., 204
Auctions, 176, 231, 264
Auncel, 8

Bacon; see Pigs, etc.
Bakers; see Bread, use of ovens, 217
Ballad Sheets, 177, 239
Bamford, Samuel, 244
Barbers, 169–71, 188, 231, 265–6
Bargaining; see also Prices, fixed. med., 30, 237, 17th C., 102, 105–7, books,

Bargaining (continued)
174, pedlars, 237, 240, quakers, 152, wine at fairs, 138, 18th C., 182–3, 19th C., abandoned in good-class drapery, 291, with wholesalers, 256
Barnet, 65
Baston, T., 221
Beans, 11, 41, 48
Bedford, Duke of, 17th C., 76, 94, 18th C., 196
Beds, med., 34, 35, 17th C., 118–9, 131, 134, 145, 18th C., 198
Beef; see Meat
Beer; see Ale
Belchier, cabinet maker, 231–2
Belts; see London, girdlers
Bertold de Ratisbon, 2
Beverley Town MSS., 5
Birmingham, 147, -ware, 154
Bishop Stortford Market, 263
Blacksmith, 131, 265–6
Bon Marché, 288
Bone Ash in Bread, 208
Boodles Coffee House, 164
Booksellers, 61, 105, 122, 140, binders, 175, cash sales, 187–8, country towns, 266, London, 171–8, provinces, 171–2, 174, second hand, 187, subscriptions for publishing, 173–4, 234
Booth, Chas., 256
Boston Fair, 26
Boston as Wine Port, 128, 136–8
Botero, G., 57
Bottles, 136, 162
Bowstrings, 18
Branch Shops; see also Multiple Shops. 149, 155, 256, 280–1
Branded Goods, 182, 277, 284–5
Brandy, shop, 194, 195, grocers, 153, testing, 234
Brass Pots, 46, 50, 119, 121, tea utensils, 194
Brazier Under Contract, 130
Bread, med., 10–12, 24, 17th C., 64, 81–3, by City companies, 67, diet, 73, 18th C., adulterated, 207, assize of, 204, brown, 207, budgets, 209, 213,